Soap Opera

Soap Opera

Dorothy Hobson

polity

Copyright © Dorothy Hobson 2003

The right of Dorothy Hobson to be identified as author of this
work has been asserted in accordance with the UK Copyright, Designs
and Patents Act 1988.

First published in 2003 by Polity Press in association with Blackwell
Publishing Ltd.

Editorial office:
Polity Press
65 Bridge Street
Cambridge CB2 1UR, UK

Marketing and production:
Blackwell Publishing Ltd
108 Cowley Road
Oxford OX4 1JF, UK

Distributed in the USA by
Blackwell Publishing Inc.
350 Main Street
Malden, MA 02148, USA

A catalogue record for this book is available from the British Library.

Library of Congress Cataloging-in-Publication Data
Hobson, Dorothy
Soap opera / Dorothy Hobson.
p. cm.
Includes bibliographical references and index.
ISBN 0-7456-2654-8 (h/b)—ISBN 0-7456-2655-6 (p/b) 1. Soap operas—
Great Britain—History and criticism. 2. Soap operas—United States—
History and criticism. 3. Soap operas—Australia—History and criticism.
I. Title.
PN1992.8.S4 H63 2003
791.44'6—dc21
2002072835

Typeset in 10.5 on 12 pt Sabon
by SNP Best-set Typesetter Ltd., Hong Kong
Printed in Great Britain by MPG Books Ltd, Bodmin, Cornwell

This book is printed on acid-free paper.

For Gordon, Mike and Nina

Contents

Acknowledgements

I am indebted to many people for the information which has influenced my thinking about soap operas over many years. My thanks go to my friends and colleagues at the following academic and broadcasting organizations: Centre for Contemporary Cultural Studies in the 1970s, friends and colleagues at ATV/Central/Carlton, Channel 4 Television, Mersey Television and the BBC. All have helped by sharing their thoughts and knowledge with me. Thanks go particularly to Charlotte Brunsdon, Stuart Hall, the late Ian Connell, Jack Barton, the late Mike Holgate, Charles Denton, David Dunn, Jeremy Isaacs, Sue Stoessl, Phil Redmond, Michael Grade, David Liddiment, John Pike, Jonathon Powell, Matthew Robinson, Peter Salmon, Mervyn Watson, Mal Young, many actors, directors, producers, executives and all production staff who have helped me in so many ways.

I would also like to thank all those people who have let me interview them about their viewing habits for their generosity in giving up their time and sharing their thoughts and opinions with me. All my colleagues at the University of Wolverhampton have been supportive while I have been writing this book and I thank them, but special thanks go to the CITS (Campus Information Technology Services) team at the Dudley Campus: Colin Fletcher, Cham Patel, Philip Soars, Tina Underhill and Geoff Woods, who have saved me – technologically – on a number of occasions.

Finally, my love and thanks to my son Mike, his wife Nina and my husband Gordon for their love and patience over many years of research. Gordon has been subjected to more hours of soap opera viewing and deliberation than it is reasonable to expect anyone to endure – and most of the time he would rather have been watching BBC2.

Preface: Why Soap Opera?

A couple of years ago, as I began writing this book, an actress in a leading British soap opera said that she felt very privileged to have a role in a drama, which, like it or not, was at the forefront of television programmes all over the world. She was on a breakfast time show to talk about her character – eternally glamorous, but down to earth – who had been recently widowed. Her current storyline involved supporting her 'best friend', whose husband had cheated on her and was now involved with a young woman one-third of his age. A divorce was in progress. Everyone in the series was talking about the storyline. Everyone in the audience cared about the 'best friend' and knew that Audrey would support Alma through her divorce from Mike Baldwin in the British soap opera *Coronation Street*. The story has now moved on and each of these characters has had many, many more incidents in their lives. But this one tiny fragment of a storyline could be part of any one of the soap operas and continuous series which are a major element of the form which dominates national and global television at the end of the twentieth century. Love, relationships, families, women, men, babies, children, marriage, divorce, death, heartache, heartbreak, tears, happiness, laughter, violence, not a little sex – emotions and the practical effects and consequences: these are the stuff of the British soap opera. Experiences of life and also death are the themes which are handled in the series, and, more recently, Audrey supported her friend Alma through illness as she suffered from and eventually died from cancer.

The soap opera is a form which is revered by fans, reviled by some critics. Its history spans and reflects social change, artistic and cultural development and national and international broadcasting history. For broadcasters, the soap opera could be seen as the perfect television form: it achieves and retains audiences, gains press coverage, creates controversy, brings in advertising revenue, supports a public service ethos and generates discussion, dissection, analysis and astonishment at its survival and evolution. An understanding of the phenomenon of the soap opera necessitates grounding it as a part of broadcasting. It is its role within the broadcasting industry and its relationship with other broadcasting forms which accounts for its unique relationship between its producers and its audiences.

The genre of soap opera, while being the ultimate twentieth-century mass media form, embraces the traditional literary genres of drama and the novel, including the serial form popularized in nineteenth-century novels and newspapers, and its dominant theme is that of realism, which directly relates soap opera to the literary realists of the eighteenth and nineteenth centuries. In the twentieth century, when the form began, television conventions and production requirements shaped and formed the soap opera, and it is within the genre of drama series that the form advanced. Its basic material and way of dealing with its subject has become hugely influential throughout other forms of television. The soap opera has become more powerful and important within the broadcasting industry, while still attracting the sometimes derogatory connotations attributed to it by commentators who remain ignorant of any specific details of the form. While academic analysis has located soap operas and their storylines as major carriers of ideological messages, it is only by considering their role as part of the business of television that a fuller understanding of the importance and significance of the soap opera can be achieved. This book locates the soap opera in its role within the economy of broadcasting as well as seeing it as a major dramatic, artistic and cultural form.

The function of the soap opera for broadcasters is to deliver audiences. For public service broadcasters, soap operas assist in fulfilling their public service remit by appealing to the largest number of viewers. For commercial broadcasters, they deliver large audiences for advertisers. The soap opera is one of the most powerful and cost-effective genres on television. Soap operas are a clear example of the two functions of television programmes. For the audience they are entertainment; for the producers and broadcasters they are business. The two needs are inseparable and mutually compatible. When they succeed as entertainment they do good business. More than any other genre the soap opera speaks to the audience, and for this reason it is a form which is invaluable to broadcasters.

The soap opera is a global form of television. In Britain, for example, soap operas are transmitted on the two main channels, BBC1 and ITV, as well as on Channel 4 and Channel 5; on all but the latter they constantly vie for top place in the ratings. Soap operas are shown and produced across the world and the soap opera as a global form is described in O'Donnell (1999) and Allen (1995). This book will not consider the role of soap opera in a global context, nor will it examine the importance of the soap operas which are produced around the world. The issues relating to global soap operas, although similar, are very different from those which determine the nature of the British soap opera. Some of the international soap operas will be discussed briefly in this book, but I do see these programmes as having their own provenance. I will, however, include the American prime-time series *Dallas* and *Dynasty* and the Australian series *Neighbours* and *Home and Away* because these series all had an important role in the development of the British soap opera and had a great impact on the British audiences and the production of British soap operas. However, the strength of the British soap opera is that it reflects *aspects of the British character and regional identity*, and it is that specific regional element of the genre which makes it different from the soap operas which are global.

The term soap opera has been taken to encapsulate programmes which span many different aspects of television drama fiction. The term is used in a descriptive mode to denote a type of programme, but is also used as a term of derision and abuse, which reveals the perspective of the writer or speaker rather than an intrinsic value in the work. This book will categorize the elements which are essential to a soap opera and trace how some of these elements are incorporated into other drama genres. There is a specificity about British soap opera which defines the form. British soap opera is rooted in its characters, and those characters are rooted in the reality which they reflect. They also have a verisimilitude which defines them as being 'true to life' for the audience. Like Forster's 'round' characters, they create the impression that they could live and breathe and operate outside their fictional form and could be transferred to other situations and still retain their credibility (Forster 1971).

This book argues that the soap opera is developed from literary genres. The individuality of the characters in the novel has been married with the needs of television production to develop a form which perfectly fits the requirements of the electronic mass media. This book will look at the way that production demands have an overriding influence on the development of storylines and character development. The actions which drive the narrative, and the characters who carry those actions, cannot solely be determined by the creative ideas of the writers. The confines of production, the availability of actors, sets and locations are also integral to the way that the drama will develop. At extreme times, the decision of an actor to leave the programme will be *the* reason for a storyline developing in a certain way. Sometimes a character lured to a different part of the country or indeed, another country, and out of the reach of the cameras for a while, may be available to return to the series. Sometimes the producer is more concerned with a dramatic impact and death will ensue. Death is final, and often provides the most popular storylines. The decision to 'kill off' a character has repercussions for all the other characters in a drama, but these developments can be determined by the production team to enhance the future stories. The soap opera is the production of a cultural form which has to fulfil all the requirements and needs of the broadcaster and the audience. How it manages to combine these different elements is explored in this book.

Writing about soap operas – a personal note

My own interest in *writing* about soap opera grew out of an interest in audience. In the 1970s I undertook research into the lives of young women at home with children and the changes in their lives from leaving school to becoming young mothers (Hobson 1978, 1980) and the importance of television in their lives was one of the outstanding findings. The selection of soap operas and other forms of popular drama and popular programmes were not only an area of interest for these young women but also one with which they felt an affinity and a sense of connection. My own research interests followed the areas of popular television and the audience, and the publication of my study on the British soap opera *Crossroads* (Hobson 1982) began a career interest which, although I also study many other areas of television, has resulted in my being predominantly defined in media circles as an academic who writes about soap opera. This has also meant that I have been involved in two areas of interest in the genre. Indeed, my connections have spanned the whole circle of production, consumption and comment. Between 1982 and 1999 I was an independent media consultant and worked on a number of consultancies, some of which were directly related to the production of soap operas. These varied depending on the nature of the client and, while they remain subject to commercial confidentiality, the thoughts and analyses that went into that work have informed my thinking on the development of the genre over the last twenty years. During that period I also wrote a number of newspaper articles – always when a particular soap opera was involved in some sort of crisis and I was asked for my opinion on the state of the programme and suggestions for its survival. I have also broadcast on radio and television on the subject. Over the last twenty years the media itself has become more and more interested in the phenomenon. Many radio and television programmes have been made about the form, and the amount of column inches devoted to the soap opera in newspapers is vast. Magazines are devoted to the subject, and actors and actresses from the genre are at the forefront of media and audience interest. Soap opera is a major force across all media.

Ethnography of media production

My academic interest in the genre has been dominated by the disciplines of cultural and media studies and the methodology of ethnography. I have also spent a considerable amount of time engaged in ethnographic observation with the various producers and production teams of soap operas. Initially this was through work at ATV, looking at the production of *Crossroads*, and then when I was working as a consultant to Channel 4 Television, I spent time at Mersey Television observing the production of and interviewing the production team and actors in *Brookside* in the mid-1980s. I have also had a lot of contact with producers and executive producers of all the soap operas and have spent time discussing the form and their views on its development. I have also spoken at a number of conferences and television festival sessions which have concentrated on the genre and brought together members of the production teams, and these experiences have also influenced my thinking in this area. These events have involved members of the audience, and their reactions to the soap opera have also informed my thinking and fed into my comments and analysis of the genre.

This book aims to bring together various aspects of the research which I have conducted over the last twenty years and academic theories which I have developed in relation to the genre. It incorporates other academic writing, debates and analysis of the genre from the perspective of media theory. I have also brought a number of literary theories to bear on my understanding of the genre. This is because I see the form as being very close to the genres of realism and the forms of popular fiction. I see the form as directly located in the disciplines of literature, from the folk tale, telling the stories of and to

Preface: Why Soap Opera?

communities, to the novel in serial form, telling the stories of the lives of individuals. The soap opera is part of our literary tradition both in its intrinsic content and in its audience reception.

It could be said that my involvement with the genre has constituted a long ethnographic study of the production, the product and its consumption. My thoughts and theories on the soap opera have been influenced by many conversations, often of an informal nature, with soap opera producers, writers, actors and broadcasting executives. I have watched and studied thousands of hours of soap opera, spent time talking to and observing production teams as they have worked on various aspects of the genre, and interviewed and talked to many viewers across a range of age, class, gender and race. While the involvement in all these specific but related aspects of the soap opera has required a considerable degree of mental gymnastics, it has enabled me to acquire a very wide and deep understanding of the genre, its production and its audience. Lest critics accuse me of incorporation, I readily admit to being as interested in the production process as the producers, as involved in the stories as the audience, but I am totally detached in my academic analysis of the cultural significance and continuing evolution of the genre. As a viewer I have watched an inordinate number of hours of soap opera across all channels. This has been both for academic research and for personal pleasure. Soap operas remain a genre which is either loved or hated; it can be no surprise to find that I am located within the group who loves the genre.

Introduction:
History and Theories

This book tells the story of the soap opera in Britain, examining it as a phenomenon of broadcasting as well as locating its importance to its various constituencies. Soap opera is part of the history of broadcasting and an important part of the economy of broadcasting as well as being a part of popular culture, a major dramatic form, a purveyor of ideological messages and a source of great pleasure to audiences. The popularity and importance of the form is to be found in the conjunction of all these elements. This book will present the story of the elements involved in the production and reception of the major soap operas in Britain. It locates the soap opera within the economy of broadcasting and establishes an understanding of the genre which is inclusive and dynamic.

The power of soap opera is that it is immediate and historic. Soap opera is a form which began out of a need to attract audiences to the newly emerging medium of radio and has developed and evolved into a genre which is vital to the continued success of broadcasting. It has spread from radio to television and from America to Britain, Australia and countries across the world in innumerable different guises. Certain elements characterize the form and are essential to a definition which captures both the structural and spiritual aspects of the genre. At a simple level, the soap opera is radio or television drama in serial form. It has a core set of characters and locations and is transmitted more than three times a week for fifty-two weeks a year. The main focus of the narrative is on the everyday personal and emotional lives of its characters. This basic definition embraces certain programmes and excludes others. Time and continuous transmission is vital for the verisimilitude of the genre. Soap operas create the illusion that the characters and the location exist and continue to operate whether the viewers are there or not. They invite viewers to drop in and see characters and share their lives, but the illusion depends on the credibility that life goes on when the viewers are not watching. Ideally, the soap opera would be transmitted every day, but the crucial element necessary for the acceptance of the genre is that the audience does believe, albeit in a 'pretending' (Walton 1992) or 'playful' relationship with the fiction, that life goes on when they are not watching.

At any moment in time the audience of any particular soap opera is aware of the current storylines; if the soap is at one of its peaks, the storylines will have a resonance which takes on a life outside the series and becomes part of the discussions of the audience in their everyday lives. However, the soap opera also has a history of which some members of the audience are well aware. The dramas have to operate within the parameters of audiences who know every nuance and ambience of the production as well as within the parameters of viewers who are new to the particular soap opera. As the form has become established as one of the major genres within television, both nationally and globally, its reputation and influence have grown to the extent that it now occupies a major role both in its own right and by its influence on other forms of television production.

It is hard to imagine that there is anyone who has not seen soap operas and who knows nothing about the programmes, the characters and their stories. Soap opera is ubiquitous. It is part of the shared knowledge of the viewing audience, part of the fabric of other media – radio, press and the soap opera's own publishing products. It has its own history and is part of the history of television, a major constituent of popular culture, part of academic debate and, in some cases, part of a shared global cultural awareness. At any time it is possible to speak about an event which is taking place in a soap opera and members of the audience will know to which particular story the speaker refers. A shared knowledge enables the form to exist in the consciousness of the audience, and major storylines can be part of everyday conversation without it ever being indicated that a television programme is being talked about. A short example can illustrate this point nicely.

'Matthew is innocent!'

The scene was at the end of the episode of *EastEnders* transmitted on BBC1 on Friday 8 October 1999 after a special week of nightly programmes. The foreman of the jury read out the verdict in the case against Steve Owen and Matthew Rose. Each was found not guilty of the murder of Saskia Reeves. Steve Owen was found not guilty in the case of manslaughter. The clerk to the court continued: 'In the case of Matthew Rose, do you find the defendant guilty or not guilty?' The courtroom and the audience waited, tense with anticipation. The foreman of the jury spoke the fateful word, 'Guilty'. 'No', screamed Michael Rose, Matthew's father, 'My son is innocent!' 'No', screamed the audience, either out loud or in their heads, for they too knew that this was a serious miscarriage of justice. Matthew *is* innocent and Steve *is* guilty; we know because we were witnesses to the incident by privilege of being viewers of the British soap opera and we have shared the anguish of Matthew Rose and marvelled at the pure wickedness of Steve Owen. Steve Owen had killed Saskia, albeit in self-defence, when he had hit her with an ashtray as she tried to strangle him after he refused to rekindle their relationship. He had then coerced Matthew into helping him dispose of the body and held him in terror for the rest of the year. Both had spent time in prison on remand. The audience could have believed that after the trial Matthew's innocence would be proved and Steve Owen would be found guilty. However, the drama required that the serious miscarriage of justice be written into the script, and the audience waited to see how the storyline would continue. Some chose to demonstrate that they disagreed with the verdict and thus revealed their involvement with the series.

By Saturday morning, when I drove to the main road close to my home and passed houses rented by students, one window displayed a two-foot square poster which read, 'MATTHEW IS INNOCENT – STEVE IS GUILTY'. This might be seen as the ultimate evidence of an active audience, and a signal to all those who share the cultural capital with the occupier of the house that they watch the same programme and share the horror at the fictional injustice. It was an acknowledgement that such miscarriages of justice do and have happened in the British justice system and signalled pleasure in the anticipation that the *EastEnders* production team would, as they eventually did, right the wrong that had been done – not, however, until they had carried the audience in suspense for a few months longer. During that period the audience was aware that, ultimately, justice would be done, for the soap opera is the most moral of television genres. Soap operas are always moral, always on the side of right. It may take a while, but audiences have learned that ultimately evil and misdemeanours will always be punished. In the weeks that followed the incident there were more posters in adjacent windows, further demonstrating the interest the audience has in the soap opera and the playful way they engage with the production and confirm their active relationship to the scripts.

Walton has commented on the relation of audiences to fictions: 'Human beings make up stories and tell them to each other. They also listen, entranced, to stories which they know are made up' (Walton 1992: 218). He asserts that the connection between the world of fiction and the real world is a psychological interaction: 'We feel a psychological bond to fictions, an intimacy with them, of a kind which normally we feel only toward things we take to be actual' (1992: 223–4). Walton's exposition on the way that audiences relate to fiction in a playfully engaged manner is pertinent to explaining how audiences engage with the events in soap opera and share their playfulness with other members of the audience, even when they are strangers.

Meanwhile, back in the world of the production of *EastEnders*, an event of much more significance happened when Grant Mitchell, one of the leading characters, left the series. By the week beginning 11 October the storyline involved the revelation that a feud between the Mitchell brothers was heading towards a climactic disaster and that Matthew's appeal was on hold. During the week Grant was due to leave there was a spectacular scene when his car plunged into the River Thames. No one knew if he had drowned or would survive – the photograph of his car flying spectacularly into the River Thames had been revealed in the press as a 'snatch' (a photograph that appears to be taken from the transmission but which has, in fact, been released to the press by the production team in order to control the publicity – see chapter 2). For a few days the production held the audience in suspense. One day, while shopping at my local Tesco Express near Birmingham University, where many of the customers are students, I overheard and shared a further cultural moment, again typical of the way that audiences are involved and 'play' with the form. Two young people, whom I presumed to be students, were talking about a mutual friend, and then suddenly the woman, without any preamble or signal of change of subject, declared: 'I think Grant may be doing a Harold Bishop.' 'Could be', replied the man, and as I walked past them our eyes met and we all shared a silent smile of recognition, the unspoken knowledge that we all knew to what they referred, that we all watched the same programmes and that we had watched *Neighbours* years ago when Harold Bishop had been written out, presumed drowned, only to return a few years later suffering – in good soap opera tradition – from amnesia.

Audiences play with the drama of the soap opera and retain certain elements, however fantastic, to play with the form and reveal their knowledge in later cultural exchanges. It is more than a suspension of disbelief because it requires active engagement with the drama and the reproduction of certain elements of the narrative in future exchanges, whenever appropriate. It is playing with shared cultural knowledge and re-using it in exchanges with people whom you may not have known at the time of watching the programmes. The incidents in the series pass easily into conversations about people the audience know, and the interweaving of reality and fiction reveals not a confusion about the status of the characters in the drama, but evidence of the validity of their representation and their place in the consciousness of the audience. Soap opera is always of the present, immediate, engaging with its audience, providing stories for newspapers and other television programmes, and leading the way as an element of popular culture. Above all, soap opera is a powerful force within television and popular culture.

'There's nothing on but soap operas'

Every week in Britain around 32 million soap opera fans will watch up to a total of forty-five hours of soaps. Almost three-quarters of the adult population watch a soap opera in any given month. While viewers have their own favourite soap operas, there are some who watch across the range of soap operas. It is possible to watch all the soap operas on British television without missing any episodes, unless there are special weeks when a programme may be stripped across five nights. Almost the only programme which can disturb the allotted slots for soap opera is a major international football match. To try to record the number of times when soap operas are shown on British television is a futile occupation. For as soon as one set of figures are recorded, the television companies will increase the number of episodes and the figures will be superseded. All that can be done is give an example of a set of figures which are correct at one specific time, and perhaps a comparison with the number of programmes which were shown at an earlier date. For this purpose I indicate the increasing fascination with the genre by showing an example of the transmissions of programmes on the terrestrial channels only.

In the week beginning 12 March 1983 there was a paucity of soap operas. Viewers could watch only 7 hours 10 minutes per week, including daytime and omnibus editions. When the BBC produced *EastEnders* in 1985 it added to the schedules by one hour during the week and by an hour on Sunday for the omnibus edition. By the beginning of the 1990s it could be said that the magic formula for a British soap opera was the ability to deliver an audience three times a week. This had become a prime requirement for the broadcasters if they were to recoup their investment in money and airtime. By the early 1990s soaps were expected to deliver audiences to the companies by expanding to four, and on special weeks five, episodes a week. The companies continued to search for new programmes to fulfil the growing appetite for soap operas, and in 1992 the BBC developed and transmitted *Eldorado* in an attempt to deliver audiences for a nightly soap opera.

In November 1996 Granada television decided to extend their production of *Coronation Street* to four episodes a week, adding a Sunday episode to their Monday, Wednesday and Friday episodes. This was not without its problems and for the first few months it was attracting three or four million less viewers than its weekday episodes. Unfortunately, the addition of the fourth episode coincided with a particularly low point in the storyline and it took time to 'teach' the audience to watch on Sunday evening. My own view was that Sunday night was not a natural time for soap operas. In television terms Sunday night has a different 'feel' and audiences have a different expectation of and commitment to programmes (Hobson 1997). The initial transmission of *Coronation Street* on Sunday night gave the impression that the working week had already begun. Eventually, during the summer of 1997 when the storylines became much stronger, the fourth episode began to achieve the same ratings as the weekday episodes. In 2002 the presence of the fourth episode of *Coronation Street* on Sunday nights remains a crucial part of the schedule both for the controller of Network Centre and for the audience.

At various times when storylines have reached particular crescendos soap operas have been stripped across a week, showing an episode every night. These 'special' storylines have usually been to carry a specific theme of a story, but by the end of 2000 *Emmerdale* had moved to a permanent five nights a week format. Ever vigilant and anxious to keep abreast of the competition, on 10 August 2001 the BBC introduced a fourth episode of *EastEnders*, on a Friday night.

As the broadcasters try to fulfil a commercial wish to attract their audiences to even more episodes of soap operas, they must also make sure that they do not alienate that audience and also members of the audience who do not like soap operas. Taking a spot check on 1 April 2002 the number of hours of soap operas on terrestrial television was 17 hours 25 minutes of original transmission and 5 hours 35 minutes of repeats, or omnibus editions as they are called. However, the genre is expanding so rapidly that by the time this book is published it is likely that these figures will have changed.

The UK's big five

The main programmes which will form the basis of this book will be the five major UK soap operas. These are *Coronation Street* (from Granada Television for ITV), *Crossroads* (from ATV/Central – returned from Carlton in spring 2001 – for ITV), *Emmerdale* (from Yorkshire Television for ITV), *EastEnders* (BBC1), and *Brookside* (from Mersey Television for Channel 4). There is also discussion of other programmes which have been important in the development of soap opera on British television: *Eldorado* (BBC1) and *Family Affairs* (from Pearson Television for Channel 5), also form part of the history but do not have the significance of the first five. Other series will form part of the discussion and exposition, especially the American and Australian soap operas, but only in so far as they have had an influence on the genre within the UK. Programmes which have flowered briefly will also form part of the history of the genre, as will the hybrids and hydra, spawned from the main genre, and the new soap operas which have been developed.

What is soap opera?

'What *is* soap opera?' is the question which is often asked about the form. Is there a definition which can capture the essence of the genre? Are there elements which are always needed? And what are the additional ingredients which are present in some examples though not in others? Is it the frequency of transmission or the location within a domestic sphere or is it in the nature of the characters? Or is it all of those things? The soap opera is a changing and evolving form. What might have been an accurate definition when soap opera began definitely needs to be updated for the twenty-first century. Definitions for the most part must be seen as diachronic, so before constructing any definition it is first necessary to consider some of the history of the form.

Born in the USA

There are many forms of soap opera. The genre, as it is perceived, began in the 1930s in America in the guise of daytime radio serials sponsored by the giant soap powder manufacturers like Proctor and Gamble. They wanted to create programmes which would attract women listeners and enable them to advertise and sell their products. Cantor and Pingree (1983) have shown not only how radio soap opera was the forerunner of television soap operas but also how the influence of commercial interests had a beneficial effect on the development of the form. When commercial radio stations were established in the 1920s they were primarily local, but by the 1930s there was a system of national networks and the conditions necessary for the development of the soap opera were in place. Manufacturers in search of markets had the capability to reach potential customers:

> The story of the soap opera (and of all other programming) after radio became a 'mass medium' in 1930 is the story of American manufacturers' need to find nation-wide consumers for their products, and of a few individuals' applied creativity and imagination in response to that need. (Cantor and Pingree 1983: 34)

The impetus for the development of the form came because the advertisers were reluctant to pay large sums of money to sponsor daytime programmes for women. Discounts were offered and they bought smaller slots, 15-minute periods. This appealed to advertisers, including Colgate Palmolive-Peet and Proctor & Gamble who made soap products. The name 'soap opera' came from that connection but there were other major sponsors: 'Serials were sponsored by at least five brands of breakfast cereals, seven brands of toothpaste, a great variety of drug products and home remedies, plus food products and beverages' (Willey 1961, quoted in Cantor and Pingree 1983: 37).

However, it was soap powder that retained the generic sponsorship, the relationship with the name and all the connotations and allusions which surround the form – the idea that the programmes were for housewives who listened to or watched them when they were not doing the washing. The advertisers bought hour-long slots but were able to use individual products to sponsor 15-minute segments. The programmes had to appeal to housewife listeners who were at home during the day. The first producer of radio soap operas, according to Stedman (1977, quoted in Cantor and Pingree 1983: 40), was Frank Hummert and his future wife Anne Achenhurst, who were directly responsible for many of the first soap operas. Their first programme *Stolen Husband* failed, but from its failure they learned much about what was necessary for future success, including the need to slow down plots. Their first successful soap opera, *Betty and Bob*, told the story of a secretary, Betty, who fell in love with her boss Bob Drake. Disowned by his millionaire father when he married Betty, and too immature to settle down, his attraction to and for other women caused problems in the marriage and the couple were divorced, remarried, had a child and finally ran out of airtime. However, they established some of the basic tenets of the soap opera, which, although developed in different ways, provided the basis for future variations on the form. *Betty and Bob* may have started off as a love story, but according to Cantor it was 'actually about the problems of marriage in modern society' (Cantor and Pingree 1983: 42). Other themes which became the foundations of plotlines for soap operas were established at this time and these included fidelity, jealousy, divorce, child-rearing or childlessness, family and romantic love. These themes became the mainstay of American radio and television soap operas and were carried over fifty years later into the prime-time series *Dallas* and *Dynasty* and the plethora of daytime serials which form a staple diet on American television. A further feature of radio drama in the USA, which has been influential in British soap operas, was the use of drama to promote war bonds and for characters and personalities to be used in wartime propaganda that was in the national interest. This inclusion of public information fed into British soap opera, initially through *The Archers*, which is discussed below.

'I'm worried about Jim' – soap opera on the wireless

The link between the American radio and television soap operas came to the UK through the British radio soap opera. BBC radio has sustained long-running daily serials as well as shorter family serials. The first long-running series was *Mrs Dale's Diary*, which ran from 5 January 1948 until 25 April 1969. The programme was transmitted at four o'clock in the afternoon and repeated at eleven o'clock the next morning. Its scheduling reflected the times when it was expected that women would sit down for a break from their housewifely duties. The storylines in *Mrs Dale's Diary* were about the everyday lives of the heroine's family, shared with the listeners by Mrs Dale as if she were telling a good friend about the happenings in her own life. The narrative then became dramatized and the listeners shared the experiences of the family and friends. Mrs Dale was middle-class. She was so middle-class that most of what she spoke about and her lifestyle was completely alien to many of the listeners to the programme. She had a daily help and a gardener, and her family was exotic to working-class listeners. Her mother sounded like a dowager duchess and her sister, the ageless Sally, an actress often appearing in plays in the West End, had various 'boyfriends' and brought a touch of glamour to the programme.

Mrs Dale was the ultimate figure who came to dominate the soap opera form. She established the link between Mrs Dale and her female listeners. She was wife, mother, mother-in-law, grandmother, friend, neighbour and employer and she juggled her life to play every role. She may not be like your mother, or indeed like anyone you knew, but she had the same job, to be a wife and mother, and those maternal feelings which reflected the dominant cultural norm in the 1950s and aimed to unite women of whatever class or age. She 'worried about Jim', her husband, because he worked too hard, she worried about the lives of her children and her family, and she epitomized a representation of the British middle-class wife. She was unashamedly middle-class, but her role as a doctor's wife enabled her to cut across class – at least within the programme. She may have been confiding in her diary, but the device enabled her news, gossip and worries about the problems of her family and friends to be shared with listeners as they eavesdropped when her thoughts were transferred to the pages of the airwaves. No character who was so naturally middle-class has ever become such an icon in British soap operas, except for the character Meg Mortimer in the ATV/Central series *Crossroads*. However, she represented the managerial and entrepreneurial middle class rather than the classic middle-class doctor's wife. No serial has ever been so unashamedly middle-class as *Mrs Dale's Diary*, and the later move into working-class and lower middle-class representation, which has since dominated British soaps, reflected the changes in cultural awareness within all areas of art and popular entertainment.

In the late 1950s and the 1960s there was a dramatic shift to working-class dramas, particularly the so-called 'kitchen-sink' dramas in theatre. 'This was a term applied to the plays written by Arnold Wesker, Sheila Delaney and John Osborne which portrayed working-class and lower middle-class life, with an emphasis on domestic realism' (Drabble 1985: 538) and by the mid-1960s these themes were reflected in television dramas. The emergence of dramas which reflected working-class life was part of the series *The Wednesday Play*, shown on the BBC. The original producers of *The Wednesday Play* were Tony Garnett, James MacTaggart, Roger Smith and Kennith Trodd, and the plays in this series were influential and remain as benchmarks against which much drama is measured. The 1965 season included Nell Dunn's *Up the Junction*, and Jeremy Sandford's award-winning and hugely influential *Cathy Come Home* was transmitted on 16 November 1966 (Gambaccini and Taylor 1993: 504). Their concentration on working-class lives and ordinary people was new in terms of television productions and ran parallel to the soap operas. It was also at this time that the cultural history of the British working class was brought to the forefront of academic studies by Richard Hoggart in his classic *The Uses of Literacy* (1973). Soap operas were part of the emerging drama which took the everyday lives of ordinary people and put them at the forefront of popular television entertainment.

Britain's longest-running radio soap opera, which has been broadcast for fifty years, is the BBC radio series *The Archers*. Starting with an introductory trial week from 29 May to 2 June 1950 and an introductory programme on 28 December 1950, it began daily transmission from 1 January 1951. It has continued every night, now with a lunchtime repeat and an omnibus edition on Sunday mornings. *The Archers* began as a family story, but one which was located in the fictional village of Ambridge and followed the changes taking place in the country community and the business of farming. It remains rooted in a sense of community, albeit a changing one, and still retains the basis of family life in all its forms and guises. It is also a series which was specifically intended to deal with 'issues' and to disseminate information. *The Archers* still retains a totally dedicated audience who support the series by responding, often in a very voluble fashion, to any stories or incidents which met with their disapproval. The series has always stayed fresh and relevant and incorporated the ever-changing social, emotional and economic conditions of the residents of the fictional farming community.

Radio sets the scene – the move to television drama

The 1960s were the time when soap operas emerged as a new type of programme on television. Although the BBC had transmitted 146 weekly episodes of *The Groves* between 9 April 1954 and 28 June 1957, it was the advent of Granada Television's *Coronation Street*, first transmitted on 9 December 1960, which seems to have encouraged the flurry of soap operas both on BBC television and by the ITV companies. In the 1960s the BBC produced three new series. *Compact*, the story of life on a women's magazine, was written by Peter Ling and Hazel Adair, who were later to move to start *Crossroads*. *Compact* had 373 twice-weekly episodes and ran from January 1962 to July 1965. The other two serials ran on alternate nights of the week. *United*, the story of the fortunes of a football club, began on 4 October 1965 and ran until March 1967. *The Newcomers*, which turned out to be the BBC's longest-running early serial, began on 5 October 1965 and continued until 13 November 1969 – a total of 430 episodes. As with the other series, the early British soap operas were rooted in the contemporary social scene. *The Newcomers* told the story of a family moving to a 'new town' at a time when the spread of 'new towns' was becoming part of the geographic and economic changes in the new Britain. These were towns which were created to take what was called the 'overspill' from large industrial cities and where young families moved to start a new life in modern 'contemporary' surroundings.

But to become a long-running series, programmes had to have a connection with events which would be familiar to large sections of the audience, and only those which had these qualities in abundance were to succeed in the coming years. During the 1960s *Coronation Street* became nationally successful and ATV's medical series *Emergency Ward 10* and the original *Crossroads* were running on ITV. This was a time when the BBC was committed to the soap opera form, but after that early flurry they had no involvement with continuous soap operas until the advent of *EastEnders* in 1985. However, the ideas that were seen as integral to soap operas were included in many other drama series, series which had a limited number of episodes but which shared a concentration on the problems and interests of the characters' personal lives. *The Brothers*, *Triangle*, *Angels* (all produced at BBC Pebble Mill, whose drama department often produced some of the most innovative and popular drama series made by the BBC), had elements of the soap opera in their themes. The personal, the social, relationships at work (in the work situation of the hospital in *Angels*), the beginning of a concentration on the inclusion of social and moral issues and the structural intertwining of those issues with the lives of the character – this was what linked these series with the later production of *EastEnders*. They also shared producer Julia Smith, and Tony Holland, the writer of *Angels*, who went on to produce and write *EastEnders* for the BBC. *Emmerdale Farm* was first transmitted on 16 October 1972 as an afternoon programme, but it became so successful that it was soon transferred to the peak-time evening slot.

Shoulder pads and handsome men – the impact of American series

In 1978 the BBC transmitted the first episode of *Dallas* at 8.10 p.m. on a Tuesday evening. It very quickly became a success and was moved to the prime Saturday evening slot, where twenty-four million viewers watched to see the much-publicized shooting of J. R. Ewing. The American producers of *Dallas* held the audience in suspense with a cliffhanger of 'Who Shot J.R.?' over many months while a new series was made. A new series? Soap opera is supposed to be continuous with only the real time of the days that it is not transmitted separating the audience from their satisfaction. Programmes like *Dallas* and *Dynasty* are not a pure form of soap opera, but rather a form of high-quality prime-time series which bears little relation to the daytime series of American television that are now transmitted on Channel 5 and cable and satellite channels in this country. The prime-time series only have a relationship to soap opera in that the main concentration of their subjects is on emotions and everyday life, albeit of the enormously rich. The productions had huge budgets and high-standard production values and presented an image to British viewers which was far from their own everyday life experiences. Yet they do contain one of the vital ingredients for success in relation to audiences for soap operas – personal problems and emotional entanglements. They are set in exotic locations but they are still about problems, the difference being that they are about the problems of extremely rich and privileged people.

Nevertheless, because they became part of the experience of British viewers, *Dallas*, *Dynasty*, *Knots Landing* and *Falcon Crest* did have an influence on British soap opera production. They may not have improved the dress sense of the women, as shoulder pads grew to resemble the attire of American footballers, but they certainly did result in an influx of attractive male characters. The American prime-time series showed viewers perfect American males, handsome, well-groomed and well-dressed and not in constant conflict with the women in their family. Apart from the Jane Wyman character, the matriarch who owned the vineyard in *Falcon Crest*, these were not series where women ruled with the same matriarchal power as in British soaps, but they were series where women were powerful and were certainly among the main characters in the series. The series were part of the genre of fifty-minute or one-hour, with commercials, American prime-time film series. They would be shown during the 8.00–9.00 evening slot and would be expected to gain maximum viewers for the networks. They were not long running, but mostly consisted of thirteen-part series, the optimum number of programmes designated by the American networks at that time for that type of slot. While they contained elements of soap opera, they can never be judged in the same way as the British soap operas, any more than they were closely related to the American daytime serials. These were high budget; high production values and massive expectations were associated with them. While the series were strictly speaking not soap operas, as I have defined them below, they were perceived as part of the genre, in both the eyes of viewers and the opinions of critics. For good or bad, they contributed to the reception of the genre and influenced the way that it was defined.

Suburbs, sand and surfing – Australian soap operas

A second foreign import of soap operas with which British viewers were familiar were the Australian soap operas: *The Young Doctors* and *Sons and Daughters* which were shown during the afternoons on ITV during the 1970s. However, in 1986 the BBC scheduled a new Australian series, *Neighbours*, which was to have a profound effect on the BBC schedules. Michael Grade refers to the moment in his autobiography: 'Bill Cotton on a scouting expedition to Australia, recommended an intriguing soap called *Neighbours*. I looked at it and bought it. I decided to schedule it twice a day' (Grade 1999: 239).

Initially, the programme was scheduled at 9.05 a.m. and repeated at lunchtime, but when Michael Grade saw that his teenage daughter and her friends watched the series during the summer holiday, he realized that if he scheduled it at 5.35, immediately after children's television and before the *Six o'clock News*, he would gain the young people's audience throughout term-time and not only during the school holidays. The success of *Neighbours* had significance over and above its success as a soap opera. It revealed that if broadcasters scheduled programmes which were attractive to the audience, they could extend the time when high ratings could be achieved. It also showed that young people would watch soap operas if the cast of characters included young members and if their storylines were part of the series. *Neighbours* brought a new type of soap opera to British television. Created by the first producer of *Crossroads*, Reg Watson, the series had many of the hallmarks of the earlier British series. It was set in a street, which was actually a cul-de-sac, the same way in as out, and had a striking resemblance to *Brookside Close*, the location for Channel 4's series *Brookside*. Similarly, *Knots Landing*, the American spin-off series from *Dallas*, was set in a cul-de-sac. Perhaps representations of suburbia are defined through a half-closed place, open to the outside world but closed enough to retain the familiarity of community.

Neighbours was and still is different from other soap operas on British television in a number of ways. Its characters were families who, for the most part, liked each other. While the original cast members included the Ramsay family, with a father and two sons who were more working class than other characters, the original cast was more middle-class than the characters portrayed in British soap operas. Or maybe they simply appeared more middle-class. They had working-class jobs but were not represented as cloth cap wearing or dowdy; they were bright and modern and representative of a vibrant and cheerful working population. It was certainly different from the representation of so-called 'ordinary' people because this was a society without a clear definition of class. What was so striking about *Neighbours* when it first appeared on British screens was that the houses were bright, tastefully decorated, with large gardens – one even had a swimming pool. The location was an important element in the series, and the bright sunny weather meant that it was always a pleasure to view. (Not that this alone is a guarantee of success; witness the problems with *Eldorado*, discussed below.) The weather was part of the whole ambience of the series. It was a series which was optimistic, and optimism and aspirations were themes within the series and a part of the everyday lives of the characters. This was one of the reasons why the series was seen as different from British soap operas of the time, and while not portraying the fantasy world of the American prime-time series, it did show a world which was different from the everyday life portrayed in British soap operas. In *Neighbours* characters laughed, partied, enjoyed each other's company and went about an everyday life which was not dominated by problems.

What was most striking about the programme was that the interaction between the members of the family was much more natural than any representation in British soaps. Parents openly showed affection to their children, especially those in their teenage years. Children spoke to their neighbours, and the relationships between different age groups were far more natural and realistic than any portrayal that had, until that time, been explored in British soap operas. In fact, *Neighbours* still has the ability to handle child/parent and younger/older generational relationships in a much more positive way than any British soap opera. Reflecting a culture which was similar to that in Britain, *Neighbours* also revealed the different attitudes and values which were part of the culture of Australia. Most striking was the concentration on issues which were important to young people but were not all problems. Schools and the experience of education have always been a major part of the series, and not in an adversarial or alienating way. The young characters all worked to help each other through exams. These matters are handled in the excellent children's television programme *Grange Hill* on British television, but this is a children's drama series rather than a mainstream soap opera.

The different attitude to work and gender roles was also at the forefront of themes and storylines in *Neighbours*. When the series began Jim Robinson, the lead male character, was a widower with three children. He ran a successful garage/motor repair shop and provided a successful role model for a single father running a home. His mother-in-law Helen Daniels, played by Anne Haddy, aided him in this and again broke all the stereotypes for older characters. She was a very attractive woman, probably in her sixties, who had a success-ful career as an artist, a number of romances and led a completely inde-pendent life, while still providing stability within the family. Many new visions and opportunities or possibilities for representations of female characters were shown in *Neighbours*. Perhaps the most positive was the character Charlene, played by Kylie Minogue. At the time of the series the character and the actress were hugely successful. The actress was also a singer who went on to become a world famous pop singer, but it was the career choice of the character Charlene that made a considerable impression. Charlene wanted to be a garage mechanic, and she worked as an apprentice in the garage of Jim Robinson. The sight of one of the most attractive young female characters, dressed in overalls, with her cascading blonde curls tied up on top of her head, was one of the most positive images for breaking the stereotypes of what jobs are suitable for girls. The characters of Charlene and her boyfriend Scott, played by Jason Donovan, were the golden young couple of soap opera in the early 1980s and their influence in provid-ing positive images of young people was immense. They influenced British soap operas and, although there were no successful equivalents in the established series, led to Phil Redmond developing *Hollyoaks* for Channel 4, a series specifically aimed at the youth market. *Neigh-bours'* strength was that it incorporated the whole range of characters; age was not excluding and alienating but part of the flow of the action. Even in 2002 the series still retains that interweaving of generations, both familial and 'neighbourly', without the conflict which can still appear to be an overriding emotion of British soaps.

Troubled teens with hope

Not that every teenager in Australian soap opera was the perfect child. Juvenile crime and living with inadequate grown-ups resulted in some young people being forced to live in a community which cared for them. This was the theme of the Australian series *Home and Away*, which took the concept of foster parenting as the means to bring love and self-discipline to the young people. Set in the fictional seaside location of 'Summer Bay', the series again brought the stories of young people to the soap opera genre. Together with the sunny skies and everyday common sense of the characters who made up the community, this series brought a new element to British audiences and new audiences to the series. Transmitted by ITV in various early evening slots between 5.15 and 6.30, the series again showed that young people were interested in the genre, as long as it had something to offer them which connected with their own lives. Problems and possible solutions were major themes of the drama, themes that were not at that time found in British soap operas. The American and Australian series are discussed in this brief background to show how they brought new themes and styles to the genre and extended the range of what was to be included in British soap operas in the 1980s and 1990s. *Neighbours* and *Home and Away* had an effect on British soap operas because they brought young people to mainstream soap operas and led to the inclusion of more young characters in the British-produced soap operas.

Gritty and down to earth – new soap operas for the 1980s

During the 1980s came two soap operas which were to extend the genre, both artistically and as a vital tool in the scheduling armoury of the broadcasters. On 2 November 1982 Channel 4 began transmitting programmes and at eight o'clock they showed the first episode of their twice-weekly soap opera *Brookside*. Channel 4 has an important role in the history of British television. While not rehearsing the full story here it is worth noting that the terms of the creation and control of Channel 4, as inscribed in the 1981 Broadcasting Act, charged the channel to ensure that its programmes would appeal to the tastes and interests not generally catered for by ITV, that its programmes encouraged innovation and experiment in form and content, and that a suitable proportion of its programmes should come from independent producers.

It was to meet this requirement that *Brookside* was commissioned. *Brookside* was the work of innovative young Liverpool producer Phil Redmond, who had previously written *Grange Hill* (the first children's drama series, which seriously addressed the issues of modern comprehensive education) and *Going Out* (which followed a group of young people through tortuous teenage years). Redmond set up his own company, Mersey Television, bought houses in Brookside Close in Liverpool and took the innovative step of setting

the series in the actual houses. The series had a wider range of characters than the other soap operas, as the setting of a new housing
estate allowed for upwardly and downwardly mobile characters.
Two- to four-bedroomed houses also allowed for a mix of different
types of residents. The most significant early contribution which
Brookside made to British soap opera was in its production methods.
The houses were turned into permanent sets, even to the extent that
the 'real' sound that echoed around the houses when the production
was in its first few weeks of transmission caused complaints that the
sound quality was not good; in fact, it was completely natural sound,
too natural for television viewers. *Brookside* was the first soap
opera to use the Steadicam camera, which made realistic camera
moves more easily obtainable. The camera was mounted on a type
of harness, which the camera operator wore, and this enabled the
operator to follow the movements of the actor in a single movement.
It was also the first soap opera to use single video camera for film
techniques, so that it gave the appearance of film rather than the
multi-camera shoot of the other soap operas. Its characters were more
varied because within the confines of the new housing estate it was
possible to have characters from different classes. *Brookside* was
born in controversy and it has continued to flourish with the most
outrageous storylines ever conceived in British soap operas. It is the
most surreal of all the soaps in that its stories are always at the
extreme edges of 'everyday' life. *Brookside* began as it has continued,
thriving on its own special brand of drama – the *surrealistically
normal*. The formula is successful, but it has been less than influential on the other soaps. It remains unique and has evolved its own
exceptional reality, which is always saved from being 'unrealistic' by
being based on real incidents which have often been reported in the
press. And while they retain the 'sharp intake of breath' reaction of
'that would never happen!', the incidents are always based on a real
event. What is exceptional is that for the most part they would not
happen with such regularity in one small enclave of houses. But that
is what distinguishes the soap opera from real life – a compression
of events into a timescale that enables viewers to stay interested.

The BBC brings the East End to British soaps

In March 1985 the first transmission of *EastEnders* brought a new
soap opera to British television, and the first to challenge *Coronation
Street* for prime-time audiences.

In 1982 one of the terms of the granting of the ITV franchise to ATV for the Midland region, was that the ITV company were required to build a studio in Nottingham, within their franchise area, and move their production to that base. Lew Grade's company had to sell their major shareholding in the company, and at the new year of 1982 the new company Central was born. ATV also had to dispose of their production studios in Elstree, where most of the ATV productions had been made. The BBC, who had not had a soap opera since the 1960s because they did not want to tie up studio space for a continuous production, bought Elstree and began to plan for their own soap opera.

One of the most spectacular aspects of *EastEnders* was its set, which was a purpose-built East End Square surrounded by large houses, scruffy and run down, and small villas and dominated by the Queen Victoria pub, which was to become the focus for much of the drama and the embodiment of the spirit of the East End – the main focus of the series. *EastEnders* brought a high-quality soap opera to the BBC and brought the BBC into direct competition with ITV's *Coronation Street* for the accolades of 'top soap'. The competition between the two soap operas provided viewers with high-quality drama as the production teams vied to capture their attention and the necessary coverage in the press.

Flushed with their success with *EastEnders* – and with a need to find a programme to bring audiences to BBC1 in the early evening as *Wogan*, the three times a week chat show, began to wane – in 1991 the BBC developed a soap opera which was intended to attract viewers early in the evening. *Eldorado*, the coast of dreams, set in Spain, was the BBC soap opera that aimed to bring a new setting for soap opera to the screen. Its difficulties were legion, discussed at length elsewhere in this book, and although it was only transmitted for nine months it made an impression on the history of soap opera. Its contribution should have been that it brought a European cast to a British soap opera and widened the genre, but in the event it did not contribute to the development of soap opera because it was slated right from its first transmission. The lessons for broadcasters should have been that it is always going to be very difficult to launch a soap opera in the full glare of press attention. Evenings were a difficult slot, and the return to the daytime slot for the nurturing of a soap opera would seem to be a better option. This was the way that Yorkshire Television developed *Emmerdale Farm* in the 1970s, and it was only after it gained popularity and was established that it was moved to its seven o'clock slot.

Channel 5 – whose *Family Affairs?*

Channel 5 was launched on 30 March 1997, and its soap opera *Family Affairs* was transmitted in the early evening slot, at 6.30, with a lunchtime repeat the next day. The series began from the concept that it would be centred on one family, the Harts – Annie and Chris – and their relationships with their children, friends and colleagues in the area. The series is set in the fictional town of Charnworth, which is located who knows where. And therein lies one of the problems for the series. It is set in a fictional location, presumably somewhere south of London from the signs in the opening titles. The problem is that most viewers who do not live in that area have no idea where it is situated and there is very little point of reference for the audience. The concept for the series was interesting, and the idea of centring around a single family was in the tradition of the earlier soaps such as *Mrs Dale's Diary*, *The Archers* and *Crossroads*, all of which were set in small towns or villages and centred around one family. When *Family Affairs* did not get the required ratings and acclaim, the production company's way of dealing with its problems was to bring in an outside producer, Brian Park, who had been the producer of *Coronation Street* when it needed drastic changes to bring it back on stream (as discussed below). Park took the dramatic option and wiped out the whole family in one spectacular explosion at a wedding on a boat. Only a handful of characters were left, none of them from the original family, and the series was totally changed, albeit not necessarily with too much success.

New characters were brought in and the *Family Affairs* of the title seemed to take on the interpretation of *affaire*, particularly sexual affairs within and between families, rather than 'business and things to be done'. The series is now focussing on one street and the various inhabitants who live and work there. Again, work seems to be located within the street where they live, and the housing situation seems to revolve around house-swapping with as much regularity as partner-swapping. Unfortunately, although the series has always had good actors and characters, it still lacks any focus and, because it is operating with the notion that the way people live has changed to multi-occupancy and friend-orientated living arrangements, it has little to link its themes with the experiences of a mass audience. It is a pity that the series has not been more successful because one of its most positive aspects is that it has a wide range of black characters who are strong, well-integrated into the drama and have had interesting storylines which have reflected them as individuals as well as black Londoners. A problem for *Family Affairs* is that it never tops the ratings for Channel 5, and one of the crucial requirements for a soap opera is that it must lead the ratings of the channel on which it appears. In 2000 Dawn Airey, the channel controller of Channel 5, outbid ITV and bought *Home and Away*. The channel had to agree to a year's moratorium, which meant they could not show the programme until the summer of 2001, and when the programme returned it immediately moved into the top ten of Channel 5's programmes.

Crossroads returns to ITV

In the spring of 2001 Carlton Television's *Crossroads* was commissioned by ITV Network Centre to provide a new programme in the slot vacated by *Home and Away*. The news that the programme was due to be resurrected caused great interest in the press and other media, with speculation and much media coverage. The decision to bring back the programme was the idea of Lord Ali, an executive at Carlton in charge of new developments. The idea was a brilliant marketing concept, for the series already had the benefit of an audience who had been bereft of their programme since 1988. When the series began transmission on 5 March 2001, it was after considerable advertising which indicated that this series was to be very different from its predecessor. The trail concentrated on beautiful, young characters whose provocative sexual posing signified that this was going to be a very different series from the original programme. The series has a hard function to fulfil because it must address two distinct audiences. Transmitted at 1.30 p.m. and 5.05 p.m., it has the possibility of appealing to those who are at home during the daytime and to the young audience who traditionally watch *Neighbours* at 5.35 p.m. By September 2001 the programme had changed to 2.05 and 5.30 and was reduced to four nights a week. A further scheduling change set the programme directly against *Neighbours* at 1.30 and 5.30, giving the programme even more competition for viewers (currently, it is transmitted at 5.30, Monday–Friday). *Crossroads* has included a number of young characters and is clearly aiming to attract a young audience, but it must also establish a relationship with the main audience to sustain its appeal and become part of the soap 'world' on British television, and it must establish sufficient appealing characters in order that the audience will be interested in their stories.

In another interesting ploy, as a link with the original series, the production brought back Jill Harvey, the daughter of Meg Mortimer (the former owner of the Crossroads Motel), Adam Chance, her former husband and Meg's business partner, and Miss Luke, one of the motel staff. Unfortunately, Jill remarried Adam in indecent haste and was murdered before she had left for her honeymoon. The production had used the characters to bring back some of the viewers from the original series, but their appearances were short-lived and the newly formulated series progressed with its new characters. What is interesting about the return of *Crossroads* is that it fulfils the fantasy that soap opera continues to operate even when the viewers are not watching. In the case of *Crossroads*, transmissions had stopped in March 1988 and thirteen years later on 5 March 2001 viewers were able to revive their interest in the lives of the characters and engage with the fiction as if it had continued while it was off the screen. However, the programme has not lived up to its initial hype and, although it has a range of characters, the storylines have been ill-conceived. Too much sexual philandering with little evidence of love and romance, and a confused notion of their audience, has meant that the series has not fared well. However, ITV Network Centre has now commissioned a further 240 episodes and the production is making positive changes.

Academic acceptance and theories of the genre

While audiences had loved soap operas from their inception, it was only with the growth of the disciplines of television studies, the development of cultural studies and, vitally, the emergence of feminist studies as an academic area of study that soap operas became the subject of academic interest in the UK. The emergence of soap opera as a field of consideration by academics and as a part of academic thought in the UK can be dated from the work on *Coronation Street* (Dyer et al. 1981). Before their book was published the writers spoke at the 1977 Edinburgh International Television Festival and criticized the programme makers for omissions in their areas of representation. While their work was based on a study of *Coronation Street*, they established theoretical tools which could be used for analysis of other programmes in the genre. They related the series to its moment of conception and its connection with the growing awareness in working-class culture (Dyer 1981: 3–6). Written before the expansion of soap opera in the 1980s this collection includes chapters which were the first to define some of the features of the genre.

Christine Geraghty sets out to define the soap opera, which she calls a 'continuous serial', within the context of serials broadcast on

British television and radio. She argues that it is through the organization of the passage of time, the relation between character and narrative and, finally, the use of gossip that the continuous serial is both able to 'run for years' and 'preserve a basic stability while making enough changes to prevent tedious repetition' (Dyer et al. 1981: 9). Geraghty defines the continuous serial through its organization of time, the use of characterization and narrative and the way that gossip both works within the structure of the serial and as a way of linking the audience with the series.

In the same collection, Marion Jordan discusses the relationship of *Coronation Street* to the conventions of social realism when she explains the basis of social realism and its adaptation in the continuous serial:

> life should be presented in the form of a narrative of personal events, each with a beginning, a middle and an end, important to the central characters concerned but affecting others only in minor ways; that the resolution of these events should always be in terms of the effect of personal intervention. (Dyer et al. 1981: 28)

She continues with the exposition that the soap opera must work with these conventions but also include its own, inter alia the intertwining of plots and the minor resolution of problems. She identifies generic conventions that the soap opera has developed – the shared public spaces where characters can meet together and generic signs to signify the class position of its characters. She introduces the concept of stereotypes for the representation of the characters and while she claims the presence of stereotypical women characters she explains their strength by claiming them to be from a generation or profession which allows assertiveness and independence. She asserts that the programme uses conventions of social realism together with the art of the realism of the production to create a fusion of the reality of the programme. She also argues that there is a 'huge' and 'overt' use of caricature – citing Mrs Walker and Ena Sharples as examples – and identifies a sophisticated use of language to augment the comedy. Jordan's analysis provides a range of theoretical tools which form a starting point for placing the soap opera within an academic framework.

My own book *Crossroads: The Drama of a Soap Opera* (1982) was greeted with surprise and great interest by the media. The interest was that an academic could be seriously considering the form of soap opera as a legitimate subject for academic study. The genre had been largely overlooked as though it was not 'worthy' of the effort of academic analysis.

Interests in the effects of soap opera on viewers had already been part of the academic 'effects' research (Katz and Lazersfeld 1955) which examined the effects of the radio daytime soap opera on their female audiences. As the American series *Dallas* became one of the first global 'super'-soaps to entertain audiences around the world, so the academic interest in the form grew. Ien Ang (1985) conducted a study of the reaction of female viewers in the Netherlands. Through an analysis of their letters she revealed that the women had an emotional involvement with the series and that there was a pleasure involved in watching the programmes. She writes: 'It seems therefore impossible to ascertain whether the pleasure of *Dallas* that is based on a recognition of and identification with the tragic structure of feeling is intrinsically good or bad' (Ang 1985: 135). She concludes:

> The politics of representation does matter. But the fact that we can identify with these positions and solutions when we watch *Dallas* or women's weepies and experience the pleasure from them is a completely different issue: it need not imply that we are also bound to take up these positions and solutions in our relations to our loved ones and friends, our work, our political ideas, and so on. (Ang 1985: 135)

Ang recognized the pleasure in and the active involvement of the audience to the form, but she is not so sure that the pleasure that we obtain from that involvement is paramount. But: 'Fiction and fantasy', she says, 'function by making life in the present pleasurable, or at least liveable' (Ang 1985: 135).

Some of the most interesting studies conducted about the soap opera have come from America. Robert Allen's work (1985, 1992 and 1995) has traced the global nature of the genre and discussed its importance in many academic disciplines. He has identified the aesthetic disdain with which the genre has been greeted by both early academics and critics. He has studied the form and traced it as a genre and through its narrative development and relationship with audiences. Mary Ellen Brown (1990, 1994) has shown the importance of the soap opera in the development of women's discourse and how the form is used by women within their lives to explore their notions of their own positions and strengths. Her work spans soaps in the USA, the UK and Australia and is one of the strong ethnographic works which unites women audiences with the cultural form. The strength of women as audience and their relationship to the form was studied by Ellen Seiter et al. (1989) as they worked towards an ethnography of soap opera viewers in Oregon. This study again revealed the importance of the soap opera in the context of the every-day lives of the women and analysed the way they perceived the pro-grammes as texts and the role of the programmes in their lives. All of these studies foreground the importance of the soap opera as a force within the area of media texts. The female viewers actively engaged with the programmes and integrated them into their own discourse and interests.

In his study of *EastEnders*, David Buckingham (1987) revealed that it was the fact that the audience had privileged knowledge of everything that was happening in the series that was one of the attrac-tions of the programme. His study was based on group discussions with adolescents and he concluded that they brought their own knowledge to understanding the programme and forming opinions on what is and should be happening. Buckingham looked at the insti-tutional base of the production, the programme and the audience readings, and his is one of the few studies that takes that full circuit of production in order to work towards a complete picture of the genre.

Much of the interest of the media in the genre of the soap opera has centred on the psychological connection between the soap opera and its audience. In academic study, the work of Liebes and Katz (1989) looks at *Dallas* and its reception by a global audience in rela-tion to their differing and critically and culturally aware involvement with the series. Sonia Livingstone (1990) has taken a social psycho-logical approach to the soap opera and to the viewers' understand-ing of and psychological involvement with the characters. Hers is a fascinating and valuable study and provides insights from a discipline which gives a social psychological perspective to the analysis of the relationship between characters and viewers.

In 1991 Christine Geraghty in her book *Women and Soap Opera* set out to:

> firstly examine the role of women in prime time soap operas and the pleasures and values which are offered to them as the implied audi-ence for these programmes ... but argues that their dominant role needs to be studied more broadly in terms of the thematic preoccupa-tions of the programmes and the formal conventions which structure them. (Geraghty 1991: 6)

She looked at the soap opera from an aesthetic perspective and also developed the form through genre theory. The different themes which are part of the genre, and the importance of the programmes for women in terms of the pleasures in the form, are all part of this study.

One of the strengths of Geraghty's arguments is to identify the difference between the positions of pleasure which are offered to women by the soap opera text and the 'social subject positioned through race, gender and class' (Geraghty 1991: 39).

Geraghty's comprehensive study examines the representation of families, the construction of community in soap opera and the possibilities of changing representations of sex, race and class. A major strength of the study is that it includes soap operas from Britain and America and concentrates on the themes which are common to both. However, the comparison can only be at the level of the generic features of the content and the form of the programmes, for in the matters of production there is little to compare the British lower-budget and the American prime-time filmed series. Geraghty signals the changing areas of interest in the soap opera as characters and storylines began to include issues relating to men, and she questions whether this movement will ultimately harm the relationship between the genre and its women viewers.

A study which used ethnography to explore the role of the soap opera in the perceptions of viewers is Marie Gillespie's *Television, Ethnicity and Cultural Change*. This ground-breaking and comprehensive study examines the role of television in the transformation and creation of identity among young Punjabi Londoners. While the study explores a number of aspects of their lives and their relationship to various mass media, one of its areas of interest is the role of the soap opera in the lives of the young people (Gillespie 1995: 142–74). Gillespie reveals how the young people relate to and use the Australian series *Neighbours* to fulfil functions and cultural roles in their own lives. Her informants saw a similarity between so many aspects of their own lives and the lives of the characters in *Neighbours* that they intertwined their own cultural norms with those of the characters in the soap opera. They frequently commented, in particular, on the multiple relationships between local gossip and soap gossip. Gillespie notes how they moved between 'soap talk' and 'real talk' and how this fluidity indicated the way that they understood the series. They engaged with the series, with the all-white cast, and saw its themes and characters as being intimately related to their own lives.

The value of the soap opera to the young people is also expressed as cultural capital where knowledge of characters and storylines helps to cement friendship and facilitates the discussion of ways in which similar problems have been solved by characters in the soap opera. The way that the young people make use of the soap opera spans many aspects of their cultural lives: 'Soap talk facilitates discussion of a range of topics, such as the attractiveness of certain male characters, which would be taboo in parental company' (Gillespie 1995: 147). Gillespie's study shows that many aspects of this particular soap opera are relevant to her respondents, and the fact that they move easily between the soap opera and their own lives shows the use that specific audiences make of the genre. Her findings echo my own in earlier writings about the genre (Hobson 1982, 1989) and foreshadow the findings on audiences in chapter 6. Her study is vital for seeing the importance of the genre to audiences.

Finally, in culmination of her own long-standing academic interest in soap operas – which began in 1977 at the Centre for Contemporary Cultural Studies when we first shared an interest in *Crossroads* (see Brunsdon 1981: 32) – Charlotte Brunsdon published her Ph.D. thesis in 2000. She has traced the growth, critique and celebration of the genre – and the concurrent development of the feminist scholars and studies – over the years of its development. She signals the interests of the book in her introduction:

> This book traces the development of British and US feminist television criticism through particular attention to the study of one genre, the soap opera, in the years from 1975 to 1986. It is the study of the development of a certain kind of academic television criticism, rather than television production and is thus less concerned with soap opera on television than with soap opera in the seminar room. (Brunsdon 2000: 1)

While academic theory has accurately traced the development of the genre as a women's genre – and has seen its importance in its connection with women as audience – the soap opera has also been seen as one of the main texts of popular television which has broken down the boundaries between high and low culture (Brunsdon 1990: 41).

However, while academic discourse has recognized the form, it has tended to see the development of the genre into areas of masculine concern as being detrimental and moving away from women's issues. In fact, the genre has evolved into one which is of vital importance to the industry, and this has elevated it to one which is recognized and praised by broadcasters (see chapter 1). Indeed, the genre is now the subject of numerous academic courses, both in Britain and in universities across the world, and as the form shows no sign of losing its popularity it will, no doubt, expand into other areas of academia. The genre has its own intrinsic qualities and concepts, intellectual concerns and identifiable structures. It is currently one of the most important genres within television production.

British soap opera and literature – the novel, 'realism' and the soap opera

While soap opera is studied in relation to television theory and theories of audience, it is, in fact, to literature and literary theory that I want to look for the closest relationships. Established as a modern form of drama, it is possible to see the soap opera as having its origins in oral literature, folk tale, storytelling and, more recently, the novel. From Richardson's *Clarissa*, through the nineteenth-century serials of Charles Dickens, the domestic and personal detail in the novels of Jane Austen and George Eliot, and the tales of northern life written by Mrs Gaskell to the modern literature of Barbara Pym – all tell tales and stories of the everyday lives, loves, joys and sorrows of the characters. Literary works feed into soap operas because the main credentials of their central and peripheral characters are that they are totally believable and their lives are full of incidents and emotions which are universal. Indeed, from the criticism which was levelled against the novels of the eighteenth century and the realist novels of the nineteenth century, it is possible to see the novel as the eighteenth- and nineteenth-century form which took the brunt of criticism for being about the everyday lives of ordinary people. When the nineteenth-century realists wrote about their own works, they could have been writing in defence of the soap opera.

In the early eighteenth century a new literary form developed in Britain. The rise of the novel and the works of Defoe, Richardson and Fielding instituted a break from the literary traditions, which had taken romance, fantasy and the epic as the dominant form. The novel, with its concentration on the individual, is well described by Watt (1972):

> The novel is the form of literature which most fully reflects this individualist and innovating reorientation. Previous literary forms had reflected the general tendency of their cultures to make conformity to traditional practice the major test of truth: the plots of classical and renaissance epic, for example, were based on past history or fable. This literary traditionalism was first and most fully challenged by the novel, whose primary criterion was truth to individual experience – individual experience which is always unique and therefore new. (Watt 1972: 13)

The novel was, in effect, new: it broke from literary traditions and established itself as a new form, which abandoned previously essential devices of literary forms. The main difference in the literary form of the novel was described by Watt as:

a broad and necessarily summary comparison between the novel and previous literary forms reveals an important difference: Defoe and Richardson are the first great writers in our literature who did not take their plots from mythology, history, legend or previous literature. (Watt 1972: 14)

What they did was develop and use different forms to tell the stories of their protagonists. Traditional plots were rejected and individual human experience and the way that individuals coped with their lives became the subject of the novel. Watt says that when Defoe began to write his fiction, he did not follow traditional plots but 'allowed his narrative order to flow spontaneously from his own sense of what his protagonists might plausibly do next' (Watt 1972: 14).

The individual and the universal

The theoretical perspective that developed was that the individual experience was important – a break with the previous belief that 'universals' were of paramount importance. The relationship between individual and universal experience is crucial in relation to the appeal of soap operas. However, what has now developed in the form of the soap opera is that the experiences of the individual are seen as valuable precisely because they *do* carry resonance with universal experiences. The individual is appreciated because they share experiences, feelings and emotions with the audience. The thoughts and practical experiences of the everyday way of life are the main theme of the soap opera, and it is the way that individual characters handle their lives and the way that their actions and experiences resonate with the experiences of the audience that forges the bond between the characters in the drama and the audience.

While it is not seen as a pure literary form, soap opera can be seen as developing directly from the novel. Its subject matter, characters, and individual themes are similar, and the relationship between the novel and the soap opera is clearly familial. The two forms are peopled by similar characters, situated in similar locations and with the similar concerns of everyday life. Where the difference occurs is in the structure of the forms, and the effect this has on the content of the stories. The novel, even when it is written in serial form, ultimately has to end. No writer or publisher has ever continued writing or publishing books for forty years, the length of time which Granada has continued to produce *Coronation Street*. No stories have continued for so long and given so much detail of the lives of their characters. When the novelist has to bring the story to an end it is often the hardest part of the task. E. M. Forster in *Aspects of the Novel* writes:

> Nearly all novels are feeble at the end. This is because the plot requires to be wound up. Why is this necessary? Why is there not a convention, which allows a novelist to stop as soon as he feels bored? Alas, he has to round things off, and usually the characters go dead while he is at work, and our final impression of them is through deadness. (Forster 1971: 102)

The writer of a soap opera has no such problem as to how to end a story. The form is never-ending and there is no need to construct false endings because, as is the case with the novel, the symmetry of the plot requires everything to be brought together. Soaps do not have to end, unless the broadcaster decides they no longer want the series. Even then, there is no need to round everything off, for the whole point about soap opera is that it continues even when we are not watching it. The dramatic engine which drives the narrative along is what I would term *recurrent catastasis*. Catastasis is 'the part of a drama in which the action has reached its height' (Chambers 1972: 201). With the soap opera, as one dramatic narrative theme reaches its climax, another one is still working towards achieving the same height. The audience never need to be disappointed because there is always more coming along behind. The multiple catastases also mean that there is always a reason for the audience to stay watching. While the use of the 'hook' is not blatantly prevalent in current soap operas, there is always a continuing story to bring the audience back to the next episode. The climaxes will continue and the *recurrent catastasis* is what drives the drama of the soap opera.

I have started at the end, or rather the lack of an ending, to discuss the difference between the novel and the soap opera. However, Forster (1971) in his excellent analysis of what he terms 'aspects of the novel', gives a brilliant exposition of the various elements which define the form. Applying these to the soap opera shows the proximity of the forms. Forster explores the difference between people we know in everyday life and characters in books. He is writing about the way that the novelist creates characters, but the analysis which he makes is absolutely applicable to the characterization in the soap opera and, indeed, in other dramatic televisual forms. Forster writes:

> In daily life we never understand each other, neither complete clair-voyance nor complete confessional exists. We know each other approximately, by external signs, and these serve well enough as a basis

for society and even for intimacy. But people in a novel can be understood completely by the reader, if the novelist wishes; their inner as
well as their outer life can be exposed. And this is why they often seem
more definite than characters in history, or even our own friends; we
have been told all about them that can be told; even if they are imper-
fect or unreal they do not contain any secrets, whereas our friends do
and must, mutual secrecy being one of the conditions of life upon this
globe. (Forster 1971: 54–5)

This explanation is beneficial when considering how the characters
are drawn and also how audiences 'know' characters. The verisimilitude of characterization and the ability of the novelist, scriptwriter,
actor and director to reveal everything about the characters mean
that it is not surprising that the characters appear to be so 'real' that
audiences feel that they know them. It also gives a clue to why the
characters appear to be so real. It is because, like the novelist, the
dramatist and others involved in creating the characters can reveal
far more about them than we could ever know about friends or family
or neighbours, or, indeed, about anyone we feel we know. What the
soap opera provides is *intimate familiarity* with the characters; more-
over, that intimate familiarity is shared by other members of the audiences, so that the shared knowledge can contribute towards the belief
in the 'reality' of the genre. Talking about the lives of the characters
and discussing their secrets does not constitute gossip because, in
reality, they are not our friends or neighbours. There is no betrayal
of confidentiality, no disloyalty in sharing intimate secrets, because
the drama has already shared its secrets with us as viewers.

Defining the form – variations on a theme – series and serials

Before defining the 'pure' form of British soap opera, there are a
number of sub-genres which, while having a close familiarity with the
soap opera, have significant differences from the definition of the
genre operating in this book. One of the definitions which has
changed has been in relation to the difference between series and
serials. The serial form is one which has been adapted from literature, and the series is a form which is peculiar to radio, and more
particularly to television. The serial has established characters, settings and an unfolding narrative whose plots and storylines continue
from one episode to another. Often television companies work with
adaptations of the 'classic serials'. A series can consist of self-

contained episodes, although it has the same core set of characters and often similar situations. It can also consist of a set of episodes, often thirteen, in which each episode has a story which reaches a form of closure at the end of the episode. However, there are also long-running storylines. An example of this form would be the American series *Dallas* and *Dynasty*. It is a form much less used in British productions with the exception of the BBC production *Holby City*, the hospital spin-off series from the accident and emergency series *Casualty*. Even the medical drama series *Casualty* does not have year-round transmission; thus, though it now carries more of the themes of the soap opera in that it concentrates on the personal lives of the medical staff, it does not form part of the pure soap opera genre.

With the expansion of both terrestrial and satellite television channels there are now more offerings of the original American daytime series, which are much closer to the original form. Those that are shown on Channel 5 and on the various satellite channels tend to be the more extreme and glamorous versions of the series. One of the main features of the daytime series is their setting, always small towns without any distinguishing features, 'Anytown', 'Your Town and My Town'. One of the specific features of American daytime series is that they can be anywhere and that anyone from across the vastly differing states of America can identify with the anonymity of the location. They also have links with American literature and are influenced by the 'gothic'. To understand the inclusion of the 'dream' sequence in *Dallas* – when Bobby emerged from the shower telling Pam it had all been a dream, and to see the episode when Pam went searching in the Emerald forests of South America to find her later love – as part of the genre, it is necessary to know that within the American daytime series, there are some bizarre gothic elements which are seen to be quite natural.

British series have to have a recognizable location, even if it is only recognizable from other fictional forms, and a location within a known region seems to be one of the requirements for the success of the form. While all the previous drama series can be seen as being within the wider family of soap opera – and certainly contain many of the necessary elements for being considered as part of the genre – they are variations on the basic form. The main differences which determine whether drama series are soap operas are connected with the number of episodes and, thus, the production process and the regularity of transmission. While this book touches on other forms of series drama, it does, for the most part, concentrate on the specific form of British television drama which I have defined as being the soap opera.

Definitions of the soap opera have changed historically as the form has evolved. What was an adequate definition in 1982 needs to be refined to reflect the changes in the genre which have taken place during the last twenty years. Writing at the beginning of 2002, a brief definition would be: 'Soap opera is a radio or television drama in serial form which has a core set of characters and locations, and is transmitted at least three times a week, fifty-two weeks of the year.'

This, however, is a very basic definition and an expanded version can incorporate some of the other necessary ingredients and a reminder of the historical specificity of the definition. My 1982 definition was adequate for the genre at that time but it needs to be expanded to bring it up to date and indicate how the genre has expanded and evolved during the last twenty years. At that time I wrote:

> Soap opera has a specific location and core set of characters around whose lives the main storylines are woven. There are additional characters who may come and go and whose lives in some way touch those of the main characters. Each episode has a number of themes and stories running through it and there is a cliffhanger at the end of the episode to hold the audience in suspense until the next episode, and to encourage them to watch again.
>
> These serials have traditionally offered a range of strong female characters and this has proved a popular feature of the genre for its audience. They show women of different ages, class and personality types and offer characters with whom many members of their female audience can empathize. They also include male characters often for romantic interest, sometimes as comic characters or 'bad' characters, but in the main the men do not have the leading roles within the serials. (Hobson 1982: 33)

It is now essential to see the soap opera as a form which includes a wide range of representations of modern men. The expansion of male characters has transformed the genre and they now share the personal and emotional elements which were previously seen as the preserve of women characters. The developmental element of men's characters, including their talking about problems and decisions, was crucial from a dramatic point of view. The soap opera is a form which is driven not by action but by dialogue. Since many of the male forms of drama are driven by action and dynamism, if the male characters were ever to appear as more than peripheral or subsidiary characters, they had to develop characteristics which allowed them to *talk*. So men emerged as central characters when they began to talk to their friends and loved ones, both female and male.

Again, in 1982 it was perfectly accurate to say: 'There are few children in soap operas, which does tend to detract from their representation of "real life", but this is caused by the difficulties in sustaining babies and children in a long-running serial' (Hobson 1982: 33). That too has changed, and now children and young people are a major part of the genre. Many started as babies and children and have grown within the series. Children and young people form a major element both within all the soap operas as characters and as members of the audience. In fact, it is now apparent that the series can be seen as a *Bildungsroman* of the development of the characters of many of the young people: Michelle and Mark Fowler and Ian Beale and Sharon Watts in *EastEnders*, Jackie and Mike Dixon in *Brookside*, and certainly Sandy and Jill Richardson in the first series of *Crossroads*. The audience has watched these characters grow up and learn through the experiences with which they have been confronted. Of course, the longest-running example of this aspect of characterization is in the 40-year life-time learning experience of Ken Barlow in *Coronation Street*: the character emerged from his experience at Teacher Training College to return to his working-class family, and he has continued to learn, albeit very slowly, through the forty years of transmission. This ability to follow a character from teenage years is unique to the soap opera. It enables the characters to reflect a longer period of development – which also relates to the period known to the audience. It is again the *intimate familiarity* with both the characters and the period – running contemporaneously with the experiences of the audience – which heightens the unique relationship which the audience has with the form.

The vital ingredient – engaging the audience

The genre has expanded both in the number of soap operas and in the range of characters and subjects which form the narratives. While it is relatively easy to define the structural elements which form the basis of the soap opera, that is not the whole story of the genre. Soap opera has an additional element, one that is vital for the form to survive as a long-running continuous part of the history of television: soap opera has to engage its audience. Its stories must be the stories of the audience and its predominant emotion must be that of recognition – recognition of the characters and recognition of the stories they tell. It must be ordinary. There are new forms of programmes which have taken many of these features from the soap opera and evolved into hybrids and hydra of the genre. These are discussed in chapter 7. They are not, however, soap operas, and while the form expands and extends, it still requires certain elements to be truly defined as a soap opera. Some of the elements which make up the soap opera are discussed in the rest of this book, but at this point a definition of the genre which emanates from British television productions would have to adhere to the following definition:

Soap opera is a radio or television drama in series form, which has a core set of characters and locations. It is transmitted at least three times a week, for fifty-two weeks of a year. The drama creates the illusion that life continues in the fictional world even when viewers are not watching. The narrative progresses in a linear form through peaks and troughs of action and emotion. It is a continuous form with recurring catastasis as its dominant narrative structure. It is based on fictional realism and explores and celebrates the domestic, personal and everyday in all its guises. It works because the audience has intimate familiarity with the characters and their lives. Through its characters the soap opera must connect with the experience of its audience, and its content must be stories of the ordinary.

This simple definition aims to include all series which can be strictly defined as being part of the genre and attempts to exclude those series which do not qualify for the form in its purest sense. This book sets out to examine the aspects of the cycle of production and reception of the soap opera on British television. It looks at the various elements which form the phenomenon of the soap opera and combine to make it a major form of television art, whose importance both to the television industry and the audience shows no sign of decline.

Part I
The Soap Business

1

Soap Opera and the Broadcasting Industry

The essential soap

Popular journalism encourages the belief that soap opera is essential for the audience. It is the fix for their daily habit, which can spread across a number of different addictions; some may be addicted to one soap, some to two, three or even four soaps. While soap opera viewers may take pleasure from the form, it is, in fact, the broadcasters who really need the dramas for the success of their channels. For having the right soap operas brings audience share, and audience share and ratings are what soaps deliver to the broadcasters. Getting high ratings gives overnight, if not instant, satisfaction. But then they need to do it again and again, and to keep being able to get a high score week after week, month after month. Whilst it has always been recognized that soap opera is needed to bring and retain audiences for a channel, its role in a more competitive multi-channel era has and will become even more important. Soaps are essential to broadcasters. They are the lifeblood of the schedule. In his Huw Wheldon Memorial Lecture at the Royal Television Society Symposium, 16 September 1999, in Cambridge, Mal Young, Head of Series, BBC Drama Group, spoke of the importance of soap opera:

> Channel Controllers love them. So do the advertisers and the schedulers. They're often referred to by a channel as the flagship programme. A show that can define and identify that channel and its viewers. A good quality soap can serve as a great entry point for the viewers, when

coming to a channel. They can be drawn to other programming that they would not normally sample.

Soap operas are vital to the television industry because, as Mal Young states, they are often referred to by a channel as 'the flagship programme'. They can define and identify the channel and its viewers. While it has always been important for the 'brand' of a television channel to be strong, it has and will become more and more important as the television industry moves further into the multi-channel era. When the move from analogue to digital is complete, and electronic programme guides become the navigator for viewers, then soap operas will become not only the lighthouse to guide them to other programmes, but the home port, as the maelstrom of channels scream like sirens luring viewers to sample their wares. If the ecology of broadcasting is to be preserved in the next turbulent period, soap operas are one of the most important tools for branding and bringing viewers back to channels. This chapter will explore the importance of the soap opera from the perspective of the broadcasting industry. It will draw on interviews and discussions with leading broadcasting figures. The aim of the chapter is to establish the function of the genre within the broadcasting industry, which is essential for any understanding of the popularity and continuing and increasing importance of the genre.

Traditionally, the soap opera has been a form which, although vital to the health of the television channels, has not been one that has been hugely respected by all members of the broadcasting hierarchy. This attitude has undergone a radical re-think, as is revealed in my discussions with the programme executives. When I first wrote about soap opera in the 1980s the form was seen by controllers as essential as part of the broadcasting range, but it was certainly not held in the high esteem which is now apparent across all the broadcasting companies. Formerly, the function of a soap opera was to deliver high audiences to a channel, and the job of the channel controller was to keep that audience watching for the rest of the night. The role of the soap opera is now much more complex and integral to the overall shape of the schedule throughout the evening.

At this point I need to explain the context of the interviews which are used in this chapter. In the winter of 1999 I interviewed the broadcasting executives whose comments form the basis of the information in this chapter. I knew all of them fairly well and we had talked about soap opera and other forms of popular television on many occasions over a number of years. The interviews lasted from one to two hours and only a tiny proportion of their opinions are given in this chapter.

Soap opera and the schedule

It is the spine of the schedule. It's at the heart of the ITV proposition.
David Liddiment, Director of Programmes, ITV Network Centre

The importance of soap opera for all broadcasters was articulated by the executives who control the schedules on British television, and each one cited the importance of soap operas in their schedules and stressed their crucial role in planning the whole evening's viewing. The Director of Programmes at ITV Network Centre, David Liddiment, discussed the main function of *Coronation Street* for ITV:

> I think it is the spine of the schedule. It's at the heart of the ITV proposition, which is television at eye level that connects directly to its audience. . . . It's not television you look up to, it's not television you look down at, it's television that speaks your language. Looks you in the eye. It directly connects to a large part of our audiences and its concerns. It echoes our audience; it's very true to life. . . . If we as a channel are about massness, about embracing, involving, bringing people together, dispersed people together, then *Coronation Street* is absolutely bang at the centre of that proposition.

So the first importance of the soap opera to the television executive is that it *connects* with their audience. It speaks to them and it brings to the channel a regular and committed audience. For the secret of soap opera is that the broadcaster has to provide a programme which engenders in the audience an ongoing and constantly renewing interest in the characters and their stories. They have to want to know more, and in order to satisfy their curiosity they have to come back to the channel and watch the next episode. David Liddiment's *eye level* metaphor is an indication of the relationship which the soap opera has with its audience. The genre must be on the same level as the audience it addresses, and since the audience for the soap opera spans age, class, gender and race demographics, then the genre must speak of universals with which all members of the audience can empathize. It must, in David Liddiment's words, 'echo the audience'.

Once the broadcasters have found their holy grail in a successful soap opera, they treasure and cherish it and make it the cornerstone of their scheduling. Every programme controller emphasizes the importance of the soap opera in their individual scheduling plans. Speaking for ITV, David Liddiment said:

Technically it is the spine of our schedule, on which we build four evenings a week. So it's critical to the success of the ITV schedule that *Coronation Street* is healthy and strong. The strong nights on ITV tend to be the nights when *Coronation Street* is on, and the strong nights at the BBC tend to be the nights when *EastEnders* is on. Fight out Monday night between us.

David Liddiment clearly articulates the vital importance of *Coronation Street* to the ITV schedule:

Soap opera is important because it brings in a large regular audience and that provides a foundation stone for the rest of the evening's viewing. It is valuable in its own right and commercially, in terms of the audience it attracts to the channel, but it is also valuable in terms of what you can schedule off it. What you can promote around it in terms of the rest of the schedule.

Liddiment clearly expresses the *value* of soap operas as a commercial tool in the armoury of the scheduler. Liddiment is one of the British television executives with vast experience of soap opera. As a producer of *Coronation Street*, Director of Programmes at Granada and Head of ITV Network Centre, he has worked on and been responsible for soap operas and many other popular programmes for the ITV network. His views on the significance of soap operas, not just for ITV but for British television in general:

I think that Britain is unique in that each major terrestrial channel has a soap opera and they all play at different times to large audiences, or large audiences relative to the scale of the channel. I think that is unique. It may have spread, but in the 1960s and 1970s it differentiated British television to have these more ambitious soap operas. If you look at the daytime soap opera in America, which in a way they all seem to have derived from, there is something pretty cynical about them. They are all story, all event and they have a certain sort of instant gratification. You can watch them and get into them straight away and you can leave them straight away. Ours – and I include *Brookside* and *EastEnders* – are more rich and complex and sit in peak time. Soap opera in America was born out of a kind of commercial need. And I think that ours were born out of a kind of imagination, and to varying degrees I think that they still show that. So *EastEnders* is critical to BBC1's success and survival, *Coronation Street* to ITV and *Brookside* for Channel 4. In their own way, they all in some ways reflect the character of the channel, or help to define the nature and character of the channel.

A tool around which to build the schedule, but also a means of *branding* the channel, is a major function of the soap opera for the broadcaster. The notion of branding is discussed further below. Since I conducted this interview with David Liddiment in November 1999, he has commissioned the Yorkshire Television soap opera *Emmerdale* to provide five episodes per week. Running at 7.00 p.m., these aim to strengthen the ITV schedule.

> *Soap is the ultimate connecting point between BBC1 and its audience.*
>
> Peter Salmon, Controller BBC1

The importance of the soap opera to the health of the channels is a point which was stated quite forcefully by Peter Salmon, Controller of BBC1 (now Controller of Sport at the BBC). Salmon, also an executive who has experience as Director of Programmes at Granada, appreciates the importance of the genre for the channel. Like David Liddiment, he is a great supporter of the soap opera and represents that new breed of executive who admires the genre, appreciates its strengths and understands its importance in the ecology of broadcasting. Articulating the importance of soap opera in his position of Controller of BBC1, Salmon presented his initial views on the genre:

> I suppose soap is the ultimate connecting point between BBC1 and its audience. It is the point at which you judge the temperature and the well-being of mainstream channels. If your soap is good or excellent then the channel is often good or excellent. On a practical level it is the way in which the largest number of BBC1 viewers connect with the channel. So the slots around it bask in the halo effect of a good soap.

The need for schedulers to have a soap opera is perceived by them as both a business tool and an emotional link with their audience – to unite with their everyday lives, even if only to bring them to the channel. Peter Salmon articulates the relationship between the BBC, its audience and the value of their soap opera:

> We need soap operas, as compass points, as reference points in the schedule. Schedules are quite confusing, as you get more schedulers and more channels, I think that schedules are quite hard to read for the public. I'm not belittling them, I'm saying that we are not as important as we think we are, and you have to give . . . reference points in your schedule that they can see from a way out and that tap into the

rhythms of their own lives. And I think soap operas, alongside the news, probably, are some of the few moments in a week's schedule, that people are instinctively drawn to. And we exploit them in that in a benign way. They are the reference points across the week. We build our schedules, literally build our schedules, around them. We build whole nights around them, and I think they largely communicate whether the schedule is well or ill. And good soaps are really good indicators as to whether channel controllers, like me, and drama executives are paying attention to the schedules. Because if you are neglecting soaps, you are likely to be neglecting other things.

The building of schedules around the soap opera provides a new function for the soap opera. In earlier periods, certainly in the 1980s, the function of the soap opera was to bring the audience to the channel, and it was then the job of the succeeding programmes to retain the audience. The 'inheritance factor' was important, but it certainly was not the responsibility of the soap to carry the channel or alter the evening's viewing. Salmon acknowledges the important role which *EastEnders* has for BBC1, as does David Liddiment for the soap opera on ITV. He also touches on a vital difference in the broadcasting world in which the terrestrial channels are competing. Schedules are more confusing, and there are, indeed, more schedulers, but scheduling is not necessarily as good as when some of the individual schedulers scheduled their channels in the past. Schedules should never be confusing; if they are, the schedulers have not done their job properly.

> *Scheduling is what I call window-dressing.*
>   Michael Grade

Michael Grade, who has worked as Director of Programmes at the BBC and Chief Executive of Channel 4, is one of the television executives who has worked in television both in the UK and the US. He is not a programme maker but a television executive who has a wide overview of the television industry in both countries. He knows how to recognize a good idea for a programme, support the programme makers and then use it to the very best advantage for success in whichever broadcasting organization he is working. He is renowned for his scheduling skills and is one of a handful of executives who had an instinctive knowledge of how to schedule programmes and link with the everyday lives of their audience. His knowledge of all types of programmes is vast, but he is particularly strong on entertainment and that includes the soap opera. Grade believes that scheduling is the vital art of television, as he and I have discussed at other times. Here he confirms this belief:

> Well, scheduling is what I call window-dressing. You go to one of the big stores, big successful department stores, you know like Harvey Nichols, and the people who do the window only come in after the buyers have been out and bought the product, and the scheduler is essentially the window-dresser. You have got to put the goods in the window in an order and in a shape and style that will attract people in.

Grade does not use the expression 'window-dressing' to mean superfluity or frippery but rather in the sense of 'displaying wares', arranging them in the most attractive fashion to attract audiences. For it is in the arrangement of the available programmes that lies one of the most successful skills of the programme executive. Grade continues by talking about the function of the soap opera for television companies. His explanation coincides with that of Peter Salmon and locates the soap opera, alongside news, as a major tool in the scheduling and, importantly, the *branding* of channels. Grade explained:

> The primary function [of the soap opera] is to distinguish your channel from other channels. There are a number of landmarks which you have in your channel. One is news, and your style of news and your news presenters give you a brand differentiation. The importance of the news for branding your channel is that it's there every night, and soaps really fall into that same category, they provide the same branding opportunity. Obviously there is the loyalty factor and so on if the show is successful, but just as *Coronation Street* brands ITV, so *EastEnders* brands BBC1 and *Brookside* is a very big part of the Channel 4 brand.
>   The importance of soaps is that they are fifty-two weeks a year. There are very, very few shows, other than news, which are on the air fifty-two weeks a year, in multiple episodes per week. They are the landmarks that distinguish your channel from others and, therefore, they are very, very important. Now they have to work to be successful and if they are, then obviously they are commercially very valuable.

In these extracts Grade highlights some of the major functions which the soap opera performs for the broadcaster – vital functions in the success of their business. Crucial is the role in the *branding* of the channel because it is to the brand of the channel that broadcasters think that viewers react. *Frequency and regularity* are also functions which are fulfilled by the soap opera and, like news, they are always part of the output of the channel. Some might say they are omnipresent. What this means is that there is always a familiarity, there are programmes which the audience know and, as Grade says, these are *'landmarks that distinguish your channel from others'*. And the more distinctive your own brand, the more successful your channel.

The cost of soap operas

One of the benefits of soap opera for broadcasters is that they are a very cost-effective programme. While broadcasters do not give out detailed budgets of their programmes, they are willing to give ball-park figures to indicate the costs of different drama productions. Mal Young gave me ballpark figures for various BBC drama series and discussed the other relevant information regarding costs. Examples of figures are:

- *EastEnders* approximately £130,000 per half hour
- *Casualty* approximately £450,000 per hour
- *Holby City* approximately £370,000 per hour
- *Doctors* approximately £40,000 per half hour
- *Dalziel and Pascoe* approximately £700–800,000 per hour

Clearly *EastEnders* and the newly developed daytime series *Doctors* are the least costly of the series under Mal Young's control, but there are other factors which affect the cost of production. Mal Young explained some of the differences in costs:

> Shows like *EastEnders* or *Holby City*, which are high-volume, year-round productions can be made for less because the set-up costs can be spread over many years. Standing sets can be re-used, as opposed to short-run series or one-off dramas in which set-up costs have to be absorbed into only, say, three or four hours of television.

The more frequent the programmes, the more the costs can be spread across the number of episodes. Both *EastEnders* and *Holby City* are made at the BBC studios at Elstree, where they have their own sets which can be used for many episodes. A further advantage of the continuous series is that it enables broadcasters to strike deals with writers and actors for longer-running series. Mal Young explained:

> Deals can be struck with acting and writing talent giving them a year's contract, security and a constant wage. An actor in a shorter run may

be paid more per episode, but may do only five or six episodes. A long runner can be quite lucrative to talent, even though the individual slot cost to a channel is much lower than usual drama costs.

So the financial benefits of the soap opera and long-running series are experienced both by the television channels and by those who are involved in writing and acting in the series. Longer contracts and assured income are of great attraction to writers and actors whose income is so often precarious and spasmodic.

However, the impact of lower budgets is not necessarily obvious to viewers; its impact is on the work of the production teams in the production of the various series. Basically the more money that is available, the more time can be spent on each scene. Mal Young articulates the basic difference which budgets have on very different productions:

> The biggest impact of costs and lower budgets is on time. *Doctors* have to complete around 15–20 minutes of screen time per ten-hour day. *Dalziel and Pascoe*, on the other hand, has to complete only 3–5 minutes, giving the production much higher 'filmic' production values. *EastEnders* is slightly different as 60% of it is in a traditional studio on multi-cam, so it's difficult to compare. On single camera days (on location and on the exterior back lot) they can achieve around eight minutes per day and on multi-cam studio days it's about fifteen minutes.

While different budgets may provide continuous 30-minute dramas like *EastEnders* and *Doctors*, or the 90-minute high-quality filmed single-dramas of the four episodes of *Dalziel and Pascoe*, according to Mal Young all series hold the same value to the BBC. *EastEnders* is different from both of these dramas because it is filmed in a different way, using both fixed studio sets and outside shooting on the back lot at Elstree.

> Both *Doctors* and *D&P* hold the same value to the BBC and its audience. One provides the daytime audience with a quality five days a week lunchtime drama all year round. The other is a much loved 'crime' brand, seen as an 'event', a treat of 4 × 90 minute films per year, with top quality cast and locations.

The cost-effective nature of soap operas is a major factor in their appeal for broadcasters and the expansion and development of the genre makes it of vital importance to the future of popular broadcasting.

Public service and the soap opera – the broadcaster's view

You can use soaps which are popular and accessible to connect BBC1 public service audiences with other genres which are sometimes a bit less accessible.

Peter Salmon, Controller BBC1

The notion that the soap opera is a form of public service television is one which would not readily be recognized. These are normally defined as the more serious programmes in the schedule, but there are a number of ways in which the broadcaster can perceive that soap opera is a genre which fulfils their public service brief.

Peter Salmon, Controller BBC1, identified the role of the soap opera in attracting viewers and leading them to other programmes:

> On a practical level it is the way in which the largest number of BBC1 viewers connect with the channel. So the slots around it bask in the halo effect of a good soap. It's where you hope in a mixed channel like BBC1 that you can connect large soap audiences to, for instance, the *Dinosaurs* audience. So you can use soaps which are popular and accessible to connect BBC1, public service audiences with other genres which are sometimes, perhaps, a bit less accessible, a bit more difficult for people to penetrate. Hence, the way I scheduled *EastEnders* and *Dinosaurs* this autumn, back to back, was on purpose. It was to help both programmes and they both benefited from it. So soaps are the ultimate access point for big audiences into mainstream channels.

During the autumn of 1999 BBC1 transmitted their science programme *Walking with Dinosaurs*, a programme which traced the story of dinosaurs and used computer-designed animatronics and filmed locations to tell the story of dinosaurs. Scheduled on a Monday evening, when *EastEnders* is transmitted 8.00–8.30, Peter Salmon scheduled it immediately afterwards so that it benefited from the inherited audience and, as Salmon said, 'basked in the halo effect of a good soap'. He wanted the *EastEnders* audience to feel that there was something 'good' to watch after their soap opera had finished, and he believed that *Dinosaurs* would fulfil this role. Audiences have an intimate knowledge of the schedule, of the nuances of scheduling and of the ambience of the programmes which are offered by a good scheduler. Hence, if *Dinosaurs* was scheduled after *EastEnders*, it was reasonable to expect that they might be interested in it. Conversely, the team who made *Dinosaurs* used the theme of a series of family sagas in their narrative structure of each episode. The first episode of *Walking with Dinosaurs* attracted audiences of 15 million viewers and the average audience over the series was 13 million, making it the highest-rated science programme on British television. As it was not a series that would normally have been transmitted on BBC1, it was vital that it attracted audiences which would justify the amount of money spent on it. I asked Peter Salmon if he had expected the series to do so well.

> I knew it was original and innovative and I knew it had potential to be popular and I waited to schedule it until we had four or five episodes that week of *EastEnders*. It was a special week – it was the court case, the Steve Owen and Matthew case – so I waited until we had a very big episode and very big storylines and I knew there would be raised heat and temperature around *EastEnders*, and I thought that what I could probably do was make the heat greater and stronger by putting that block together. And I think that *Dinosaurs* being that successful owes an awful lot to a brilliant run of *EastEnders*. We launched a very important popular factual phenomenon by bouncing it, by kind of radiating it out of some of the strongest storylines on *EastEnders* for years.

However, at the same time as the strong storyline with Steve Owen and Matthew Rose, the series was about to lose perhaps its most popular star, Ross Kemp who played Grant Mitchell. The build-up to Grant leaving had been going on throughout the summer and the popularity of the actor and the character was such that his loss to the series was likely to be very serious. Planning for this loss was also important, but is here played down a little by Peter Salmon. As he spoke of the importance of the court case, I brought up the storyline which was to result in 'losing Grant'. He explained his strategy:

> I knew it was a big autumn. I had been running up to a very big autumn for six months. I obviously knew the talent [viz. Ross Kemp] was moving on and that's sad on the one hand, but it is an opportunity. You know that departures are often the most dramatic moments in soaps. It's like losing a member of your own family, or a twenty-first birthday party or a wedding, it's those high spots. So I had been planning, we had been planning a great marketing campaign behind *EastEnders* for six months; it was a very cunning strategy, where we knew we had got a good team, good talent, good writers, good storylines to bring people back to *EastEnders*. You know, people who had been defectors, to get people literally talking about *EastEnders* again, so we managed that campaign some way out, which came to a climax this autumn with the biggest storylines for years. And I decided I would launch *Dinosaurs* in the heat of all that.

The campaign to which Salmon refers was a concerted advertising campaign which centered around the lines 'EastEnders, everybody's talking about it'. It worked on the basis of simulated 'real life' observation of ordinary people talking about the storylines running in the series. This explanation from Peter Salmon brings together many of the elements involved in the planning of the soap opera storylines – the planning of the advertising campaign, the capitalizing on a strong storyline as an actor leaves the series, and the careful scheduling to enhance the potential audience of a popular factual series and give it the benefit of the high and committed audience.

So a popular drama series can act as a *conduit* leading the audience to a programme which they might not have known they wanted to watch. And for the controllers of popular mass audience channels that is a vital asset to help them achieve their aim to reach the largest number of viewers, or to gain the biggest share of audience.

Soaps then have a value over and above their own intrinsic value to the broadcaster, and they have a vital role in the armoury of the channel controllers as they plan their scheduling strategy right across their channel.

Soaps, social issues and the channel controllers

Although the television executives have similar views on the role which the soap opera plays in their schedules, their attitude to the content of the programmes can differ and in that difference can be detected some of the elements of public service which is more specific to the BBC. Peter Salmon articulates the role of the soap opera in its relation to current society. He sees the series as reflecting social conditions which exist in society and which are then *re-presented* to the audience in the series.

> I think they are a wonderful way of taking the temperature of channels, but also a way of taking the temperature of your society.... *EastEnders* is a social barometer; it's not just a soap, it's a way of taking a health check on society and its issues as well. And it is absolutely the weave and life-blood of *EastEnders*, probably more than any other soap. It's not there as graphically as *Brookside*, where you feel people walk through the door with labels on them saying 'Issue of the week'. *EastEnders* is that sort of pivotal thing which is both imaginary and comforting but also relevant and topical, and I think we on BBC1 see it as a showcase for good performance, cracking writing and stories of the day. Not 'issues of the day'. I think we are very careful not to overload it with issues, it's always got to be story and character led.

For Salmon it is recognizable that the series carries social issues but that they always follow naturally from the characters and the stories; however, he also sees the series as having a social role in acting as a 'social barometer'. Mal Young, on the other hand, sees the series as carrying a much greater force of social relevance and operating as a vehicle for handling relevant social issues and stressing the accessibility of the genre:

> I think that any form of popular drama is a very good access point for your audience. An access point for the channel. They speak to the widest possible range of audience from an 8-year-old to an 80-year-old, because of the themes which they explore. I do say that they have become the replacements for *Play for Today* because when you look at some of the plays for today . . . *Cathy Come Home* was basically an issue, a homeless issue, that would fit directly into *Brookside* now or *EastEnders*, and probably has been done.

The ability to attract an audience right across the age range and right across the demographics is one of the unique qualities which the soap opera has. And in this sense Mal Young correctly identifies the genre as being the vehicle which handles many of the social issues which were the domain of the single play in former years.

Soap opera connects directly with the audience.
     David Liddiment, Director of Programmes, ITV Network Centre

'Connecting with the audience', from Peter Salmon; 'connects directly to its audience' expressed by David Liddiment; and from Mal Young 'a good quality soap can serve as a great entry point for the viewers, when coming to a channel' – this shows that all controllers see the function of the soap opera as connecting the channel with its audience and providing points in the schedule around which they can build an evening's viewing. They are crucial in their strategy to bring viewers to a channel and to lead them to other offerings. Television executives *need* soap operas.

Saving the channels

It may seem far-fetched to suggest that the strength of a channel's soap opera is integral to the well-being of the channel and is part of the planning for the future. The importance of *EastEnders* to the BBC may have been perceived as simply being necessary to provide a soap opera for the channel. But its role was much bigger. *EastEnders* was launched in the midst of the 1980s Conservative government, which prowled like a stalker looking for prey to be devoured. The BBC was, once again, under attack from the government. Michael Grade, who was at that time Director of Programmes at the BBC, articulated the importance of the serial to the future health of the BBC when I asked him how important it was that *EastEnders* was successful when it was launched:

> To have failed with *EastEnders* would have been absolutely . . . The government were baying for the BBC. You had a market forces driven government who believed in privatizing and taking all of the great institutions and confronting them. The BBC had been through a bad time which is why they bought me back from America, because they were going through a terrible time and any excuse to bash the BBC, and a very hostile right-wing press and so on. To have had a high-profile launch for *EastEnders* and then to have failed would have been very, very difficult.

Defining the show – the business view

While the academic definition of a soap opera, including my own (see Introduction) may strive to include all elements of the genre to ensure that nothing relevant is left out, practitioners have much more succinct definitions, which reveal their own particular interest in the genre. Their opinions on soap opera are always related to its role in the schedule, and the role that the genre fills in the broadcasting business. A selection of views can be condensed into a relatively simple formula. In answer to the question 'Do you have a definition of soap opera?' the following answers were given.

- *David Liddiment* 'Continuing story, continual story, it just goes on forever.'
- *Michael Grade* 'I think it's frequency. I think it's the permanence in the schedule. It has to be fiction and it has to be permanently in the schedule – that's soap.'
- *Peter Salmon* 'It must be multi-episodic; I think they must be on several times a week. It feels to the viewers like you're on all the time, and I don't mean in the sense of being ubiquitous. I mean in the sense of being one of the few things that gives their lives some rhythm, regularity, stability, loyalty and you can't do that once a week.'

What is obvious, from all the professional programme makers and executives, is that it is the frequency of transmission which they see as the prime ingredient in the make-up of the soap opera. This is not simply a cynical business definition, because they *need* the programme for their schedules; behind it lies a far more complex reason which unites the channel, through the soap opera, with their audience. The audience is needed both for the soap opera and for the channel itself. It is the soap opera and its frequency and permanence which gives the audience an anchor point within the schedule and provides the broadcaster with, in their own opinion, their most valuable scheduling tool.

Learning the trade – soaps as a training ground

The continual process involved in the production of soap operas means that there is always the opportunity for creative staff to work on the programmes, both trainees and experienced programme makers who wish to spend a short time on a specific soap. When *Crossroads* was in its first incarnation, and from its inception, it took actors from the Birmingham Repertory Theatre to provide the first cast members for the programmes. Now soap operas often take young actors straight from drama schools, and their apprenticeships are played out in full view of an audience of 15 million. Executives also see that the turnover of actors in soap operas can be beneficial. Of course, they are unlikely to admit that losing an actor is a real body blow to a production. However, with the huge turnover of actors from the soap operas, there is always an opportunity to bring in new characters and established actors are often more than happy to join the cast of the ongoing series. Michael Grade spoke of the creative opportunities offered by the seemingly difficult situations when established actors/characters are lost to a series.

> Where soaps score is that ultimately actors get tired of doing it so you have to refresh. I don't know how many cast changes *Coronation Street* has been through or *EastEnders* or *Brookside*, and you think, 'Oh, my God, when they have gone it will be the end', but it isn't. When Den and Angie left *EastEnders* you would have thought that was it, and when Elsie Tanner and Ena Sharples left you think that is the end of it, but it isn't, and that is because it requires you to be inventive by restoring and creating new characters.

When Phil Redmond created *Brookside* he also used a number of young unknown actors, taking some from the theatres in Liverpool and Oldham and mixing them with experienced actors. Not all the inexperienced actors were young: Ricky Tomlinson, who played Bobby Grant, was a building worker who also had experience as a night club entertainer, but he immediately made the role of Bobby Grant and created a major character. When *EastEnders* began they also used young actors from some of the stage schools as well as a number of actors who were relatively unknown. The series provides vast numbers of jobs in a very unstable industry. To get a role in a soap opera means that if your character is successful and you choose to stay in the series, you can have the rare luxury of job security in an acting job. The genre has also been a training ground for actors, and many have gone on to star in other series after they have left soap operas.

For writers and directors the genre is also seen as one where they can practise their skills. For writers the structure of the soap opera provides the characters, the set, the locations, and new writers can concentrate on writing the dialogue to already created characters and situations. Directors also have learned from and progressed through their experiences working on soap operas. At Granada there has always been a tradition of their trainee directors wanting to work on 'The Street'. Some of those directors have gone on to become world famous television and film directors. David Liddiment emphasized this aspect of the value of the soap opera to the broadcaster.

> Young directors have always and still are queuing up to go on the *Street* at Granada and everyone knows, of course, about Mike Apted and Mike Newell and Charles Sturridge, but actually we now have got the next generation. People like Julian Jarrold, who made the film on Sunday night with David Jason, *All the King's Men* (BBC1). He came to Granada from being a trailer maker like me and he did some wonderful *Coronation Street*. Also Richard Sydney and Julian Ferrino, both are now making their names as leading drama directors in British television and film and they all came through the *Street*. It's a wonderful learning process for people because it provides them with a format and a structure and the sets are a given; so you don't have to think of everything from scratch, your characters are given, so you can concentrate on your craft and what these guys bring, the ones who go on to be brilliant directors, what they bring is an eye that the *Street* benefits from, because they try things. They have a particular imagination that they bring to bear on the show and the *Street* benefits from that.

It was remarkable how each of the executives to whom I spoke gave almost identical answers to all the questions about the role of soap opera in the business of broadcasting. In the following extract, Jonathon Powell, Controller of Drama at Carlton, encapsulates all the elements of the soap opera which are important to the broadcaster.

> I think they have got two, maybe three, things of major significance. They have a function and their function is to deliver ratings on a consistent basis and that's why they are in the schedules and they can deliver those ratings at a relatively low cost, particularly for drama. The cost of producing a soap opera once you have got it up and running is minimal compared to the cost of producing a standard hour of drama. . . . And once you have drama into your schedules in a very cost-effective way, you've hooked an audience in and they become involved in the lives of the characters; soaps do provide something that is ever present in the schedules, they guarantee the audience will turn up week after week and that is particularly important to any scheduler in the early evening, 7.30–8.00. Because that starts generating the audience for the channel throughout the rest of the evening. Now there is a lot of stuff talked nowadays about audience inheritance and stuff, and yes the audience do have a lot of choices but they are very sophisticated and they won't stay with a channel if the programme following is a bad programme. They will just turn off and go somewhere else. However, if you put a good programme that they really like after a soap you can really increase your audience. You can increase your audience by 25–30 per cent with something very strong. So they have a very strong functional purpose.

Jonathon Powell identifies the first value of the soap opera as *functional*, to bring an audience to the channel and to deliver that audience for other quality programmes and to do this on a regular basis. His next comment articulates why soaps have this ability to work for the broadcasters:

> Also the audience's connection with the characters is an emotional connection and that gives them an emotional relation with the channel and they become symbolic of the channel. All channels have programmes which represent them to the audience, where if you say to people 'What do you think of that, what is your favourite programme? Why is ITV better?' And they say, 'Oh, because of *Heartbeat, Coronation Street, Emmerdale, The Bill.*' Those programmes will always be at the top of the audience's mind and there really aren't any other kinds of programmes that generate the kind of perception in the audience's mind that drama does. And there are strong subsidiary reasons why they are important to broadcasting organizations, and that is to do with talent. On-screen talent, and behind the scenes talent, directors, writers, increasingly a lot of writers. . . . Increasingly you are

looking for writers who have learned how to and wish to engage emotionally with the audience in a kind of head-on way.

What Jonathon Powell goes on to explain is the emotional relationship which soaps engender with their audience and how the
ability to create that emotional relationship is increasingly needed in
the demands of a multi-channel era. What is interesting is that the
soap opera as a form is working in a practical sense for broadcasters by forging an emotional link with the audience. What Jonathon
Powell and the other executives show is that they have a deep understanding of the value and range of functions which the soap opera
performs for the broadcaster. Their responses were all similar; from
the point of view of the different channels they all articulated that
the soap opera was of vital importance to each channel.

Soap opera and the docusoap

*People were getting a bit bored with documentary styles and
they learned that character and narrative are two powerful
factors in any television show, so that was a direct steal from
popular drama.*

Mal Young

In the late 1990s a new form of television genre developed which was
directly influenced by the soap opera. The so-called 'docusoap'
started as a small bubble which lathered across screens on every
channel and seemed to be ubiquitous. This form (discussed in chapter
7), had a crucial function for television executives and television
schedules. It also meant that the soap opera was influential in the
creation of another television form. While it may have been seen by
critics as a retrograde step, for the executives searching for new ways
to attract audiences the emergence of the new genre was seen as beneficial. From the perspective of the soap opera executive, the influence
which the genre has had on other dramatic forms is perhaps more
important. While executives from the drama department saw one
of their genres having an influence on another area of television,
they also saw it as a way of revitalizing other forms of drama. So a
reciprocal set of influences took place. Mal Young explained the symbiotic relationship:

I think we have seen it [soap opera] influence other areas, particularly
over the last few years, in that 'documentaries' [the department] real-

ized that people were getting a bit bored with documentary styles and they learned that character and narrative are two powerful factors in any television show. So that was a direct steal from popular drama and now we have seen some fantastic documentaries because of it. Oddly enough I am now pushing a lot of my producers and writers to steal back. I think documentaries stole ahead of us and I think maybe the audience think 'well hold on, I can see "real", "real life", you're telling me that your soap opera is "real" and I can watch the "real" thing'.

The 'reality' which was taken from soap opera to documentary was the concentration on using 'ordinary' as a feature in the content of the form. To necessitate the illusion that the programme was being filmed in a natural way, light-weight cameras were used to take shots which gave the impression of unmediated production. The documentaries were to appear as if they simply caught the action as it happened. The use of this technique was brought into other forms of drama, but rarely used in soap operas. What was important was that the personal nature of the storylines and the 'reality' of the characters were seen to be related to the soap opera. In fact, the docusoaps were as constructed as the real soap operas. The genre had variations and while some programmes imitated the best of the soap opera, much of the output was shallow and sensationalist.

A soap too far . . . away! The *Eldorado* story

The vital importance of the soap opera to broadcasters has been illustrated by the comments which controllers have made. While the form is essential for the broadcasting business, if a soap opera does not meet the necessary requirements of the broadcaster and the audience, then it can have a spectacular demise after a high-profile launch. The story of a soap opera which was born and killed off within a period of nine months threw into high relief the importance of the genre and its political as well as creative role in the broadcasting industry. In July 1992, amidst a blaze of publicity, the BBC launched its new soap opera *Eldorado*. 'Welcome to Eldorado: a coast of golden dreams and deep dark secrets; a world of hedonism, hope and heartbreak – and the sun-drenched setting for BBC-TV's new three times a week drama serial', enticed the BBC's glossy publicity brochure. On 12 March 1993, nine months after its launch, *Eldorado* was axed by Alan Yentob, his first major act as the newly appointed Controller of BBC1. The story of what happened in the nine months, and indeed in the six months prior to the launch, brings together a number of business and creative elements which need to be present to make a successful soap opera. It did not fulfil any of the requirements of the soap opera, as identified by the executives above. It was vital for the health of the BBC, but it did not deliver what was required of it. *Eldorado* was not successful, but it was not only the content and the characters which caused problems; a number of issues of wider broadcasting policy and planning eventually all combined to effect the demise of the programme. Indeed, some of them could be seen as built-in self-destruct mechanisms, which were almost certain to destroy the programme. By examining the way that the programme developed and the problems which it experienced, it is possible to see the elements necessary for successful soap opera. In the case of *Eldorado* too many of them were missing. At first sight it may have seemed that *Eldorado* had many of the ingredients necessary to make it a success, but the overwhelming power of the other factors meant that it was impossible for it to succeed.

The BBC wanted, indeed needed, a programme, which would take over the seven o'clock slot which was to be vacated three nights a week by the axing of *Wogan*. The viewing figures for *Wogan* had dropped and Jonathan Powell, Controller of BBC1 and producer of the prestigious drama series *Testament of Youth* and *Soldier, Sailor, Tinker, Spy* was determined that any new soap opera after *EastEnders*, would need to be 'different', to prevent criticism that the BBC was only copying ITV by having more soap opera. The BBC were required to take 25 per cent of their programmes from independent producers, and the offer of a soap from one of the leading independent producers seemed to present something completely fresh and different. Powell wanted a permanent set and a soap which would tackle contemporary issues. The magic formula was offered by Verity Lambert through her independent production company, Cinema Verity. Lambert was a respected producer with experience in popular drama over thirty years. She offered a package which must have seemed irresistible. The programme was to be set in Spain, on a purpose-built set, in the mountains, with spectacular scenery and sea, and offering the bright light and sunshine which was one of the ingredients which had attracted viewers to *Neighbours* and *Home and Away*. Although its characters were to be mainly British, it offered the opportunity for a European cast and potential overseas sales. Seemingly best of all, it had Julia Smith and Tony Holland, the team who, as producer and storyliner, had created *EastEnders* and many other popular drama series. The series had potential – experienced executive producer, independent producer, experienced and successful producer and storyliner, interesting and visually appealing location, varied cast of characters. Only the latter was an unknown quantity.

The commission was awarded to Verity Lambert at the beginning of 1992 and at first it was expected that the series would be needed for an autumn launch. According to Julia Smith, in the BBC publicity brochure:

> Someone said very casually one day that the new serial would be going out three times a week rather than twice. Tony Holland and I just said, 'Forget it then, we don't want to know, we are resigning'. We had been concentrating on a bi-weekly soap. When they told us they wanted half as much again our initial reaction was that it was not possible. (BBC Enterprises 1992)

Not only did the soap need to be created but the set had to be built from scratch on a hillside in Spain. The decision to launch in July caused many of the problems which the series was about to experience. The whole production had to be moved forward at a frenetic pace, and it would appear to have been inconceivable that the earth could be moved from a mountain side, a complete set built, storylines and episodes written, actors cast and technical equipment installed, tested and operated. All this happening 1,000 miles from the known production base in London, and the whole production to be ready for transmission by early July.

After the supreme effort the decision to launch a soap opera in July was seen as a major scheduling mistake by some, including the arch-scheduler and ex-BBC Controller of Programmes Michael Grade, who wrote to confirm my assertion in a *Guardian* article that the problem with the launch of the programme was that it was at the wrong time of year (Hobson 1992). We agreed that it was the most significant feature in the problems which the series experienced. To launch a new soap opera in July is madness. The audience is moving into a time of disruption on many levels. A large proportion of the potential audience was on holiday or would be over the next few weeks. Three weeks after the launch they were watching the Olympic Games, from Barcelona. The schedules were interrupted. There was no chance to get into the habit of watching a new programme. If they had time for a break in the early evening at 7 p.m., they were sitting in their garden enjoying the sun. They were certainly not watching television and they did not have the available time, nor the inclination, to get involved in a new soap opera.

July is a period which is also known as 'the silly season' in press terms. There is so little happening which can be constituted as 'newsworthy' that journalists will jump on any story that becomes available to fill their column inches. In the case of *Eldorado* they had been courted by BBC publicity, and a number of them had been taken to the location in Spain. They were well informed about the series and they were vicious in their attack when it did not deliver what the publicity had promised. However, there was more to the attacks than a simple criticism of a new soap opera. This was a period when the BBC was itself under scrutiny. In November 1992 the government published its Green Paper on *The Future of the BBC*. Everything they did in the months leading up to the paper and in the months after its publication was subject to press comment, and the criticism of *Eldorado* was part of that adverse publicity.

The criticism of *Eldorado* as a programme was not without cause. The enthusiasm and energy which carried the production team through the early period suffered a blow when the early episodes fell short of the standard which any of those involved would have wished. A rescue package was put in place when the Executive Producer, Verity Lambert, brought in a new producer to replace Julia Smith. Corinne Hollingsworth had worked with Julia Smith on *EastEnders*. When she joined the production the series had recorded up to episode 27 and sixty further scripts were completed. She took radical action and virtually scrapped everything that had not been recorded and had the scripts rewritten. Characters were written out, not necessarily because of the actors but rather as a rationalization. Thirty-one characters to start a new soap opera is far too many for any series. Further changes were made and the programme was considerably strengthened by these changes.

Once all the changes took hold, the series began to improve considerably. Viewers were watching with more interest and the story-lines were vastly improved. However, in the end the series was axed, more because of matters of BBC politics than to do with the performance of the programme. It had not fulfilled any of the needs of the broadcasters, and it had not provided a contribution to the building structure of the schedule because it did not bring enough viewers to BBC1. It did not connect with the audience because, for the most part, they did not have experience of living permanently abroad and had no points of reference. It is, of course, a different matter to be spending time abroad on holiday and that was the reason that the idea seemed attractive to the programme makers, but the reality was not there for the audience and they did not have any empathy or shared knowledge with the characters. The programme was a victim of many mistakes on the part of the executive: too little time to remedy shortcomings was given to the production team, and the programme did not have the necessary ingredients to connect with the audience. What its spectacular failure illustrated was the importance of the genre to broadcasters and the high-profile criticism to be aroused by every problem which such a programme encountered. Michael Grade told of how the introduction of *EastEnders* had to be a major success and how it was crucial to the BBC, at the time of the launch of *Eldorado* to be seen to be delivering a successful programme. Jonathon Powell, one of the most talented executives and drama specialists, left the BBC.

As has been shown by their comments soap opera as a genre is important to broadcasters. How the genre has managed to develop over forty years as a major part of the broadcasting industry is the subject of the rest of this book. The story of the soap opera is as fascinating as some of the storylines which hold the audience and continue to bring them back to the programme, however many additional programmes they are offered. The genre has retained its position at the top of the ratings by reflecting the issues of interest to its audience and consistently delivering high audiences. How has that been achieved and what is the future of the genre for broadcasters and for their audiences?

2

Elements of Production: Features of the Form

Many different elements are required for the production of a soap opera and many features are common to all the series. These various elements of production form the main part of this book, but there are some which do not fit easily into a narrative form. For that reason I am indicating their importance in brief summaries of their function within the production of soap operas. These elements are in addition to the major issues addressed in this book, and while space does not permit extensive discussion of their importance, they are vital ingredients in a comprehensive consideration of the genre. They are aspects of the productions which should be part of the understanding or analysis of the form, and although they have different degrees of visibility, they are all vital elements in the production of the programmes.

A producer's medium

Television is a producer's medium and the soap opera is the form which clearly demonstrates their power. The strength and impetus for the soap opera comes from its producer. The original story may be the work of the writer who created the characters but once the series is commissioned and moves towards production, then the producer is the controlling and creative force who ensures the success or failure of the programme. While the original style and 'reality' of any series is created by the writer, once it is established the soap opera takes on its own reality and it is the producer who has the power to change the style or direction of the series and who holds the creative spirit of the show in their power. When they create a new show, producers can be benevolent parents who guide their charges, picking the best route for them to travel. The first producer of a soap opera is both the parent and the midwife, delivering the infant and planning every part of its passage into the tough world of television production. It is a genre in which the writer who creates the series works with the producer who brings it to the screen. There are producers who can be seen as being the leading exponents of the development of the soap opera. Granada's *Coronation Street* was created and written by Tony Warren, whose creation of characters has never been surpassed in soap opera production, but even Tony Warren has said that it was Harry Elton, a Canadian producer at Granada, who persisted in encouraging him to create the series and then persuade the executives at Granada to go with the idea (Nown 1985: 24). *Coronation Street* has had many famous producers who have nurtured the programme over its years in production. Bill Podmore was a producer in the 1970s, Mervyn Watson from 1982–91. Each was responsible for the series during periods when it was particularly strong. More recently, Jane Macnaught brought some of the most socially aware storylines to the series.

Crossroads was the idea of Lord Lew Grade, who wanted a soap opera to reflect the Midlands in the same way that *Coronation Street* reflected the north of England, and it was his idea to have the character of Meg Mortimer as the owner of the motel, but it was Reg Watson, the first producer, who created the production which became the soap opera. After Reg Watson went to Australia to create the equally successful *Neighbours*, Jack Barton took over as producer and nurtured the programme through its most successful years.

As Jeremy Isaacs began putting in place the commissioning editors and initial commissions for Channel 4, he was approached by Phil Redmond, who asked him if he would mind a soap opera which included 'so-called' bad language. Isaacs replied that he had no problem with this, and the concept of an entirely new soap opera was developed. What was new was the fact that, in *Brookside*, Phil Redmond hoped to use the natural language which the characters would use in their everyday lives. This was just one of the innovations which Phil Redmond brought to the genre, together with the use of filmic techniques while using video technology. Until this time all soap operas had been made in studio settings using the technique of multi-camera shooting, whereby the director cut between the shots offered by each camera – unless they were shooting scenes on location when film was used. What Phil Remond did was to use the techniques of film, whereby a single camera records the action from one point of view and then reverses to shoot it from another point of view. The video was then edited using what was then very new technology. He also used the Steadicam to include long moving shots which had previously not been possible. (Steadicam is a camera mounted on a harness which the camera operator wears and this enables the camera to be held and move in a natural way to follow the action.) Redmond was one of the producers at the forefront of using the new technology and this made him one of the most innovative producers in the early 1980s. Much of the innovation of *Brookside* is covered in other parts of this book, but recognition for the initial creation of the series, and indeed the spirit of the series, has to be credited to its creator and executive producer, Phil Redmond. One of its subsequent producers, Mal Young, carried the series through some of its major dramatic storylines but Phil Redmond retains control as Executive Producer and, ultimately, maintains the direction which *Brookside* takes. Keeping control as Executive Producer is a skill which Mal Young first learned from Redmond, and one which he took to his role of Executive Producer of BBC Drama Series. Mal Young has since developed the genre of soap opera within the BBC and created new series which took aspects of soap opera and incorporated them into other areas of popular drama.

In the 1980s, when the BBC set out to create its own soap opera, it turned to Julia Smith, who has a successful history of producing other drama series – *Angels* and *District Nurse* – with writer Tony Holland. Her attention to every detail of the series has been praised by executives, and she and Tony Holland have documented the process in their book *EastEnders – The Inside Story* (1987). Until her death she was regarded as the top female producer of British soap operas.

There are, of course, many other producers who have been part of the development of the genre, and what is important is the recognition that it is the producer who is the main driving force behind every soap opera at any time that it is in production. Production staff progress within one soap opera and they also move between different soap operas. Matthew Robinson was the lead director at the beginning of the first episode of *EastEnders* and has worked on most of the British soap operas. Mervyn Watson has produced *Coronation Street*, *Emmerdale*, and now *Casualty*. Moving between productions is now more and more common for producers within the genre. When Mal Young left *Brookside* he was headhunted by Greg Dyke, then Chief Executive of Pearson Television, and for a short time was Executive Producer of *The Bill* and *Family Affairs*. Headhunted again

by the BBC, he was appointed Head of Drama Series and is responsible for both the soap operas and the other continuing series shown
on BBC1 – *EastEnders, Casualty, Holby City, Dalziel and Pascoe.*

Just as the producer of a Hollywood movie is the vital element in
the film, so the producer is the key to the soap opera. The producer,
even if for a short period of time, is the overall controlling influence
in the genre and in the day-to-day, week-by-week development of the
series. A director may work with a programme for only one week at
a time, and may be vital for that week, but the producer holds the
continuity of the series in their control. For that reason, when a soap
opera goes wrong, it is always the responsibility, and usually the fault,
of the producer. To begin a soap opera is exhilarating and exciting,
but to take over a soap has specific implications depending on
whether it is doing well or badly.

New brooms – lifesavers or exocets?

When a new producer is appointed to an existing show it is for one
of two reasons. Either the previous producer has left to go on to a
better job, and left the soap in good shape, or the new producer is
appointed because the previous incumbent has left or been removed
and the soap is in peril. In the first option, the programme may have
been very successful and the producer may have left it at the top of
the ratings, but the new producer will still feel that they have to make
their mark. If the latter is the case, the programme may be in
desperate need of new ideas and changes are called for.

Even the most successful soaps can have peaks and troughs, but
they also have times when they fall into serious decline. It is not part
of the normal waves of production variations but part of much more
serious problems. It is not a rapid descent and by the time the series
has reached what could be called a crisis point, it takes a long time
to appoint a new producer and even longer to turn the series around.
When things begin to go wrong, it usually takes a certain time for
the broadcasting executives to see that the soap opera may be going
out of control. However, when a new producer is brought in to a
show he or she may become the wicked step-parent, taking over
control and trying to impose their own ways on their new charge. To
improve an ailing soap is not easy, but it is welcomed as a positive
creative contribution by the production team and the audience. To
intervene in a successful soap is much more difficult. And yet new
brooms always want to sweep clean and new producers always want
to make their mark on a show. This can result in serious problems

and, importantly, serious drops in audience figures. A soap opera is a slow-moving production and, despite its frenetic production schedules, to turn around an ongoing machine which constitutes all aspects of production, one needs to go back to the basic ideas of the original script meetings. This means that it can take a few months to bring about the changes. If a programme is in a particularly successful phase, it can take a while before the problems caused by a 'new broom' are seen on screen and, conversely, it takes time for the rescue plan of a producer brought in to save the series to take hold.

Actors and actresses

Actors in soap operas, and the characters they portray, are the main attractions that bring audiences to the genre. However, the actors and actresses have not always been held in the highest regard by critics and producers, even though they are by audiences. The nature of the relationship between the actors and the audience means that audiences do feel that they 'know' the actors and their characters. This is not a confusion of actor and character, but rather recognition that the character is so familiar that the audience also 'know' the actor. It is an aspect of the intimate familiarity which surrounds the characters and their audience. It is also true that while writers create characters, after the actor has appeared in the part for any length of time, the writers pick up on the natural characteristics of the actor and incorporate them into the character. For the most part, actors in soap operas have to produce performances that are understated and low-key, always less than 'actorly', for it is their job to create the illusion of the ordinary. Although some characters can appear 'larger than life', as in real life, it is usually because their performances are understated and enable audiences to connect and have empathy with the ordinary people they represent.

Some actors have stayed in soap operas for most of their professional lives; others have moved out and pursued successful acting careers in other areas of drama. Some have been confused into thinking that the success of their character within the series means that they are more important than the programme; they have left and then found it very difficult to find other work. In the past it was almost impossible for actors who had appeared in soap operas to find work after they had left a long-running series. This was mostly because producers were reluctant to cast actors who had been associated with a particular character in soap operas – believing that audiences would not accept them in other roles. But those days have gone. Now, because of the importance of the soap opera to broadcasters – and because the changing perception of the soap opera means that it is certainly held in higher regard – a number of actors who have appeared in soap operas have gone on to have series written for them and to have roles in other popular drama. What they bring is an ability to connect with the audience and to draw an audience to the new programme. Actors have always been capable of playing a number of different parts; that is what they do. But the attitude of the producers has changed, thus expanding the forms of popular drama in which actors can move around and create new roles.

Costume and make-up – creating the ordinary

The construction of a character through dress and appearance is an important aspect of the fictional representation in television soap operas. It is partially through their appearance and clothes that the audience comes to understand the style and personality of the characters. Costume helps to create personality and register the changes in a personality. Costume can create the 'ordinary' or the most glamorous. The clothes have to be completely 'in character' for the soap opera and its style. They range from the hairnet that characterized Ena Sharples in *Coronation Street*, which was almost a prop and became an integral part of the character, through Hilda Ogden's perpetual rollers and headscarf, to the shoulder pads in the designer wear of the women stars in *Dallas* and *Dynasty*, which characterized the series and, later, the 1980s. The youth culture which features in some of the Australian soap operas, particularly in *Neighbours*, gave rise to a fashion that reflected the surfing clothes worn by the young stars. Long, baggy knee-length shorts, first worn by Jason Donovan as the character Scott, led to shorts becoming a major fashion item for young men.

Costume needs to be either unobtrusive or dominant, depending on the character or the soap opera. Even in the less glamorous British soap operas, when a character wears clothes that catch the eye of the audience, they are the subject of requests for information as to where they can be purchased. In British soap operas the costumes are much more subdued than in the American series, but since the 1980s many of the characters have become more glamorous and there has been much more fashionable costume. As Jackie Dixon in *Brookside* progressed from normal teenager to Merseyside mogul, her dress and certainly her hairstyles revealed the buying power she had. At one stage a storyline designated Jackie Dixon, Lyndsey Corkhill and

Suzanne Farnham as being 'high-flying businesswomen', and their designer suits and sleek hairstyles signified their changing status and their different perceptions of themselves. When one of the characters, Lyndsey Corkhill, lost her money and her status and was reduced to working in the garage, it was not simply the lesser job she found humiliating; but the fact that she had to wear the sweatshirt uniform of the garage was, for her, the symbol that added signification to the loss of her status. Every character has their own costume; this is part of the illusion that creates the representation, and the connotations of the reading of the visual are part of the characterization. Consider any soap opera: certain elements of the 'ordinary' are shown through the unobtrusive nature of the costume; anonymous and indistinctive signify the ordinary.

One of the differences between American and British soap operas is that American soap operas are much more aspirational. Reflecting the 'American Dream' that hard work brings financial success and status recognition, the series are cast with so-called 'beautiful people' whose clothes are a reflection of the glamour and success that they have achieved and to which the audience can aspire. In American daytime series the characters are always 'dressed up to the nines' and often totally unsuitably dressed for daytime occasions. Most women characters are dressed in clothes which might be perfectly suitable to go out to dinner or lunch or for special occasions, but they hardly look appropriate when visiting your neighbour or best friend for a cup of coffee and a chat. Conversely, some of the characters, maybe a daily help, are dressed in clothes that can only be described as bizarre: wild checks and bright tops, which are completely out of keeping with everyone else in the cast. When I asked the Creative Director with the American series *All My Children* why this was the case, she told me that clothes were integral to creating character in the daytime series. Their characters had to be expensively dressed during the day because that was what the audience expected. As lower class positions cannot be indicated by accent, they are portrayed through costume, the wearing of flamboyant and unfashionable clothes and a certain hairstyle being used to indicate a character of lower status who does not have any dress sense.

Cliffhangers

The cliffhanger (a.k.a. The Hook) is the device at the end of the soap opera that leaves the audience in suspense and draws them to the next episode. While there are a number of storylines running at any time, it is the main storyline of the day which either reaches a climax or point of high tension in the cliffhanger. Not all soap operas operate with the cliffhanger but it is one of the most self-conscious references within the genre. When a cliffhanger is used at the end of a series of a soap opera, the audience can be left waiting for many months for the resolution. The most famous cliffhanger was 'Who Shot JR?' in the American supersoap *Dallas*. The audience had to wait until the next series to find the solution.

In the spring of 2001 *EastEnders* ran a similar extended 'cliffhanger' when Phil Mitchell was shot in Albert Square. There were five suspects and each one could have committed the crime. The series held the audience in suspense until the perpetrator, Lisa, was revealed by Phil himself, who had seen her commit the crime. The series capitalized on the cliffhanger for maximum publicity. Various actors appeared on other television programmes declaring that they did not know who the guilty party was, and the press ran features speculating on the identity of the attacker. The self-conscious cliffhanger is far less common in current soap operas, but nevertheless every episode has to end with an ongoing story or situation which feeds the desire to know what happens next and to ensure that the audience watches the next episode.

Now that the soap opera has become such an important part of the schedules, the BBC in particular trails the forthcoming episodes of *EastEnders* in a way that was never done before. Also ITV runs trails that indicate important storylines which are continuing in forthcoming episodes. All this is part of the need to entice the audience to continue watching every episode.

Locations, sets and the semiotics of dramatic space

Every soap opera has its own visual style, which is closely associated with its location. For the most part these are constructed sets that represent the area in which the series is set. They may look exactly like the 'real thing' but they are carefully designed to create the right conditions for filming the series as well as the illusion of the drama that is being portrayed. Locations for soap operas are more likely to be purpose-built sets with outside lots and studio sets. The sets are a very important part of the drama because they create the physical space in which the drama takes place. But the location and sets are also major characters in the creation of the dramatic realism of the production.

Coronation Street – with its original terrace houses, small modern houses, corner shop and public house, The Rover's Return – contains all the signs of the north, both as it was in the 1960s when the series began and as it is now, even allowing for changes to accommodate new characters and locations for fresh storylines. It signifies a version of the north of England which is both familiar to those who live there and representative of the 'idea' of the north to those who may have never travelled to that area.

The set for *EastEnders* is as much a star of the programme as any of the members of the cast. It epitomizes the East End of London, both to those who live there and to those who have never visited the area and only know it from other films. The *EastEnders* set, created by Keith Harris, is a magnificent work of design and craftsmanship, creating an illusion of the reality of the houses, shops, gardens, the Queen Vic pub, the market stalls and every part of the physical space that is the fictional Albert Square.

When Phil Redmond proposed his idea for a soap opera to Channel 4 Chief Executive Jeremy Isaacs, it was based on a plan to purchase a number of new houses on a housing estate in Liverpool which would form the permanent location both for the setting for the drama *Brookside* and for the administration and production offices. It was an innovative decision, and for the first time real houses were converted into television locations to help create the reality. 'The Close' then became a major part of the drama and as the houses were occupied and the characters began the natural attempts to personalize the gardens, and nature performed her own part in enabling the flowers and trees to grow, so the basic outdoor setting became gradually transformed.

For series set in rural locations, the actual countryside is a major element in the production. *Emmerdale* has the Yorkshire countryside as a given as well as its own purpose-built village of Beckindale, and the location is what signifies the region as much as the accents in the series.

Music – the siren call to view

The signature tune of every soap opera is as much a part of the programme as the characters and storylines. The music is written to suit the series and the composer is involved from the very beginning. The music is the *siren call to view* to the audience and has to be recognizable from outside the room where the television set is located as it heralds the beginning of the programme and calls the viewers into the room to watch. The signature tunes of all the soap operas are recognizable even from the first note of the tune. Composers also make

different arrangements to suit any episodes which end on a particularly poignant incident and where the mood needs to be different
from the normal mood suggested by the signature tune.

One of the major differences between the soap opera and other
drama series, and certainly the high-cost prime-time American series,
is that music is not part of the soap opera. *Dallas*, *Dynasty* and
other American prime-time series have music as an integral part of
the programmes; music is a major part of the dramatic ambience and
runs throughout the episodes. In the Australian series *Neighbours*
music stings are used to separate scenes and punctuate the drama,
and even sometimes as part of the actual dramatic content. British
soap operas do not use music as part of the drama. Sometimes, CDs
will be playing in the background in The Queen Victoria public house
in *EastEnders*, or more rarely in a house, but again this is part of the
creation of a realistic representation of the scene. What is not audible
is the presence of a musical soundtrack throughout the drama, as
would be the case in other dramas and cinema films. It is a feature
which is often not noticed, but it is a crucial element both in the way
that audiences perceive programmes and in any debates about
realism. In 'real life' we do not walk around with a musical soundtrack accompanying our actions, punctuating and accentuating our
thoughts, even if some of us may have a soundtrack running in our
heads! So it is in fact more realistic not to have music, but it is something which signifies an absence of one of the major elements of the
grammar of television. However, it does mean that every aspect of
the drama has to be created without the considerable assistance of
music.

Opening titles

The opening titles are a significant part of the creative illusion of soap
operas. The titles encapsulate the essence of every series: the rooftops
and terraced houses in *Coronation Street*; the Yorkshire moors with
lambs leaping in the spring-time and the idyllic Yorkshire village in
Emmerdale; the aerial shot of the River Thames winding its way
through London to the curve in the river where Albert Square nestles;
the famous opening titles of *Brookside* which show the city of
Liverpool, the housing estate and other features of both the city and
the soap opera. All of these are part of the creation of the illusion of
the soap operas and signify to the audience the nature of the drama
that will unfold.

Press – the ultimate symbiotic relationship

The relationship between the press and soap operas has changed and evolved over the years. While I will not explore this relationship in detail, it should be noted that the relationship between the press and other media and the soap opera is almost symbiotic. The interest in soap operas as a form, rather than as a source of gossip about stars, came when *Brookside* began its transmission on Channel 4. As the press began its onslaught on the channel (Isaacs 1989; Hobson 1987) the soap opera gave them a taste for stories that concentrated on the genre. For the first time media correspondents on broadsheet newspapers and tabloids had found themselves with the facility to write stories which reached the front page and had a number of column inches inside their papers and one of the genres about which they wrote was the soap opera. From a standing start they moved to rampant coverage and the relationship between the two has increased ever since. The two forms now exist in an almost symbiotic relationship: the newspapers definitely need stories from the soap operas and, equally, the broadcasters need the newspapers to carry coverage from their series. Look at the range of newspapers – tabloid and broadsheet – and glossy magazines and the myriad of television programmes that all rely heavily on reporting the celebrity status, the storylines, the relationship of the storylines to everyday life. Daily television programmes also rely heavily on stories from the soap opera and their actors for a major part of their own content.

The relationship between the press and the soap opera producers is now seen by the broadcasters as one which has to be carefully managed. Stories are given to the newspapers when the production wants coverage, but at times they also need to protect the privacy of their stories from the press. One aspect of the 'revelation' from a soap opera is when a shot is supposedly 'stolen' from the production and leaked to the press. A 'fuzzy' shot, the snatch, is reproduced in the press and it looks as if it has been 'snatched' from the production. In fact, the photographs are released to the press by the press office of the broadcasters in order to manage the version of the storyline that they wish to be revealed.

Resolutions – a never ending form

A rare ending to an episode is the resolution of a storyline. This can happen, and if there is a happy ending, or even a satisfying moment, it leaves the audience feeling content; a sad ending can have a cathartic affect. There is never a complete resolution to all storylines in soap operas. Even when a series is axed by the broadcaster, as with *Crossroads* in 1988 and *Eldorado* in 1993, they still finish with the illusion left intact that the lives of the characters will continue with the cameras or microphones keeping watch. In fact, the illusion that life carried on while we were not watching was finally confirmed when Carlton brought back *Crossroads* in March 2001! The significance of the never-ending form is discussed in relation to the narrative structure of the soap opera in other parts of this book, but it is important to see the form as a useful tool in the plans of the broadcasters, who have shown that they can always revive a soap opera if necessary.

Topicality

While soap operas purport to represent reality, while they give the impression that they continue to exist even when the audience is not watching the programmes, and while they have a relationship to the time and reality in which they are located, there are a number of occasions when that reality is outside the range of possibilities of the drama. 'Pretending' that the fictional stories are part of the 'real' world is made extremely convincing by relating the characters, stories and emotions to what is currently relevant in the world as it is represented. Some incidents are ignored because the production cannot take the chance that the expected event might not happen. One year *Brookside* decided to include a storyline that involved the Grand National horse race, and everything went according to plan. However, if they had included the same storyline a few years later when the Grand National was cancelled because of a bomb scare, then the series would have looked rather stupid. In 1981, when Prince Charles and Lady Diana Spencer were due to be married in July, Jack Barton, producer of *Crossroads*, took the decision to include mention of the wedding in the episode to be transmitted on the day. As it happened the marriage did take place, but the possibility of such events not happening is a serious – and calculated – risk that producers have to take, especially since the programmes are all recorded around three weeks before transmission. With digital production now the norm, it is possible to make last-minute changes, but this is not something any producer or director would relish. Soap operas have to run the fine line between including topics that are prevalent in 'real life' and excluding those that it is not possible to incorporate into the drama. This is sometimes evident as an omission, particularly in the everyday conversations that characters have with one another. One of the main topics of conversation that is part of everyday life is conversation among members of the audience about the television characters and storylines. These can hardly ever be part of the series; inter-textuality does not stretch to that.

Again there have been many occasions when if soap operas were relating stories as they happen – if they were a 'fly on the wall of everyday life' and not created by a drama department production team – they would include events which happen in reality. Massive disasters, such as bombings in the capital and major cities, general elections and, in particular, royal weddings, birthdays, births and deaths – would be mentioned in communal conversations in the pubs. However, these are rarely included, either because it is too risky (in case they do not happen) or because the programme was recorded before the incident happened.

However, the difficulty arises when events in the real world become so universally significant that they *need* to be included for their absence could seriously question the 'realism' of the drama. To include such events is very difficult for television productions and highlights the fragility of the representation of reality. But sometimes it is essential that they are included. This is where the radio soap opera can be completely topical and include incidents which would be essential to the people represented in the soap opera. The radio series *The Archers* showed the strength and speed of their ability to respond to topical events in the week of the outbreak of the foot-and-mouth virus in February 2001. The first case was diagnosed on Tuesday 20 February and a ban on all exports and movement of animals was instigated by the Agricultural Minister. By the end of the week *The Archers* production team had rewritten the opening scene of the Friday episode so that the outbreak became part of the drama. The scene involved farmer Tony Archer and his son Tommy, who has his own pig business, inspecting their livestock and looking for signs of the virus. The script involved talking about the signs of the virus, reference to previous outbreaks and speculation at the horrors which will result if the virus spreads around the country, as indeed it went on to do. It was a perfect example of how the series can and does respond to such events and how it can incorporate aspects of the reality which it represents and fulfil the expectations of the listeners. The series then continued to carry elements of the outbreak with completely new storylines and adjustments to the lives of the characters, including the drastic measure of David and Ruth isolating Brookfield Farm in order to keep out all visitors and avoid any movement to and from the farm. They even sent their young child Pip to stay with relatives in the village. The series incorporated the practical actions which were being implemented throughout the country, the fear of the economic disasters which could ensue, and the emotional consequences for all the characters. In this way the series acted as a melting pot for all the events which were taking place in Britain during the time of the outbreak and incorporated many aspects of the emotional as well as the practical elements into the drama. Topicality and absolute public service combined in the radio form of the genre.

The television series *Emmerdale*, which is also set in a farming community, had an episode on the same evening at the end of the first week of the crisis. In one scene Jack Sugden, the owner of the only working farm in the series, is awaiting trial for the murder of his wife Sarah and he asked another character, Kathy, to put his farm on the market. In an unfortunate coincidence of timing the meeting at the farm to put the farm on the market did not mention the livestock, even though the week before it was said that the livestock might have to be slaughtered before the farm could be sold. On the night there was no mention of the foot-and-mouth virus, which would definitely have been part of the discussion. Indeed, even within The Woolpack there would have been discussion about the outbreak. By the next week *Emmerdale* had included reference to the outbreak in their storylines, and the topicality of the issue was able to enhance the 'reality' of the series. Whereas to respond to topical events would have been impossible in the earlier methods of production, new technology has enabled changes to be made and given productions the ability to deal with events which would inevitably be talked about within the situations reflected in the dramas.

However, there was little evidence in the other television soap operas that the crisis was prevalent in Britain. In *Coronation Street* Fred and Ashley continued their competition for the best sausage recipe, and in the newly transmitted *Crossroads* the angry chef slapped down a piece of meat on the counter of reception and questioned the quality of the meat, without even a line about the difficulties of obtaining meat and the need to increase prices in line with rising wholesale prices. For television soaps the whole process of being absolutely topical is much more difficult, and it is these rare moments when an event is dominating the news on radio, television and in the press that it becomes apparent that soap operas, although based on reality, are only a representation of the many different experiences of real life to which the audience can relate.

One such rare moment was included in *EastEnders* and ensured the cultural awareness of the series. When Queen Elizabeth, The

Queen Mother died in April 2002, the programme reflected the event during the episode on Friday 5 April. Sonia was watching television and the sound of the BBC coverage as the Queen Mother's body was moved to Westminster Hall to lie in state was played into the episode. The event was also referred to in the drama, with Sonia sharing her grief at losing her baby with the grief of the nation at losing the Queen Mother. On the day of the funeral the episode included a scene with Dot and Pauline listening to a portable radio in the laundrette and holding a copy of a newspaper with the Queen Mother's photograph on the front page. The voice of Tom Fleming gave the commentary on the funeral and the two characters spoke with affection and respect about the death of the Queen Mother. The series acknowledged the moment of shared national mourning and reflected the events of the day in an episode which was transmitted at 7.30 on the night of the funeral.

Writers – the lifeblood of soap operas

The writers of soap operas are the lifeblood of the series. They are the people who create the characters, think of the storylines and write the everyday dialogue which both tells the stories and gives the characters their personality and individuality. Many writers of soap operas are not known for their individual contributions. Although much of the work which is done in the creation of the storylines is collective, there are exceptional writers who have worked on individual soap operas for many years. Some have been outstanding and their episodes are visible even within the established conventions of the individual soap operas. Some have gone on to be the leading writers of major drama series. Jimmy McGovern, Kay Mellor, Paul Abbot and Tony Jordon all worked on soap operas and went on to create their own drama series. And while continuing to write within the genre, Peter Whalley, Julian Roach, John Stevenson and Adele Rose have all produced drama scripts of the highest quality and created some of the most outstanding dramatic works among the thousands of scripts which have to maintain the fiction of the ordinary and the everyday. Some episodes stand out, maybe for their dramatic events, maybe for the sheer quality of the fine writing, comic or poignant. Some characters are created with such skill that they immediately form a relationship with the audience and fit easily into the soap opera. All are created by writers who both provide the words for the actors to say, and then pick up on many of the actors' personal skills and mannerisms and write them into the characterization.

As with any other form of drama, writing remains one of the most important elements in soap opera, and high-quality writing and exceptional acting and directing unite to make the form one of the most outstanding on television.

Part II
The Content of Soap Operas

3

Soap Stars: Actors, Characters and Icons

Soap operas tell stories. The stories are told through the medium of the characters in the series. Characters are the most important element in any soap opera. If the characters do not appeal to the audience then the best storyline imaginable will be wasted. If an important storyline is given to a character too soon after they join a soap opera, the story will be wasted because the audience will not care about the character. When a new soap opera is launched, it needs to have a slow opening, so that audiences get to know something about the characters before any big story which relates to one of the main characters breaks. Characters have to be introduced; the audience needs to know who they are before any major stories evolve.

This does not mean that there cannot be dramatic events early on in the series. *EastEnders* began with the death of an elderly man, Reg Cox, but he was a dispensable character whose only function was to be the catalyst which brought all the characters into one place so that they could be 'seen' by the audience and their role in the community could begin to be revealed. This is completely different from single dramas, where a dramatic occurrence often happens immediately the drama begins; or from police or detective series, where sometimes the main event, a crime, has happened before the drama begins. Most producers believe that it is the characters that form the main strength in the soap opera. These characters in British soap opera are representations of people who are recognizable to the audience. This is essential if the stories they tell are to be believable. They must portray a form of realism and explore the aspirations and experiences which satisfy the wants of the audience. Since audiences watch across a whole range of soap operas, comparisons are made across programmes and characters have to be able to stand out for their verisimilitude.

There have been so many outstanding characters in British soap operas that it is impossible to do more than give an indication of who they have been and why they have been so integral to the series in which they appeared and to the genre overall. Many questions can be asked about characters in soap operas. What are the main character types and how have they been represented? How have they evolved and changed? Are there similarities between different soap operas and could characters move between series? What sorts of representations are made and how have these changed? Why do we need the characters, what is their function and how do they work? (Geraghty 1991: 19–20) It would be easy to fall into the trap of indicating that soap operas are 'peopled' with 'types', but this is too facile. The reality is that the characters and the people they represent are so much more than the categories into which we attempt to fit them; they could all fit into many different categories. If a character is defined as the 'good woman' or the 'young tearaway', that is never the only way that they can be defined. These are dangerous ways of describing characters and can only be shorthand for what they are meant to represent. When thinking about the characters in soap operas it is always necessary to look at their total function and see how they are developing as a character. For the development of characters is one of the main features of the soap opera; and their ability to respond to different life events builds into the cumulative narrative of the soap.

Soap stars

Stars are identification figures, people like you and me, embodiments of typical ways of behaving.
                                                          Dyer 1979: 24

Characters in soap operas have to be individuals who represent character types that we recognize. Some are destined to become icons. They are manifestations of what we know about our times and ourselves. Dyer defines the relationship of stars to 'ordinary beings' when he writes: 'Stars articulate what it is to be a human being in contemporary society' (Dyer 1987: 8). In tracing the historical development of stars, he explains the development from 'gods' to 'mortals':

In the early period, stars were gods and goddesses, heroes, models –
embodiments of *ideal* ways of behaving. In the later period, however,
stars are identification figures, people like you and me – embodiments
of typical ways of behaving. (Dyer 1979: 24)

Dyer was writing about film stars, but his thesis can be applied to
the actors in soap opera, perhaps more than in other television
dramas. The notion that 'stars' are 'embodiments of typical ways of
behaving' is one which perfectly describes the requirements of actors
and characters who appear in soap operas. They have to be natural,
normal and exceptional enough to provide the trigger of recognition
between the audience and the character. The characters and the actors
who portray them are the component parts and the fuel that drives
the dramas along. Without them the stories would be of no interest.
Soaps as a form of drama are the stories of the lives of their characters. But as we shall see in the next chapter, their stories also have to
be our stories. We have to be able to identify with them; whether or
not we like them is another matter. What is necessary is that we feel
the surge of recognition when they appear. Even if that surge is a
recognition of the negative, it still sets in place that intellectual and
emotional engagement as to how this character will behave and how
well we recognize their behaviour, for good or evil. Over the years
the most powerful and dominant characters have changed, not only
as individuals but also in the representations they portray.

Soap characters can never be stereotypes, because we know them too well

Characters in soap operas are sometimes defined as stereotypes.
Stereotypes are necessary because they encapsulate features – and
qualities or deficiencies – which we use as a shorthand way of recognizing what the drama is portraying through certain characters. It
might be thought that stereotypes are only a negative form of characterization. However, they are neither good nor bad; they are
simply a tool of the dramatist. Soap operas do contain certain stock
characters that will be found in all series, but they will differ in their
importance depending on the function for which they are necessary
to the drama. The notion that soap operas are full of stereotypes is
clearly not correct. Soap characters cannot be stereotypes because we
know the characters too well. They have to contain aspects of ourselves, or of those we know, in order to connect with the audience.
     Stereotypical traits may be included as the first clue when a
character is introduced, but, as the audience learns more about the

character the stereotypical cipher disappears and the individual character emerges. When you first meet someone in 'real life' you may form an instant opinion of him or her, but you know that there is, in fact, much more to know. How often have you met someone and only when you have known them for a while have you discovered some of the more interesting aspects of their character? Your first impression may not have been wrong, but there is so much more about them to be discovered. In the soap opera there can be an initial reaction to a character, but as the audience begins to 'know' a character, the complexity of the individual is unfolded. In the soap opera, the stereotype is a brief moment in time rather than a long-standing part of the character.

When a character is introduced, the shorthand way of defining them is by including characteristics and outward features which indicate to the audience the features and characteristics which are represented by and represent the new arrival. These signs of a character are both visual and aural. The way they look, dress, stand, move, speak and react all denote what we need to know about the character when they first appear in the series. The connotations of these signs are, of course, what inform our individual opinions of the characters and our anticipation of how they will perform in the drama. So while the initial representations might be an indication, it is in the unfolding and never-ending stories that the characterization is developed. Because of the ongoing nature of soap operas, characterization can never remain at the level of the stereotype. Audiences expect character development, and producers and writers have to move their characters along or the audience will not develop any relationship with them. There is a vast difference between the stereotype and the representation of familiar characteristics. The visual and verbal clues alert the audience to what they should expect, but they can be confirmed or rebuffed in their expectations depending on the way the character develops. Stereotypes are only indicators of what to expect. They quickly disappear when the characters take on their full potential and find their place within the fiction of the series of which they are a part. Understanding the nature of representation is the key to understanding the characters in soap operas. Understanding the characters and having empathy with them is the way the audience connects with the soap opera, and rejecting the notion of the stereotype as a feature of the characters in soap opera is a necessary step to understanding the appeal of the genre. No audience can stay interested in a stereotype for very long, certainly not for the period of time for which the current soap operas have held audience appeal. The characters have to have the ability to appear to be representations of real people and be recognizable for the individual characteristics and emotions which link them with our subjectivities. Therefore, the way that I am approaching characters in this book is to see them as the conduit of the dramatic storylines and the representations of what we know about our culture and ourselves.

Strong women in all soaps

Soap opera has traditionally been a genre which is perceived as being for women. Its major characters have been women and its subject matter has been focused on domestic issues and themes. Not that such issues and themes do not have relevance for male viewers; but until comparatively recently the soap opera was not a form which majored on male characters and their concerns. In 1982 I wrote what was an accurate assessment of the characters in the programmes at that time:

> These serials have traditionally offered a range of strong female characters and this has proved a popular feature of the genre for its audience. They show women of different ages, class and personality types, and offer characters with whom many members of their female audience can empathise. They also include male characters often for romantic interest, sometimes as comic characters or 'bad' characters, but in the main the men do not have the leading roles within the serials. There are few children in soap operas, which does tend to detract from their representation of 'real life', but this is caused by the difficulties in sustaining babies and children in a long-running serial. (Hobson 1982: 33)

The idea that soap opera would become a genre which was also about men's issues and in which men took major roles was almost unimaginable. Men were in all the series, but the male characters were never a major driving force of the narratives. By 1991 Christine Geraghty was asking whether soap opera was 'women's fiction no more?', and signalling that men were becoming an important part of the genre (Geraghty 1991). And throughout the 1990s the changes in the fiction continued. Now male characters are major elements in all the soap operas and their rise is part of the changes in the productions and of the changes in the cultural and social life of the population. Similarly, babies and children are of major significance in all the soap operas, and the series have developed to become far more representative of the 'real lives' which they aim to portray. But that is for later; first we must look at the way that the strong female characters dominated the genre throughout its formative years. Men were there, but they never ran the show, nor carried the narrative, nor did they create much of the trouble that now dominates the soaps and, it could be argued, has resulted in major changes in the genre.

Traditionally, the main characters in British soap operas centred round matriarchal figures. On radio, Mrs Mary Dale presided over her family in quiet and concerned control. Mrs Mary Archer supported Dan and ran the family while the family ran the farm. For fifty years the series has flourished and, unlike other soap, has had equal numbers of female and very strong male characters throughout its fifty years. When *Coronation Street* was first transmitted in 1960, it exploded with female characters across a whole range of ages and types. These women were predominantly northern working-class women, based on real people who were known to the creator Tony Warren. But they were not only based on women he knew; they were enhanced by other writers and by the creation of the characters on the part of the actresses who played the roles. Strong powerful women who were usually, but not always mothers, were omnipresent in the soap opera. The opening episode of *Coronation Street* immediately revealed the wide range of women characters representing women who were familiar and who carried the cultural references of the age. The trio of older women, widows one and all, who reigned supreme in the 'snug' of the Rovers Return – Minnie Caldwell, aged 60, Martha Longhurst, aged 61 and the redoubtable Ena Sharples, aged 61 – all appeared at the time as if they were at least in their 70s. Think of Audrey Roberts, born 23 July 1940, now the same fictional age as the trio of older women, and there is no comparison with her appearance, lifestyle, attitude and representation of women in her age group as they exist in 2002. The age range of the characters may be the same, but their lifestyle, appearance and attitudes have changed to reflect the changes in contemporary behaviour and thought. Along with Albert Tatlock, the three women represented the working class who were born at the beginning of the century, had lived through the First World War, the Depression and the Second World War and were now left alone but for their tenuous friendships with each other. The narrative function for Minnie, Martha and Ena was not for their maternal instincts, but rather for their role as a combination of a Greek chorus and a Shakespearean comic trio who commentated on the action from the snug of the Rovers Return. Many of the characters from the *Street* have become part of the history of British television – Annie Walker, the landlady of the Rover's Return, whose pretensions were tempered by her down-to-earth husband Jack; Ena

Sharples, the street busybody, caretaker of the Glad Tidings Mission; Elsie Tanner, the street vamp and its first single mother; Hilda Ogden, who took over from Ena as the street busybody and was the cleaner at the Rover's Return, hugely popular and loved; Bet Lynch, blonde bombshell barmaid; and Raquel Wolstenhulme, shop assistant and part-time model, later barmaid – all incorporating different representations of working-class women and essences of northern life. But all have strong and individual characters which define them as believable and 'round' (Forster 1971: 85). Easy phrases give a shorthand description of their function but only tell parts of their character.

In *Emmerdale* the character of Betty Eagleton perfectly embodies the representation of the older woman who is a busybody and looking for gossip, but the stereotype fails when you realize that she is living with Seth Armstrong, her partner, but that she refused to get married. She forages for information but has the kindest heart and rallies to support anyone who is in need of help. In *EastEnders* Dot Cotton may be interested in learning and spreading the gossip of the Square, but her own life has also been the subject of other people's gossip, as she has coped with her wayward husband and criminal son and, more recently, as she has aided her friend Ethel in her request for euthanasia. These characters may have a narrative function of spreading stories and creating comedic moments, but they are always characters who have their own problems, troubles and vulnerability.

When *Crossroads* began in 1965 it was based on the story of Meg Richardson, a recently widowed woman with two teenage children. Her aim was to provide a home and an income for herself and her family. The actress Noele Gordon, like her character Meg, was decidedly middle-class, which was reflected in her clothes, her manners, the furniture in her 'sitting room' and her social attitudes. The character was interesting, and one of the fictional representations which illustrate the perceived proximity of the actress to the character portrayed. Most actors and actresses are middle-class, but there are a few who appear in soap operas who find themselves portraying characters who closely resemble themselves. Noele Gordon never married and had no children, and yet for many members of the audience she epitomized the middle-class mother of the period, one who was standing alone and running a successful business (Hobson 1982: 88–9). She owned the motel and, although she took on male business partners, and even married, she was always seen as a strong middle-class woman who combined motherhood with a demanding career. She combined motherhood with strong business acumen and provided what Brunsdon (2000: 66–82) has defined as the 'housewife's fantasy'.

In the Yorkshire countryside, Annie Sugden, the matriarch in *Emmerdale Farm* had been left a widow before the series began. She was left with a farm to run, with the help of her three sons, Jack, Joe and Matt. She was responsible for the continuation of the business and the provision of jobs for them and their families. She was also representative of the Yorkshire woman who was tough, down to earth and possessed the qualities which might be seen as positive aspects of being a woman. Annie's domain was her kitchen, her skills were domestic; she was always cooking a meal, making tea, providing sustenance, displaying conventional feminine qualities. This may have been out of kilter with the times, but it certainly had a resonance with the target audience. She represented strong domesticity, 'getting on with it' and in fact celebrated the skills of the modern 'domestic goddess' with a hob and a scrubbed wooden table.

Brookside, although it set out to reflect the remit of Channel 4 and be 'different', began with a set of characters out of which emerged the iconic Sheila Grant, played by Sue Johnson. Sheila Grant embodied the characteristics of a working-class woman and, though living in Liverpool, spoke to any mother of teenage children. She was married to Bobby, an active trade unionist, and her three teenage children were both a joy and a source of worry to her. As the series began, Sheila, Bobby and their family moved from a council estate into the four-bedroomed house in Brookside Close, courtesy of the money left to her on the death of her mother. It was the biggest house on the close, and this immediately brought her into class conflict with the middle-class Collinses, downwardly mobile because of the redundancy of their bank manager breadwinner father, Paul Collins. Sheila Grant was a woman who embodied the physical duties and emotional worries that were addressed by women of that time. Her children presented her with a range of problems and worries. Barry was verging on petty crime; Damon's life with his teenage friends Ducksie and Gismo was a constant cause of worry for her; her daughter Karen was in her mid-teens and encountering problems with her periods – she created guilt for Sheila when she was put on 'the pill' for medical reasons as this clashed with Sheila's strong Catholic convictions. When the series began her husband Bobby was one of the leading union members who were striking at the factory where they worked, and the fear of redundancy was a constant part of her day-to-day experience. She had a small part-time job in a bread shop which gave her a little independence but no freedom. Sheila's religion was her strength but even this was a cause of conflict between her, her husband and her wayward family. Sheila Grant's storylines were many, but will be remembered for two in particular. The first was when she was raped and the aftermath of that, when the response of her husband was almost more dreadful to bear than the rape itself. The second was when she became pregnant for the fourth time in her 40s and how she coped with having a child at that age. This was no story of a career woman who was making a choice to delay her family, but that of a woman with grown-up children who had to cope with the unexpected fact of her unwanted pregnancy. Her Catholicism ruled her response to the knowledge of the impending child, but was no comfort as she dealt with the reality of her position. In the event when the child was born, she became a joy to Sheila and added to the power of the representation of the woman the character portrayed.

The character left the series after a passionate affair with a neighbour and after some spectacular displays of uncontrolled testosterone on the part of the two men in her life, Bobby Grant and Billy Corkhill, her lover. Sheila Grant was an ordinary woman. As much as any character in a soap opera, she has carried the unspoken but tolerated gnawing despair of disappointment in her married life. Bobby was not a demonstrative man. He was perhaps more passionate in relation to his politics than his marriage. He did his best. He never knew what it was that he was not doing and he muddled on in his relationship. When things went wrong he truly did not know what to do to make them right, and he railed and grieved when he could not make things better. For some women, life with Bobby would have been enough, but Sheila Grant was a representation of womanhood rather than motherhood, and as a 1980s woman she knew that she must look for more in her life. When she lost her youngest son, Damon, in a stupid random stabbing attack in Newcastle, her grief was paramount and united mothers in the shared agony of the loss of a son. Her life was so touched with the tragic; but it was not a tragedy for it was not of her own making and she fought against the adversities which attacked her family and her own life. Sheila Grant was never downtrodden, never sorry for herself and never self-sacrificing. She saw that she had the strength to have a life of her own as well as being a wife and mother. Sheila Grant, like many of the characters in soap opera, links the genre to the realism of the nineteenth-century novel. They carry the individual stories of the characters but unite them with the universal feelings and experiences of the audience.

Being a woman – Elsie Tanner, mascara and movies

Dip into any period of stories in soap operas and some characters stand out for their representation of what was the essence of the experiences of the life of women at that time. Two examples of characters from *Coronation Street* epitomize the representation both of northern working-class women and of the universal characteristics which link those women with members of the audience. Elsie Tanner was a character who was in the series from its beginning. When the series began she was between husbands, although she had been married at 16 and remained married for twenty-two years. Her daughter Linda had a difficult marriage to a young Czech engineer; their cultural expectations clashed in the early days of her marriage. Dennis, her son, skirted around the law and she did her best to keep him under control. Her life was a struggle. She defended her children – and her reputation – in public and screamed at them behind closed doors. And if she didn't, the audience thought she did, because they knew that was how she would have behaved. She strove to maintain the standards necessary to keep her in the respectable working class, but at the same time she epitomized the glamour of those women who had been young during the Second World War. She brought memories of nylon stockings, American servicemen as boyfriends and Max Factor mascara applied with a tiny brush from a blue flat mascara case. She made up at the kitchen table, sometimes dressed in her underwear, and she offered an image of femininity and strong womanhood which captured memories and created dreams across generations of women. It was not a conscious identity which was shown, but the connotations of the everyday mixed with the screen glamour of Hollywood – memories of our mothers and black and white movies.

Raquel – the creation of an icon

More recently, the character of Raquel Wolstenhulme was a representation of an innocent, beautiful and glamorous young woman. The story of the creation and characterization of Raquel was elaborated by David Liddiment when we talked about the way that characters were created. Raquel first appeared in the series as a shop assistant in the local supermarket Bettabuys. She was created by the writer John Stevenson. David Liddiment spoke with enthusiastic affection about the creation of the character:

> The idea of Bettabuys in the world of *Coronation Street* means like 'everyman', 'every-supermarket'. It isn't Sainsbury's, yes? So it's probably a northern chain and the name conjures that up for you straight away – before you even see it. And then when you start to improvize and populate Bettabuys, then you start to invent characters that are

rooted in that imagined place. I remember well the idea of a Miss Bettabuy, which is such a wonderfully funny idea. Why is it funny? But it is. It's a sort of contradiction that there is something prosaic and mundane about Bettabuys, and the idea that Bettabuys would have a beauty competition is a wonderfully rich comic contradiction. Now at first this is just a conversation in a writers' conference – it's in someone's head. And then you come up with that wonderful name, Raquel Wolstenhulme, so you end up with Raquel, which is glamour – Raquel Welch, Hollywood superstar, glamorous world of film, Cannes Film Festival – all of those connotations and Wolstenhulme, which is a mouthful, a down-to-earth northern name. And, of course, that name is then reflected in the character, and the casting director casts Sarah Lancashire, who does something wonderful with it, but she probably hasn't got much to go on, except those things, Bettabuys, Miss Bettabuys, Raquel Wolstenhulme and immediately you have got a picture, you have got something to hang your hat on. And of course, she brought that wonderful characterization to it that, I have to say, didn't come out of the ether, it came out of the scripts and she brought something extra to it. And then the writers, three months later or ten months later, finally see what they have written on screen and seeing something magic happen and out of that the whole of the character of Raquel blossomed, and before you know it again the comic imagination of the writers had the wonderful French lessons with Ken.

What David Liddiment gives is an explanation of how a character was created. From the idea of a new location for storylines, through the idea of a beauty contest within the shop, and the creation of a character whose name was to encapsulate her character and whose character was to encapsulate a representation of a young woman in 1990s Britain. After her initial introduction as Miss Bettabuys, her character became more central to the drama and she moved to a job as barmaid at the Rovers Return. Always looking for romance which would end in a happy marriage, Raquel articulated the hopes of many young women in her position. The character was complex; one that the whole audience loved, she was naive, gentle, and although she looked as if she would break men's hearts, for the most part it was her own heart that was broken. Every romance which she had was a disaster, and eventually she married the equally gentle Curly Watts, who had loved her for years, on the rebound from a betrayal by Des Barnes, the local bookmaker and sometime love-rat. The scene at the registry office as she waited for the marriage to take place was one of the most poignant and heartbreaking of any scene in a soap opera, or indeed in any other dramas. Raquel knew that she was not marrying Curly because she was in love with him; she loved him as a friend and she felt that she would never let herself be hurt by anyone else ever again. She would marry not for love but for comfort and security and to try to protect herself from ever being hurt again. She went into the ladies toilet and wept uncontrollably, and many members of the audience wept with her as she revealed the depth of her self-knowledge and an awareness of her own situation, and through that she united with the audience. She spoke of the young working-class women, bright, intelligent, who had been failed by the education system, thus uniting the shared cultural knowledge of the audience as she wept for herself and millions of other women like her. And then she 'put her face on' and went out to greet the world, looking wonderful and weeping inside.

Women did not watch these and other characters and think 'Elsie Tanner is a representation of a certain class, and in later years of the series, of a certain age, who looked and behaved in a certain way'. They saw the representation of that northern woman, but it was through how she felt – revealed in the more intimate moments of the series when she reflected on her life, when she showed her vulnerability – that the shared feelings of feminine consciousness were revealed. Similarly, twenty years later when Raquel broke down in the ladies toilet at the Registry Office and revealed the level of her self-knowledge, she brought into play the recognition of the shared experiences of the audiences. She unleashed emotions of vulnerability; grief and sorrow for what could have been in her life had she been born into a different class. Women audiences shared the knowledge of what she felt – maybe not a recognition of their own experiences, unless they were in a similar age group, but certainly a recognition of what it had been like to be a young woman in Britain over the period of representation.

To capture aspects of a culture is one of the functions of successful soap opera, and it is through the characters that this is achieved. The stories may tell what is happening, record or reflect the history of events, but it is through the history of the emotions of the characters that the cultural history is recorded and the reality of soap operas is achieved. In fact, the themes and concepts incorporated into soap operas have significance only if they are part of the stories of life as experienced by the characters.

Mothers as stars – 'my kids come first'

If there is one characteristic which encapsulates the representation of motherhood in soap operas, it is that their children are of paramount importance. The concept of motherhood is seen as a quality which gives women status and unites them, whatever faults they may have or whatever they may do. While the concept of motherhood has always been important in soap operas, in recent years some characters have stood out as representations of current images of women. The rise of single mothers within society has been reflected in the representations in soap operas. The character Carol Jackson in *East-Enders* first appeared in the early 1990s. She had four children, Bianca, Robbie, Sonia and Billy. When the character was introduced, she was living with Alan, the father of Billy; although Carol was to marry him in a later storyline, her image was always that of a single mother. She had had Bianca when she was 14 and had never told David Wilkes, her boyfriend at the time, that she was pregnant. Keeping her family together and having a life of her own was Carol's role in life. She followed in the tradition of Elsie Tanner, but because she was a woman of the 1990s, her children were from a number of fathers and her strength as a mother was that she had kept her children together. Life was hard for Carol, and while she experienced a varied life she always struggled to maintain her independence and her sexuality. One always felt that Carol Jackson was a smouldering sexual woman for whom the experience of motherhood and the time spent looking after her children had necessitated her leaving her sexuality 'on hold', ready to be reignited at sometime in the future. Eventually, the drama delivered her the ultimate contradiction: when she thought she had at last found love with Dan, she found out that he had earlier been the lover of her daughter Bianca and had continued the affair on meeting her again. Ultimately, Carol lost Dan and, far more serious, her daughter.

The power of motherhood, and the strength of the needs of children for their mothers, continued as part of the storyline after the actress Lyndsey Coulson had left the series. In a new storyline her youngest daughter Sonia became pregnant after her first and only experience of sexual intercourse. Ignorant of the fact that she was pregnant until she gave birth, Sonia then struggled to accept her own motherhood and her baby, and when Robbie, her brother, tries to persuade her to let him contact their mother, she refuses. The character and the production cried out for the guest reappearance of Carol Jackson; you knew she might be judgemental towards Sonia, but she would have sorted out her problems and supported her as a mother. The characteristics displayed by mothers were missing just when Sonia needed support and guidance. Unfortunately, the actress had left the series and the ending was unsatisfactory in terms of a realistic resolution. The audience may well have felt that while Sonia was in such a difficult situation someone should have contacted Carol or at least Bianca, her sister, who was in fictional terms living in

Manchester and studying for a degree in fashion design. It is a nice example of the limits of the realism of characters; ultimately they are always at the mercy of the availability of the actors. I do not know whether the actress was available, or, in fact, whether the production did not want the mother or sister to be available to support Sonia, but it would have certainly been more realistic if one of them had come back to Walford, even if only for a short period of time.

The power of motherhood remains one of the greatest strengths in the soap opera and there are countless examples of the way that the concept is a major force within all the dramas. One of the most poignant representations is the story that mothers love their children whatever their faults. It is a positive image and is often in contrast to the weakness of the children. Dot Cotton remained loyal to her son Nick regardless of his criminal activities, his drug addictions and the personal attacks he made on her. She supported him and attempted to get him to reform. She is the embodiment of saintly motherly love and will never abandon the child she prays will one day show that he returns her love. Similarly, Vera Duckworth in *Coronation Street* dotes on her wayward son Terry, and can never believe that he is as devious as he appears to be and that his activities have included both petty and serious criminal behaviour and selling his own son to his rich maternal grandparents. In 2000 Vera made the ultimate sacrifice of giving one of her kidneys to save the life of one of her grandsons, fathered by Terry, after Terry was too frightened to donate his own kidney. Terry appeared to be heartless, but after the operation he crept back to the hospital to peep through the window of the hospital ward and check that Vera was recovering from the surgery. This action reveals that despite all his faults Terry does love his mother and, unlike Nick Cotton, he does return her love. More recently, Terry proved his redemption by taking his father to hospital at peril of his own arrest, and Vera was vindicated in her belief that Terry was a good boy at heart.

Female representations – minor and major characters

One of the reasons for the popularity and predominance of soap opera – as a form that is watched by women and studied and lauded by feminists – is that it is a form which is fecund with female characters. Traditionally every soap opera has had a major female character as its lead, and this has been one of the determining features which has defined the form. The ubiquitous matriarchs are the leading characters in British soap operas, but there is also a legion of women who have been both the spine and the nerve ends of the soap operas. The function of many of the characters was vital to the progression of gossiping, both as part of their character type and also as a means of transmitting information to the audience by talking about what has been happening. This and other dramatic devices are standard tools of the dramatist and can be seen in dramas throughout literature. See the way that Shakespeare introduces and imparts information to the audience by way of gossip and joking between characters.

Soap operas are not generally noted for their outstanding humour, except for the comedy of manners in *Coronation Street*, but these older female characters often have the function of providing comedy. The most famous trio and the ones that set the standard, are the three friends, Ena, Minnie and Martha in *Coronation Street* (discussed above), but there are many examples of this character type. Dot Cotton and Ethel and her dog, 'little Willie', provided the similar characters in *EastEnders*, and when Ethel left the Square, the production attempted to provide a number of 'friends' to fulfil the same function of a female friend for Dot and the series. More recently, Ethel was reintroduced into the series, with the specific reason of containing a story which focused on euthanasia and is discussed in chapter 4. An interesting aside on this point is that it is much more difficult to replace these characters, because, far from being complete stereotypes, their relationships depend on them being longstanding friends with the ability to share stories and reminisce. For the characters to 'work' there is a need for unspoken intimacy and a shared knowledge of each other's lives. They carry the internal knowledge of the narratives and share that knowledge with the audience.

The major female characters in soap operas may have changed but they have always been a feature of the genre. In the beginning the matriarchal characters were either married or widowed and were usually a mother. They had the experience that would enable them to advise members of the community or comment on any matters that might come up within the soap. They were usually over 40 and had children who also appeared in the soap opera. They were well respected in the neighbourhood and often held a position of authority. They would listen to problems and give advice. As the soap operas went on over many years, some characters who began as one type of character progressed to a different position as they aged and acquired a different status.

Soap operas in the UK have traditionally also had characters who could be defined as older ladies. They would never call themselves or each other 'women'. For the characters represented by this type of female, 'woman' denotes your gender, 'lady' connotes your position. Widowed or unmarried, they are often friends within the series. The genre began in the 1960s with a relatively high number of unmarried women. Some were young and had expectations of finding partners; some were a little older, were defined as spinsters and were seen as unlikely to find partners. They were defined as 'looking for love' and the liberation which came with the 1960s had little effect on them, although the dramas usually had surprises in store for them all. Men were necessary but 'tricky'; particularly in the reflection of working-class life in the north of England, the women were in control of the domestic sphere and men had their uses but were not in control in the home or in the neighbourhood. Many of the female characters reflected the social and economic situation of women in the north at that time. Miss Emily Nugent, who began as a young unmarried shop assistant, looked as if she was destined to remain a spinster, but she did have her own 'Shirley Valentine' moment when she had a romantic fling with a Hungarian building worker. Later, Emily married Ernest Bishop but domestic security was denied her when he was shot in a wages raid at Mike Baldwin's factory and Emily was left a widow. Emily suffered again when she chose another husband, Arnold, who was in fact a 'con man' and a bigamist. She threw him out and scrubbed her house clean to rid herself of his memory, and in recent years she has settled down into good works and quiet respectability, though tinged with a revolutionary streak, and often acts as a mother figure to young male characters in the series.

What is interesting about Emily, and indeed other older characters in the various series, is that their history is known to certain sections of the audience but not necessarily to the new members of the fictional characters in the soap opera. We may know that Rita was a nightclub singer and has had numerous romantic liaisons, and that Deirdre's life with Ken was seriously disrupted when she had an affair with Mike Baldwin, from which Ken has never recovered, but these elements of the history of the characters remain part of the interest and 'shared secrets' of the genre, known by the audience and by some of the characters within the dramas.

The concept of a strong woman who copes with problems, brings up her family, supports and enjoys life with her friends, survives when men betray her and sometimes lives happily with a male partner, has been a major tenet of the soap opera since its inception; and women remain a major strength within the genre. However, men have always been integral to the soap opera.

Male characters – fathers, brothers, sons and lovers

In the early years of *Coronation Street* there were very few male characters who were not married or soon to be snapped up. The stable,
responsible, long-suffering Jack Walker, licensee of the Rovers Return
was married to Annie Walker, the first 'queen' of British television
soap operas, but his role was always secondary to the women in the
series. Uncle Albert Tatlock was a widower and represented all the
older men who had been part of the 1914–18 war and had those
stories to tell to the younger generation. Ken Barlow and his brother
David were almost the only characters who represented younger
men and they were in their early 20s. Dennis Tanner was the potential
'juvenile delinquent' son of Elsie Tanner, and his appearance in the
first episode signalled his character as a problem and the forerunner
of many 'bad boys'. Soap operas have always had a number of male
characters, and even leading men, who were seen as handsome and
attractive characters. David Hunter and Adam Chance in *Crossroads*
always had a strong female following and represented clean-cut,
handsome, middle-class managerial material. For many years the men
in *Coronation Street* were not as important as the women, but their
presence was integral to the drama. They caused trouble or bother;
they provided sexual intrigues, but with the best will in the world it
would be difficult to describe any of the men in 'Corrie' as 'sex
symbols'. Ken Barlow went through a series of wives and girlfriends
but he could hardly be described as an early 'Dirty Den'.

The rise of male stars came in the 1980s with the two new soap
operas *Brookside* and *EastEnders*. By this time, the influence of the
American series *Dallas* and *Dynasty* had shown British audiences that
men could be attractive to look at, not very attractive to know, have
feelings and emotions and even take the lead as the major characters
in the series. In *Dallas*, a patriarchal series, it was the power of the
father, Jock Ewing, that dominated the series, and the only saving
grace of the arch villain J. R. was that he strove to please his father
and longed to feel his father's love. In *Dynasty* the two major women
characters, Krystle and Alexis, fought metaphorically and literally
over the main male character Blake Carrington. While both series had
major female characters, they also needed leading male characters
because these were prime-time series that needed to attract the lucrative audiences of night-time television. Family relations were always
at the centre of both of the series and were one of the major reasons
for their universal appeal.

In 1982 Channel 4 began transmitting *Brookside*, and the first episode began with a scene with Damon and his two friends, Ducksie and Gismo, 'up to no good' in some of the unfinished houses on the Close. Their behaviour, natural for young men, involved 'messing around' and the odd use of so-called 'bad language'. 'Bollocks' was written on the wall of a bathroom in an empty house and this contributed to the press designating the channel as 'channel swore'. These younger characters began to attract young male viewers to the programme and the channel, while Damon's older brother Barry and his friend Terry were certainly the beginning of the attractive, unmarried male characters who were skirting on the boundaries of minor criminal activity. (Barry was later to be a major underworld player.) They were attractive, they provided sexual chemistry in the series. But, above all, these young male characters brought a young male audience to the channel.

The breakthrough for 'grown-up' male characters came with Dirty Den, landlord of the Queen Vic in Albert Square, played by Leslie Grantham. The character of Den was the first male soap star and, some might think, the most charismatic of any who have appeared since. He had the secret of sexual magnetism in his relationship with those he loved or after whom he lusted. Unknown before he appeared in the series, the actor became a star by portraying an ordinary man who epitomized a sexually smouldering personality which was almost never fulfilled in any relationship. His relationship with his wife Angie was the cornerstone of the series, but it was not the sexual chemistry between them which drove the series. They were business partners who ran the pub and put on a dramatic show for the customers and the viewers. His romantic attachment was to his mistress Jan, but his eye would rove, sometimes alight on and sometimes devour other characters. The actor portrayed the character with total conviction. Den would speak, move, stand, look and act in a way which was cool, detached, powerful and inscrutable and yet totally fascinating. His faults were many but his attraction was paramount, and he became not only the male star of the series but also the template for a number of characters that followed, in particular, the Mitchell brothers who came to the Square and the Queen Vic and wreaked havoc whatever they did.

Recently there has been a massive expansion in male characters and the genre can no longer be seen as solely foregrounding women's issues, women characters and a feminine perspective on emotions and events. Male characters now include boys, youths, young men, twenty-somethings, thirty-somethings, older men, sons, fathers, brothers, husbands, lovers – every manifestation of the masculine has become a major part of the genre. Men have not only become major players; they are now portrayed as complete characters whose story-lines can be as personal as those of the women characters. They are no longer adjuncts; they are activists in the dramas and their presence in soap operas has moved through different development phases to their current leading status within the genre.

'It's good to talk' – Men behaving well

The change in male characters came in the late 1990s when men in soap operas began to talk to each other. While the changes may have happened earlier, examples from *EastEnders* in the summer of 1998 can serve to illustrate the changes in characters and how this reflected changes in the status of men within the genre. Something began to happen in Albert Square which changed the foundations of the genre. A number of the male characters began to spend time talking to each other. Not just talking in a socially expected sense, but having conversations with each other. Talking about their *feelings*.

One of the main protagonists of encouraging other men to talk has been the character Mark Fowler. Being HIV positive may have meant that Mark has developed his own communication skills, because he has talked about his own life and the implications of the fact that he is HIV positive. In order to advance the storyline, only Mark could talk about the issues involved and hence the needs of the production could only be met if the character developed and displayed the ability to talk.

Another early example of the move towards male conversations came in association with the story of Sanjay and Gita, an Asian couple. Sanjay had had an affair with Gita's sister. The marriage was reconciled but it was always stormy. After a particularly bad time, Gita left the Square unexpectedly. After being away for a number of months – Sanjay had thought she was dead – she returned with a baby, and Sanjay was not the father. The conventional dramatic 'soap opera' response which might have been expected on the part of Sanjay was that he would have gone to the pub and drowned all his sorrows. Sanjay did go to the pub with Mark, but he refused to get smashed and instead preferred to talk to Mark about how he felt. A scene ensued when he talked through all his problems and then decided he would carry on with his life with Gita and accept the baby as his own. The point was that the production allowed the character to talk through his feelings and the storyline progressed through talk rather than action.

Another storyline in *EastEnders* when men talked about their feelings concerned Simon, who was bisexual, and Tony, who was gay.

They had had a relationship with each other and with others on the Square. They attempted to solve their problems by discussing, with both men and women, the various aspects of their relationship and the difficulties they each experienced with the dreaded concept of 'commitment'. The Italian di Marco brothers walked around the Square, stood in the restaurant, and talked about their dead father, their feelings, and their concern for their mother and their sisters. The Mitchell brothers, Grant and Phil, always talked, usually after a great deal of pent-up aggression had been let loose, when they needed to resolve their many crises. Men moved into the position of being characters who are involved in sharing their emotions with other men in the series. The move was unprecedented in British soap operas. *EastEnders* was again at the forefront of reflecting reality, because it picked up on the cultural moment when men in other parts of the media were learning that it was 'good to talk'.

Young people – growing up in a soap opera

While *Brookside* could be credited with bringing a young male audience to Channel 4, with the introduction of teenage and young male characters to the British soap opera, the credit for making girls and young women major characters has to go to *EastEnders*. That is not to say that there have not been young characters in the other soaps, but to introduce them and include a long-term development of their characters was a definite move made by Julia Smith and Tony Holland when they planned the series. From the beginning they included a number of teenage children – Mark and Michelle Fowler, Ian Beale, Kelvin Carpenter, Sharon Watts – all around 15 or 16. They immediately indicated to audiences that this was a series which wanted to attract a young audience by including stories which were relevant to them and their interests. The relationship between parents and children and young people, and young people's relationships with each other, were introduced into the series and were a conscious part of the forward planning for the programme. The response of young people to the soap opera is discussed by Buckingham (1987).

Michelle's story

When *EastEnders* began Michelle Fowler was a teenage girl living with her parents and her grandmother and her older brother Mark. Mark was the rebel, and Michelle was her father's favourite and got on well with her grandmother, Lou Beale. She was conceived by Julia

Smith as a young girl who would evolve through the series and realize her potential through education. From a teenage girl who made a number of disastrous mistakes, Michelle progressed through teenage motherhood, marriage, an abortion, divorce, re-entering education and gaining a degree (which the producers never capitalized on), getting involved with a number of completely unsuitable men and eventually becoming pregnant again by another unsuitable man. Her character development took her through formal, and life, education and brought her out as a strong and independent woman. As in all good nineteenth-century fictions, Michelle was rescued from her own actions by moving to America where her career and personal life have blossomed. The character of Michelle Fowler can be seen as representing the way that soap operas have taken young characters and let them grow up within a series and also carry the storylines which encapsulate the social and cultural issues of the day. Michelle had one important relationship in the series which was to have repercussions throughout her life. Sharon, adopted daughter of Angie and Den Watts, was her best friend. When Michelle and Sharon were young teenagers, they spent time together, formed the ubiquitous 'band' and discussed and went out with the available young men on the Square.

Michelle's first romantic involvement was with Kelvin Carpenter, her young black friend who lived with his father Oscar. Very soon after the beginning of the series, Michelle lost her virginity in an unguarded spontaneous encounter with Den Watts at the Queen Vic. In order to introduce a story of teenage pregnancy after one act of sexual intercourse, Michelle became pregnant. She refused to admit who the father was and the production engaged in a mystery cat-and-mouse episode when a number of suspects all left the Square for unknown liaisons, but only one was to meet Michelle. The final meeting revealed that Den was the father. Michelle decided to remain pregnant, she named her baby Vicky, after the Queen Vic, and the character embarked on a new phase of her life as a single teenage mother. She began a relationship with Lofty but always knew that to marry him would be a mistake. She jilted him at the altar, although she later married him. Pregnant again, but definitely not in love with Lofty, she had an abortion. Lofty left her and she embarked on a series of disastrous love affairs, including one with a married computer salesman, and one with Clyde Tavernier, who lived in the Square and was a single father. A disastrous one-night stand with Jacko, a weird student friend, resulted in her being stalked by an obsessive. Later she formed a relationship with Geoff, a university lecturer old enough to be her father and definitely more boring than the average father. Finally, she had another ecstatic encounter at the

Queen Vic with landlord Grant. While their relationship had always been one in which Michelle had been fiercely critical of Grant, especially during his marriage to Sharon, after an evening of mutual hostility they were both overcome with passion – and Michelle again became pregnant. Michelle had the dubious pleasure of two sexual encounters under the bar of the Queen Vic with the two most interesting and sexually smouldering men in *EastEnders*, and as a result had two children. Michelle then went to America, when the actress wanted to leave the series, and now has a research post, and a new husband of whom we know nothing. When her baby was born she named it Mark, and Grant was never told that they had a baby.

While Michelle's 'love' life dominated many of her storylines, there were other aspects of her life which emerged as she developed as a young woman and while she was coping with the results of her encounter with Den. Michelle's time at university was a wasted opportunity by the producers. They fell into the trap of creating stereotypical student friends, and her studies seemed to add little to her life. In fact, this is a clear example of why the majority of characters in soap operas are not stereotypes and why on the relatively rare occasions that such characters become part of the fiction they fail to register any sense of realism. Far from highlighting the difficulties she would have experienced as a single mother studying in higher education, the production team almost let the strains of studying for a degree wash over her. Far from offering a positive image of the benefits of education, for the most part Michelle's studies were presented as having almost no effect on her outlook and indeed were perceived as having been a negative experience. Michelle attained a third class degree and was positively apathetic in her efforts to find a job. Eventually she did go to work in the housing department of the local authority, but her education was never explored or exploited.

The character of Michelle Fowler is an interesting example of the strengths and weaknesses of the soap opera. Michelle's efforts were never fully recognized, her opportunities were never explored. Although Julia Smith had included plans to develop the character through education, by the time that would have been appropriate a new producer was in control of the series, and he never adequately recognized or rewarded her achievements. Eventually, Michelle finds fulfilment in America, although we never see it, and she remains a memory in the series. Her strength as a character was that she was a young girl who grew up in the series and faced problems that were faced by other young girls in her position. Perhaps her choice of men showed serial ineptitude, and she never really found very much happiness in her life except through her child Vicky. But to those of a similar age, the character portrayed that the consequences of teenage pregnancy lasted throughout one's life and while children brought emotional and practical difficulties, they also brought lasting pleasure. Michelle Fowler was one of the characters in soap opera who – like Elsie Tanner, Raquel and others discussed in this chapter – were representations of young women of her age and class and who communicated with the audience fragments of their own lives.

Ian Beale, Thatcher's child – young, ambitious, rich and unhappy

The story of Ian Beale is the story of a character who also conveys the spirit of the time within the 'real' world and shows how political and social conditions affect the development of the character. When *EastEnders* began Ian Beale was a schoolboy, the son of Pete and Kathy Beale. Pete ran the family market stall and was portrayed as an East End male, macho and mouthy. Ian found himself drawn to the domestic arts and was interested in following a career in catering. He suffered the slings and arrows of his father's bigotry but pursued his interests and over his working career he has developed many catering businesses and expanded into property development. The character is described in the *EastEnders' Who's Who* as:

> A bit wimpy, perhaps, not what you'd call a man's man, but he was caring and pleasant and spoke politely to people. Recognise the description? . . . The fish-and-chip magnate trying to turn Walford into the capital of Capitalism? . . . Somewhere along the line, Ian evolved into an obsessive, obnoxious money-monster. . . . Ian's always pretended to be magnanimous, doing things for the community (the residents' association, standing for the council, throwing street parties) but it's inspired by self-interest. (Lock 2000: 36)

His personal life has been difficult and his marriage to Cindy was one of the most tempestuous in any soap opera. She arranged to have him shot and ran away to Italy with their children. Eventually, however, she died in childbirth, in prison. His relationships with women have always been difficult and his love life has verged on the disastrous. However, his saving grace is that he is a passionately caring father and devoted to the well-being of his children. He has always fought to keep them and their well-being has been one of his motivations. Ian Beale is a character who is representative of the age in which his own development has taken place. The significance of the Ian Beale character is in its perfect rendering of the influence the political climate had on the development of young people during the 1980s. Developing entrepreneurial skills, making money, ignoring the consequences for others – after all they had been told that there was no such thing as society – was a praiseworthy effort for young people during the mercenary go-getting prime-minister-inspired 1980s.

Ian Beale is a perfect creation of a character who reflects the spirit of the age. He strives to achieve financial success but is unable to find any personal happiness. He is successful but is surprised when no one likes him. He is confused by his own position in life. By the year 2000 Ian had overstretched his financial position and in a dramatic climax to a period of intense effort to secure funds to save his businesses, Ian approached everyone who had the money to assist him. Some obliged but Phil Mitchell blatantly refused, even as Ian begged on bended knee for help, and Ian was made bankrupt. The presentation of the character and the pain and shock of bankruptcy was a reflection of the financial plight of many people who had believed the siren call of the financial promise and the cruel lie that there is no such thing as society, that as long as you looked out for yourself and worked to accumulate money the rewards would be assured.

Ian Beale is a character as strong as any nineteenth-century Dickens character in reflecting the spirit of his age. Not a very likeable character – because he has always been interested in progressing his own financial gains – he represents the naive confusion of those who have been socialized in the period of economic individualism. His personal motivation has always been to make money, and his ineptitude with personal relationships can be seen as the result of the ambivalence with which these two functions can be managed. Ian Beale is one of the major creations which capture the personification of political attitudes taken up at a personal level during the 1980s. Told by the prime minister that there was no such thing as society, the character could only believe that he should pursue his own interests for personal and professional success. In the year 2000, having lost his two wives and devoid of respect among his family and community, he was brought to a dramatic and harrowing low when he was bankrupt. The character, sensitively portrayed by the actor Adam Woodyatt, is perhaps unrecognized but is a major representation of a young man of our times. His life has been transformed by his relationship with Laura, his children's nanny, who has developed as a strong female character who has seen the potential for Ian to be saved – and, of course, because she is in love with him, she wants to rescue him and spend her life with him and his children. They have now married and Ian is rebuilding his life and, importantly for him, his business. How Ian will develop is in the hands of the production team, but his character has the potential to continue in its reflection of the realization that everything that he was led to believe was the correct way to behave does not in fact bring the success and happiness that was promised.

Ian Beale, Michelle Fowler, Sharon Watts and many other young people across the range of soap operas are not only representative of characters; their function is to show how similar young people may have reacted as they grew up and dealt with the different aspects of their everyday lives. They use the literary convention of *Bildungsroman* and continue to develop as they experience different phases of their lives.

The function of characters – their stories are our stories

The characters in soap operas are the key to why audiences watch the programmes. The chemistry of a soap opera and its audience is one which involves a considerable commitment on the part of the viewers. Perhaps more than any other television form, viewers are investing their continued time and support to a soap opera and their contribution to the communication has to be recognized. Viewers 'know' characters so well that they expect them to act in a way that is appropriate. That is not to say that characters cannot change, but it does mean that they have to change within the realistic parameters of how that character would behave. Characters must be predictable but capable of a surprise, capable of a change which elicits from the viewers the *assurance of recognition*, the 'mm, I can see now why he or she did that'. They must be vulnerable but able to show their depths and strengths when needed; in fact, as we would like our friends to be. They must be like Forster's round characters, about whom he writes: 'The test of a round character is whether it is capable of surprising in a convincing way. If it never surprises it is flat' (1971: 85).

Just like Forster's 'round characters', the characters in soap operas have to be capable of surprise and of giving the illusion that they could exist outside the soap opera. The characters carry the verisimilitude of the soap operas. It is they who have to cope with the vicissitudes of life; they who link the realism of the dramatic with the reality of the everyday life of the viewers. And why would you want to spend time with these characters? Their stories are our stories and what happens in their lives must have a resonance in our lives, so that the audience is willing to embrace the drama of the soap opera.

Good characters and bad characters seem to be a redundant concept in relation to this genre. As in 'real' life, people are more complex than merely being good or bad, hero or villain; they are not that simple. The characters are multi-faceted and we see their different characteristics and their interaction with a number of other characters so that we can judge their behaviour and understand their motivations. The acceptance of different characters and an understanding of their psychological complexities is something that is possible because the nature of the genre again enables the production to develop and reveal many aspects of major characters. In soap opera everyone has the possibility of being redeemed. This chapter has not so much been a comprehensive representation of the myriad of different characters that appear in soap operas on British television as a glimpse at some of the most outstanding. There are hundreds of these characters, and perhaps the best way to understand them and the role they play in the popularity of the genre is to take each as an individual and attempt to see what aspect of our lives and the lives of those we know they are portraying, and how that contributes to the strength and durability of the genre.

4

Soap Opera and Everyday Life: Decades of Domestic Drama

A child of their times – stories of social change

The reality of soap operas is fictional. Soap operas may be *based* on a representation of reality but they are always from the imagination of their creators. The soap opera is a constantly evolving form, which can be changed and developed, expanded and renewed. It has a never-ending narrative form, which enables it to respond to nuances of change in the lives of its characters as they reflect changes in society. Indeed, its storylines have to respond to the 'reality' on which the soap operas are based. All soap operas reflect the time when they are conceived and are first produced, but their capacity to evolve is the secret of their longevity. The fictional reality which is created comes from the ideas which are incorporated into the programme when it is first transmitted, and the reality that constitutes the programme comes from that time. It is an intricate pattern woven with the structures that are the warp and weft of the series – the locations, the sets, real or constructed, and the characters, enhanced and developed through storylines which can incorporate changes in the personal lives of the characters and their environment and reflect changes happening in the 'real' world on which the soap operas are based. It is both a diachronic and a synchronic approach to the representation of reality and fiction. The historical reality is the history of the soap opera, of the fiction, as well as of the world which is represented. Soap operas reflect the 'structure of feeling' (Williams 1971: 64) of the time of the writing in the drama, and the drama then becomes part of our own structure of feeling in our experience as audience.

Once upon a time in a soap opera – forty years of stories

To look at aspects of the history of the soap opera on British television is to offer a glimpse of the social history of the British society on which the series are based. Forty years of storylines in
Coronation Street, and the accumulation of storylines from the other
soap operas discussed in this book, make it impossible to do more
than simply give indications of major themes and issues which have
formed the drama in the various soap operas. The most obvious are
the universal themes which are common to the genre both in Britain
and in soap operas around the world. The family, women, young
people, love, marriage and sex may be prevalent in all the soaps, but
the concern with class, men, work, sexuality, education and regional
identity have their part in soaps in specific countries. Social class is
one of the major features in British soap operas, but social identity
as constructed through regionality is also a major theme of all the
soap operas. The selection of areas of most interest must also reflect,
to a certain extent, those areas which have made the most impact on
audiences. But the point about the need to be both individual and
universal means that every viewer/reader can select what they have
seen as the most important elements within all aspects of the genre,
and so there can be millions of different views on the most important themes which have been covered in the series.

Every soap opera reflects the conditions which are contempora-
neous with its birth, and these elements continue to be a part of
the dramatic creation throughout the series. *Coronation Street* was
steeped in the working-class community which it represented and held
in high regard. When it began in the 1960s its representation of reality
was based on the northern terraced community, and it reflected the
working-class values which had existed through the 1930s, 1940s and
1950s, immediately before the series began. The characters may have
first been seen on screen in 1960 but they had fictionally been 'born',
their beliefs had already been formed, and these were the dominant
values which were part of the drama when it began. It reflected
the belief among the working class that hard work and gaining and
retaining respectability were important qualities to be sought. Some
characters spent their life trying to achieve the elusive respectability.
Hilda Ogden scrubbed, cleaned and kept other people's property
clean, and she longed to be seen as 'respectable' herself. When she
won a competition to find the most happily married couple, an ironic
storyline if ever there was one, it was the sheer luxury and respectability of the hotel, and the fact that she was part of it, even for a short
period of time, which gave her such pleasure. Janice Battersby strived
for years to retain her head above the financial parapet and avoid

being 'looked down on' by other members of the street because of Les Battersby's criminal and anti-social behaviour. Remaining respectable is one of the constants for the working-class characters in soap operas. In *EastEnders* the pursuit of respectability is a major concern of Dot Cotton and the fragile thread with which she maintains that respectability was threatened by her wayward husband Charlie and her criminal son Nick. Now Dot has achieved a new status married to Jim.

Crossroads in its first incarnation began life in 1965, when the first motorways were being built in Britain. Along with the motorway came the idea of the motel, a concept which was previously only known through the American films, in which the motel brought connotations of illicit meetings or the psychological horror of the Bates Motel in Hitchcock's *Psycho*. The soap opera concentrated on the lives of the staff of the motel, because for the guests, the whole concept of staying in a motel was that it was an anonymous time. Famous guests had their own storylines but for the most part it was the staff who formed the basis of the drama. In that sense, the series did reflect the norms and nuances of behaviour of the various representations of class which were included in the series. But for most of the audience it was the everyday life of the characters to which they related, for many of them had no experience of staying in motels. What *Crossroads* did was create a soap opera which was based on a workplace, where the concentration on the everyday life of the staff was different from any soap opera before or since – until *Crossroads* returned to ITV in 2001.

Emmerdale, *Brookside*, *EastEnders* all have influences from when they began, and their storylines and reflections of attitudes and behaviour have changed over the decades that they have been in production. *Emmerdale* has shown how the rural economy has changed, how farming has become less at the forefront of the business and how the gentrification of the area has meant a growth of more restaurants, stables and stud farms and an increase in the land owned by richer families from outside the area. Outside companies brought in management and different approaches to farming and this has all been reflected in the storylines from its inception and up to its current position as one of ITV's leading soaps. *Brookside* and *EastEnders* both began by reflecting the social conditions in their particular region and have reflected changes through their storylines. Common stories are for the most part those which reflect the themes of the everyday, the ordinary and these are addressed across all the soaps.

Soap operas explore a practical and social world and the emotional world of their characters and these are reflected in the themes and concepts which are handled in the dramas. The history of the genre incorporates norms, values and changing behaviour which is a reflection and representation of what is happening in the world outside the soap opera – the world of 'so-called' reality, the 'real world'. Changing values and norms have to be reflected in the drama, but the values and beliefs have to remain true to the integrity of the characters. So how does soap opera reflect an everyday life which is familiar to its audience and yet keep the drama realistic and compelling? Soap opera makes the ordinary fascinating and elevates the minutiae of everyday life to popular art. The soap opera is at the heart of popular culture. Understand the significance of the drama of the soap opera and you will understand how soap opera works through the celebration of popular culture and everyday life. The significance of the drama is not only realized through major themes and concepts; there are tiny moments which together work to create the DNA of the form.

One example, from millions of tiny moments, can illustrate how the minute detail creates the reality. In the series *Coronation Street*, after her experience of schoolgirl motherhood (discussed in detail in chapter 5), Sarah Louise started to go out with a new boyfriend, Glen. Wary of her vulnerability and of not making any further mistakes, Sarah Louise is very careful to maintain her sexuality as her own and is not ready to commit to a sexual relationship with the new boyfriend. Although she agrees to spend New Year's Eve with him, she is not prepared to have a sexual relationship. When she is challenged by her best friend, Candice, for not sharing the most important news that she has slept with Glen, Sarah Louise is horrified to think that Glen has lied about her to his friends. Candice is horrified that Sarah Louise has not shared this important moment with her, and Glen, when confronted, sheepishly admits that although he did not actually tell his friends that he and Sarah Louise had had sex, neither had he denied it. This is a tiny incident in a major and ongoing storyline but one which encapsulates important and recognizable issues for the young audience and resonates with women of all ages. The universal concept concerns the reputation of the young girl: having had one baby, is she now sleeping with another boyfriend? And, importantly for her, what will people think of her? So many tiny elements fuse in this storyline: the notion of the missing chivalry of the young man who did not deny their involvement; the pressure which he felt at not being able to admit that no sexual activity had taken place, thereby losing face with his friends, and the vital importance of the issue of the total sharing of secrets between 'best friends'. If Sarah Louise had slept with Glen, then her first duty according to the codes of honour between best friends was that she told Candice that it had happened. A simple collection of codes of human relationships, perfectly formed into a tiny moment in the series. This is one of millions of such moments that reflect the changing historical reality which soap operas reflect. It is the ability to reproduce these known values and changing norms which keeps the soap opera at the forefront of popular culture. These are not major issues in the storylines; they are moments when the writing team will have said, 'and then, and then', and will have added to the verisimilitude of the storyline. These are the moments to which audiences relate and which incorporate the minutiae of everyday life; audiences know this means that the writers are 'in touch' with both their own characters and the reality on which those characters are based.

Characters, themes, issues and dramas

Traditionally, soap operas have been perceived as being one of two types. They have either been character- or story-led. All soap operas handle 'issues' in their storylines. The significant difference is whether the drama is driven by its characters; in this case, only if the issue grows naturally out of the personality of the character will an issue be part of the storyline. In some soaps, it was the issues which were to be handled which were more dominant; they were sometimes grafted on to characters, so that the issue in the story could be seen as dominant and not always seen as growing naturally out of the characterization. Of course, most of the time soap operas combined these two different approaches, but for the most part the different soaps have been characterized as being character- or issue-led. *Coronation Street* and *EastEnders* have always been character-led, and their stories and issues have grown naturally out of the personality of their characters. *Emmerdale* has handled fewer issues and has always been character-led, while *Brookside* is definitely perceived as being issue-led and at the forefront of socially aware drama. The colloquial term for issue-led drama is 'gritty'; thereby suggesting that only 'gritty' life is 'real'. For a moment we will run with the 'gritty' reality of our lives. But it is important to remember that soap operas also deal with those parts of our lives which are neither 'gritty' nor emotionally uplifting; they just are parts of our lives. The title of the American daytime soap *Days of Our Lives* is perhaps the most apt phrase to describe what soap opera is about. It is about all the days of our lives, whether they are exciting or mundane, and the stuff of soaps is the minutiae of those days and how we deal with whatever is a part of them.

A genre of life's problems and pleasures

However, it is wrong to assume that gritty, realistic drama, which handles contemporary issues only, came into being in the 1980s with the coming of *Brookside* and *EastEnders*, for such themes were part of British soap operas in their earliest phase. Indeed, the radio soap opera *The Archers* was started as a means of getting government information about farming over to the audience and has always had a farming advisor. In its first inception the long-running ITV series *Crossroads* handled serious issues within its storylines. One woman talking about the series in the early 1980s said:

> It brings in every aspect of life, the poorer part and the rest, like *Coronation Street* as well. It does involve people getting drunk, having babies without being married and all this, that and the other. It is an everyday programme; you get involved in it. I mean, they have brought mugging into it now, haven't they. I think it's because they bring everything into it that it is so good. (Hobson, 1982: 131)

These comments illustrate the inclusion of issues which were relevant at that time and also show the differing attitudes which may now operate in views on social behaviour. It would seem unlikely that in a similar interview an interviewee would now comment on the inclusion of stories about 'having babies without being married'. What is significant enough to be mentioned changes with the social conditions which obtain at different times. Pregnancy is still a major theme of the soap opera, but it is unlikely that it would be referred to solely in terms of the woman not being married. Now it is unlikely that the pregnancy would merit the comment that the character was not married, and if negative comments were made they would certainly reveal more about the views of the speaker than of the majority. In fact, this woman was not making a negative comment; she was seeing the inclusion of the storyline as being a recognition of the myriad of everyday events which the programme reflected.

Crossroads was always at the forefront of social issues, and storylines which were based on various areas of social concern were included from its inception. The programme reflected the commonly held views of the time when it began, and presented the consequences of those attitudes for the characters. Although it was never revolutionary in form, it did include stories which were not readily discussed in other areas of popular television. An example was the storyline of Diane, a waitress in the motel. She had a baby she could not keep and he was taken to America by his father. How she experienced life without her son was a major part of her storylines and her character development. An unseen character in the soap opera, 'Little Nicky' was a presence in the drama because of his absence from his mother's life. Pregnancy wanted, unwanted, expected, unexpected, the liaisons which resulted in pregnancy, the children that are born of such liaisons, and the repercussions throughout the lives of all the characters – this is one of the major themes across all the soap operas.

Crossroads also handled the question of disability when one of its major characters, Sandy – Meg Richardson's son and part of the management team of the motel – was confined to a wheelchair after an accident and had no possibility of recovery. The storyline was written because the actor, Roger Tonge, suffered from a condition which made it difficult for him to stand for long periods of time, and the series handled the disability in an extremely positive manner. In the early 1980s *Crossroads* included a storyline where a young woman with Down's syndrome became the friend of one of the characters. The series was also one of the first to include black characters: Mac, who worked in the garage, and his wife and child were secondary characters in the early 1980s. So the inclusion of 'so-called' issues was handled in the series, although it was not seen as an issue-based programme.

Coronation Street was not seen as a series which handled strong social issues but this again is a misconception. However, its handling of issues was much more integral to the characterization within the series. Its issues 'grew' out of what was completely likely to have happened to the characters; an issue was not 'given' to a character because the issue was important and the producers felt that it should be included in the programme. From its inception it did handle problems which were part of the contemporary social world. Elsie Tanner was the single mother of a teenager, Dennis, who cruised on the verge of crime and encapsulated the view of the newly discovered teenage problem. It could be said that for the broadcasting industry based in London, the very existence of the world of the north was one huge 'issue'. Look at the first episode of *Coronation Street* and see the characterization and the issues of their everyday life writ large within the dialogue. It does not have to say, 'We are going to show you how tough life is in the north; how a woman without a husband will find it hard to deal with a teenage son who tries to outwit her at every move; how a young man who has been to grammar school and away at teacher training college will have difficulty coming to terms with life back home; how corner shops need to recognize that customers may have difficulty managing their money but they will keep them longer if they do not allow them to get into debt.' It does not have to preach or teach its audience, because these are issues that they recognized and about which they knew as much as the producers. *Coronation Street* has never been obvious in its social stories, but it has traced and reflected the stories of its region since its inception. In recent years it has become one of the leading series for inclusion of serious issues and is now absolutely at the forefront of this aspect of the genre. Some of the most serious issues which have been handled in the programme are discussed in chapter 5.

Emmerdale had a tradition of dealing with storylines which were reflective of the problems of living in rural England. Teenage pregnancy was also part of their storylines, and in 1983 Sandy Merrick, a teenage character in the series, became pregnant and went to Scotland, where her father lived, to have her child. She decided to have her daughter adopted, returned to Beckindale where she lived with the extended family of the Sugdens and resumed her life without her child. This storyline from *Emmerdale Farm* might not be remembered, because the programme was not always included in serious debates about the genre, but it illustrates that soap operas have always included stories which were part of the universal concerns of its audience. In 1987 *Emmerdale* tackled the issue of nuclear dumping in rural Britain. The storyline involved the prospect of a nuclear dump being sited near the village and the programme raised issues concerned with the prospect of nuclear dumping. Although the issue was resolved when the plans for the dump were abandoned, it did bring an environmental issue to the notice of its audience. In this and other storylines *Emmerdale* did handle serious social issues, but their production team would insist that it was a character-led series which only included such a storyline if it could be seen as a natural development of one of their characters – or, as with the nuclear dumping story, was pertinent to their specific location. *Emmerdale* is often overlooked and is not recognized as one of the major series on British television, but it has always been at the forefront of issues which both affected its own constituency and linked it with the wider audience.

The soap operas which changed the perception and the reality of the genre were born in the 1980s. In 1982 when Channel 4 launched its new soap opera *Brookside* it revolutionized every facet of soap opera. Conceived with one of its aims being to bring a young audience and the elusive AB males to Channel 4, it set out to be deliberately controversial and to handle social issues in an unflinching way. It increasingly took on the mantle of issue-based drama, although it also had strong and identifiable characters. *Brookside* was the cause

of much of the criticism which was levelled at the channel. When it
began it aimed to bring young people to the forefront of soap opera.
Phil Redmond was determined that in this series the characters would
speak in a normal way, and this included the fact that young people
would swear when they were in the company of their contemporaries.
Hence in the early days Damon and his young friends did swear when
they were alone together, 'messing around', and the language they
used added to the adage that Channel 4 was 'Channel Swore'. In fact,
the production was meticulous in ensuring that the young characters
only swore when they were together, never in the company of older
people. Some of the other male characters, workmates of Bobby
Grant, on the verge of redundancy, also swore, but again only among
themselves and never in front of their wives and families. It reflected
the codes of conduct which were prevalent at the time but it added
to the 'Channel Swore' epithet that was given to Channel 4.

Brookside has consistently tried to reflect changing fashions and
lifestyles in Merseyside and has included storylines that have followed
the affluence that has been part of the experience of some of the
inhabitants of the Close. It has, however, contained dramatic themes
which have not been handled in other series. Deep diversions into
criminality, sieges and shootings, cults and incest, and explosions
have not added to the credibility of the storylines, but they have been
mixed with stories which are completely grounded in the believable
everyday lives of the characters and have hence created a series which
is unique. It represents a surreal normality which is different from
any of the other soap operas. And yet, surreal as some of the storylines have appeared, it is more in the nature of the condensation of
so many incidents into one small geographical area wherein the
incredulity lies. It is not that the incidents would not happen; it is
simply that it is unlikely that they would happen in that quantity and
in such a relatively short space of time. And therein lies one of the
basic tenets of *Brookside* in particular, and to a certain extent of all
the other soaps. Their 'reality' works by a condensation and compression of time and events, so that their dramatic storylines consist
of stories which may happen in the world of the audience but would
not all happen to such a small group of people, living in a small area,
and in such a small space of time.

Similarly, *EastEnders* has consistently handled issues, but these
have been part of the natural lives of their characters. They have
always concentrated on the lives of their characters, which have been
varied and multi-faceted. One of the strengths of this series has been
their concentration on the stories of changing family relationships
as families have grown, changed, fragmented and evolved into new

forms. The basic extended family represented in the series has been one of the major ongoing themes, with new families entering the Square and then moving on.

Characters and issues – families

Tell me a story. The strength of soaps is in the narratives, which talk back to the audience about their lives. The stories chosen to be told in soap operas are infinite, and across the range of soap operas thousands of stories have been told. There are, however, certain themes which have been prevalent in all the series and versions of these have been explored across all the soaps. One way to categorize the themes is by accepting that they are all aspects of everyday life. Within that overall theme are the subsections of aspects of social life, aspects of emotional life and examples of the practical elements which have to be dealt with.

The central concept of soap operas is the family and life within and between families. The drama of the soap opera is the way that the family in various forms survives the forces which attack it. The family is a universal theme, dominating the series in Britain, America, Australia and many other countries. This may sound obvious but it is only confirmed when other genres are considered and it becomes clear that family life is never one of the central tenets of these genres. It is in the difference that the specificity of the genre is confirmed. Traditionally, medical and police shows, the 'Cops and Docs' series, have been marked by an absence of family life in their storylines. Themes are concentrated on work situations, and the effect work has on personal lives is sometimes part of the drama but is not normally integral to the genres. Marriages may break under the strain of the demands of work, or long-suffering partners may try to 'understand the demands of the job', but it is usually only peripheral to the drama. Families are portrayed as an absence in the lives of the protagonists, or contribute to the stress which they have to experience in following their work duties. However, even in these series, the inclusion of personal life is becoming more integral to the dramas and this is a direct influence from the popularity of the soap operas (see chapter 7). Conversely, in the 'thirty-something' dramas it is solely the nature of relationships that dominate the storylines. The modern sit-coms and new drama series based on groups of disparate friends or 'flatmates' take the concept of sharing lives with others who are definitely not your family as their major theme. Families are seen as an intrusion rather than, as in the soaps, part of a continuum of life. Conventional soap operas have included some characters who shared a house in this manner, but always in a way that was determined by the requirements and logistics of the production. Filling an empty house with a group of disparate characters may be seen as reflecting a different way of living, but it rarely has a resonance of reality within the soap opera.

Within the overall theme of the family there has been an exploration of the relationships of both its importance as an institution and the many individual relationships between members of the families. The most family-orientated soap operas were the early radio series, *Mrs Dale's Diary* and *The Archers*, both of which developed at a time when other radio series, particularly the half-hour radio comedy series, were based on traditional, conventional families. In the post-war period, one of the major themes of radio was the return to normal family life, and series like *The Huggetts*, *Life with the Lyons* and, later, the early BBC soap opera *The Grove Family* took family life as a major theme. The representation of family life in the above-mentioned series concentrated on traditional families. When the new soap operas began, family life was not necessarily the conventional traditional version and right from the start they began to reflect different examples of family life. In *Coronation Street* Elsie Tanner was a single mother with grown-up children. Harry Hewitt was a widower with a young teenage daughter. Perhaps the most traditional family was the Barlows, with a mother and father and two sons, Kenneth and David. When the series began this traditional working-class family was experiencing difficulties faced by parents and children when their newly educated working-class son returned from his time at training college. Perceived elements of family life in conflict with the class and cultural values was one of the first themes of *Coronation Street*. Ken was 'ashamed' of his working-class roots; his father Frank, a postman, felt 'inferior' to his son's educated status, but this only comes over as rejection of and contempt for the education that Ken has acquired. David, the younger son who stayed at home, has become the favourite and his status as a northern male is confirmed when he is allowed to work on his bike in the living room.

Representations of family life in the 1980s have been a major feature of the two new series which began in that decade. *Brookside* encapsulated various forms of family life, and when it began it was perhaps more conventional in its representation than other series, although it changed over the years of its production. Because of the nature of the location for the series – a newly built housing estate in Liverpool – the production was able to incorporate various families: the working-class Grants with their three teenage children; the downwardly mobile Collinses – the father a redundant bank manager, whose change in circumstances threatened all of the family relationships. The Havershams, Heather and Roger, were newly married, a dual-career family; compromise was not an option and infidelity was not tolerated. When Roger, a solicitor, had an affair with one of his clients, Heather threw him and his clothes out of their house and the newly qualified accountant went on to pursue her life alone. As the series moved through the 1980s the storylines highlighted the changes in family relationships which were taking place in the region where the series was set. The result of the redundancy had a profound effect on the life of the Collinses whose affluent middle-class lifestyle in the leafy Cheshire suburb of The Wirral was abruptly ended when they moved to one of the smaller houses on the Close. The relationship between Paul and Doreen Collins was threatened as they tried to come to terms with their changed lifestyle. When Doreen decided to develop interests of her own, she became a magistrate and eventually had an affair with a colleague. The family relationships of the working-class Grants were also affected by the recession during the 1980s. When the series began, Bobby Grant was a shop steward whose firm was involved in union negotiations over threatened redundancies. *Brookside* in its early days was very sensitive to the cultural and political events which were part of the contemporary social history. The recession, which was so devastating to the British economy and British working class, was reflected in storylines in *Brookside*, and the effect on the family life of the various characters became part of the storylines: redundancy for the middle-class Collinses and unemployment for the working-class Grants.

Soap operas have been at the forefront of reflecting the changes which have occurred in family life throughout the periods of their existence. Because of the wide regional and class representation, they have provided different examples of those changes. The professional qualifications of Heather Haversham in *Brookside* meant that she had economic independence which enabled her to be able to get rid of her wayward husband Roger and keep their new home. She reflected the independence of the newly qualified woman who was not dependent on her solicitor husband for maintaining her lifestyle. Heather had the financial means and earning power which enabled her to become emotionally and practically independent. And while Heather had a number of men friends over the next couple of years, she retained her emotional independence until she met and was fooled by an architect, Nick Black, who she eventually married, only to discover that he had been a heroin addict for twenty years. The storyline explored drug addiction in the middle classes and, while there have been many stories of drugs and the destruction and devastation which they have brought to the lives of all who have used them, it was the first and the only representation of middle-class drug use in any of the soap operas. Drugs was one of the major themes to dominate stories in *Brookside* and *EastEnders* over the late 1980s and the 1990s. But because of the family nature of the stories the emphasis has been on the various family lives which have been affected by whoever has been using the drugs. The story of Jimmy and Jackie Corkhill's marriage has been dominated by the drugs which have permeated every part of their lives. Jimmy has been a drug addict, their son 'little Jimmy' died because of his involvement with drugs, and the effects of drugs resulted in the death of young Tony Dixon in a car accident (when Jimmy Corkhill was driving under the influence of drugs). The attitude towards drugs in *Brookside* has always been to confirm their destructive and pointless power. In fact, the inclusion of storylines connected with drugs has resulted in both series showing the effect on whole families and communities when the use of drugs is prevalent.

Many of the changes which have happened in family life have been reflected in all the soap operas, and these have been similar whichever soap is considered. What is reflected is that changes are common to all regions and classes and yet it is still the family form which remains the main source of subject for the dramas.

Class – are soap operas all about the working class?

One of the myths about soap operas is that they are watched by the working classes and they are about their lives. This myth has emanated in Britain because *Coronation Street* certainly was written to represent the northern working-class life in Weatherfield and was a creation that came out of the late 1950s when the end of class was forecast. In the 1950s and 1960s class was much more rigidly defined, and although a number of the characters in the soaps during the 1960s were working-class, there was also a number of characters who could be described as lower middle-class, or even middle-class. *Crossroads* was definitely a soap opera which was much more middle-class, its main characters being the owners and management team of the hotel. The other characters in the series – the staff at the motel – were definitely representations of the respectable working classes. The same was true of the early years of *Coronation Street* when the main characters, although living in small terraced houses, mainly had jobs which were lower middle-class: Annie and Jack Walker, publicans, running the Rovers Return; Florrie Lindley, who has just bought the corner shop; Ken Barlow, newly qualified school teacher, and his father, a postman – all were certainly at the respectable end of the working class.

In the current storylines, most of the characters are self-employed, owning their own businesses. Kevin owns the garage; Fred and Ashley own the butcher's shops; Audrey owns the hairdresser's; Rita, who also has wealth inherited from her husband, owns the newsagent's shop; Mike Baldwin owns the clothing factory, Steve MacDonald and Vikram Desai own the taxi firm, and Dev Alahan owns a number of retail businesses. While there are some characters who could be termed as working-class, it is clear that the predominance of characters are self-employed and owners of their own small and large businesses.

Similarly in *EastEnders* there a number of fairly well-heeled characters, although fortunes change at the whim of producers, and what is true at the time of writing may well have changed when this book is read. Sharon owns part of the Queen Vic pub, Ian Beale and Laura, now in much lesser circumstances, still own the fish and chip shop. Phil Mitchell owns the garage, the café and has other interests, including the Queen Vic pub. Dr Trueman was the local doctor. The lists could be expanded. Although there are a number of characters who do work for other people, most of the characters are again self-employed.

The same exercise can be carried out on *Emmerdale* and *Brookside*, both of which have professional and self-employed characters in abundance. It soon becomes clear that the soap operas should not be described as being about the 'working class' but rather as representative of a wider range of characters which span all the classes. *Emmerdale* has Chris Tate who is wealthy, and Zoe Tate, his sister, who owns a veterinary practice. It even has a rich aristocrat, Lady Tara!

The point about the myth that soap operas are all about the working class is one that is easily dismissed. The soaps span all social classes and have expanded over the years to include newly emerging social groups and to reflect the changing fortunes of existing characters. In fact, what is perhaps mistaken for class identity is the regional identity which is so expertly represented across all the soaps on British television.

Soap opera and the national identity

One of the major functions or consequences of the British soap opera is that all the series have a considerable role in reflecting the national identity through regional representation. Being conscious of a national identity does not come naturally to the English. Conversely, it is so natural that there is little self-awareness of national identity unless one is confronted with a difference. Equally, to recognize how the national identity is constructed through a dramatic form requires a move from the taken-for-granted to a conscious analysis. In this book I have been examining the nature of the British soap opera, and it would seem appropriate to consider what is the element of 'Britishness' that determines the specific nature of these manifestations of the genre. The construction of the identity of 'Britishness' in British soap operas is one that is very finely achieved through dramatic conventions and by reference to social and cultural meanings, constructed by means of representations of aspects of region, gender, age, class and race. Like all versions of popular drama the soap opera must work with already held cultural information, as well as with the knowledge which is acquired through having watched the programme over a number of years. Equally, the sense of a British national identity is so multifarious as we move into the twenty-first century that we are still confused as to what it is to be English within Britain. The sense of a national identity has always been more clearly defined and experienced by the Scots and the Welsh, who retain their national identity in a much stronger way than that experienced by the English.

However, it is clear that soap operas have an important role in the representation of our national identity. They not only reflect our identity; they are part of the cultural artefacts which construct and shape the same. Part of the idea and reality of what it is to be British is determined by the area in which you were born. Quite obviously, people who are born in Scotland, Wales and Northern Ireland have their main allegiance to their country rather than to the state of being British. But also those who are born in England, outside London, define their identity from the starting point of their village, town or city, which then extends over to their regional identity. To be English is to come from a region in England and to define yourself in relation to that area. You come from the north, the Midlands or Scotland, or from Manchester, Birmingham or Liverpool, or from Devon or the north-east. 'Where are you from?' is part of the conversation between strangers when they meet.

One of the main influences on the development of the regional nature of the soap opera on British television is the system of independent television. Commercial television in Britain has been based on a regional federal system, and the companies which have been granted franchises, and later licences, to operate are required to reflect their region in their programmes. Apart from regional news, traditionally one of the main ways in which this requirement has been satisfied has been through the soap opera. The Midland franchise holder ATV, later Central Independent Television and now Carlton, had the series *Crossroads*, Granada had *Coronation Street*, which reflected the north-west of England, Yorkshire Television had *Emmerdale* and Scottish Television offered *Take the High Road*. This reflection of regional identity also had its influence on the two other major soaps. Channel 4 television commissioned *Brookside* from Phil Redmond's Liverpool-based company Mersey Television as one of their few major productions outside London, and the BBC set their soap opera *EastEnders* in the East End of London – both conforming to a recognizable location and selecting areas not reflected in other soaps. Recognition of a location, even if it is only through known representations of that location, is a very important factor in the acceptance of soap operas. In the early 1990s, after much searching, the BBC launched a new soap opera *Eldorado*, which had a completely different genesis. It was filmed in Spain and featured expatriates from Britain and Europe living in a newly built community. The series was a failure for a number of reasons, but certainly the fact that the British audience had no point of reference, even imaginary, was one of the contributory factors. Similarly, the current Channel 5 soap opera *Family Affairs* is located in the fictional village, town or district of Charnworth. Where is it? Somewhere near London – we know that from the train service in the opening credits – but unfortunately its identity is nil.

'Up north' – *Coronation Street* and the north of England

Coronation Street is steeped in the working-class traditions of the north of England, captured in the 1960s when the series began. Its set is still the street of terraced houses in the fictional suburb of Weatherfield. Although there have been changes and additions, the row of terraced houses and the Rover's Return public house are still the main focus of the drama. The *Street* or 'Corrie' as it is colloquially known, has maintained the highest standard of drama, majoring on comedy which observes the manners of northern life. *Coronation Street* signifies the north (Dyer et al. 1981: 2–3). It embraces the qualities of being 'down to earth', 'speaking as I find', 'standing no nonsense', being honest and straightforward. It reveals qualities that are perceived to be synonymous with the north of England – blunt but honest and admirable.

Brookside: 'Being a Scouser' – the Liverpool voice

'Being a Scouser', coming from Liverpool, has a specific cultural meaning which is not only based on the physical place but also through the cultural artefacts which have come from the reality and representations of the City of Liverpool. *Boys from the Blackstuff*, perhaps the most famous BBC drama series, explored the brutality of unemployment and life on the dole and the life-draining experiences for the men and their families. Liverpool came to represent an experience of 'real life', the traditions of working-class life where the traditional working class had been torn from its means of survival. Into this tradition *Brookside* emerged in the early 1980s, as the hold of Thatcherism took over, and the newly built estate which was the setting for the series included representatives of the downwardly mobile, in the Collinses, the upwardly mobile yuppies, in Heather and Roger Haversham, and the working-class union representative Bobby Grant, who moved into a four-bedroomed house, courtesy of inheriting a small amount of money after Sheila's mother's death.

Symbols used in *Brookside* to represent the regional identity of Liverpool have changed over the nineteen years of the series transmission. Strong regional accents, mannerisms, body language and language which is peculiar to the region – all contributed to the representation of Liverpool as one of the major stars of the series. At the first 'From Script to Screen Weekend Conference' I organized at Burton Manor in Cheshire, one of the members of the public who came to the open session spoke with passion to Jimmy McGovern, criticizing the programme for not being more reflective of the unemployment at the time. She spoke with passion to the writer: 'We expect more from you. You are our voice!' She was being critical of a storyline, and her comment indicated that the audience felt such a strong affinity with the programme that they saw it as a vehicle which would voice their concerns. There was a sense in which *Brookside* was seen as expressing the voice of the dispossessed, portraying an image of Liverpool as passionate. The image of the region was expressed not only through the distinctive regional accent but also through the language, the use of phrases which are peculiar to that region, and particularly through the passionate concern of the characters vis-à-vis their own lives and events which happened in them. As the series has progressed it has attempted to reflect the changing lives of its characters and the positive changes in the economic and social conditions in Liverpool. Jimmy McGovern has gone on to create his own dramas, including the famous *Hillsborough*, which so eloquently told the story of those who lost their lives at the Sheffield football stadium.

EastEnders – regional to all but Londoners

EastEnders is the soap opera from the BBC which is based in the East End of London in the fictional location of Wolford. Filmed at the Elstree studios, in leafy Berkshire, the programme is a representation of the East End of London. To viewers who live in London, it may be representative of London, but to viewers in the rest of the country who have little or no experience of this area, save what they have seen in fictional representations, it is just another region of the country. So the representation of the East End of London is as much a regional representation as the representation of the north-west shown in *Coronation Street* or the Yorkshire Dales represented through *Emmerdale*. The characters in *EastEnders* are seen as southern, particularly Londoners. Some of them are portrayed and perceived as rather 'flash', 'street-wise' and a little bit 'dodgy'. The East End of London is well-established in drama and film and the representation of Londoners was included in *EastEnders* from its first episodes.

The Fowlers and the Beales represented the East End families and the interrelation of in-laws and legitimate and illegitimate children was prominent in the characters and the storylines. While images of the East End that were prevalent before the series began tended to show a historical version of how the area used to be, *EastEnders* has embraced the modern version of the East End and shown it to be multicultural by consistently including a wide range of Asian and black, first- and second-generation Londoners. While other series are often accused of not including enough ethnic characters, *EastEnders* has integrated good and bad characters, as representations of many cultures, creeds and colours. In fact, it is a representation of multicultural London, rather than the metropolitan view of London preferred by many other media forms. For many members of the audience who live outside London, the capital is no different from any other region in the country and is equally unknown, and while other dramas may show a middle-class, north London version of the capital, it is the multiclass and ethnic representations in *EastEnders* that provides their perceptions of the capital. Within the series it is not a vision of London as a capital city which is represented but rather a vision of a square within a district of London which is part of a regional identity, the region being the East End of London.

Emmerdale – Britain's pastoral dream

Emmerdale Farm, now re-christened *Emmerdale*, portrays a rural lifestyle and is, for the audience, based less on class than on a specific country style of living. For many years the programme was perceived as the soap opera for the middle-aged and the middle classes – the series which anyone could watch without being offended or confronted with the harsher realities of life. This was a mythical perception of the series because it had always had its fair share of social issues. However, because of the rural nature of the setting, and maybe because of the pastoral dream of the urban audience, it was always felt that it was not as gritty as the other city soaps. It did, however, always handle social issues, but these were based in the countryside and were somehow not seen as being as serious as issues in urban life. In the 1990s the series went through a number of transformations when Phil Redmond was brought in as consultant producer and set about changing the series. In a major storyline a plane crashed, fell on the village of Beckindale and wiped out a number of major characters. The story resulted in criticism and censure from the ITC because of its close resemblance to the story of the Lockerbie air crash, but the sensational storyline began the journey which set the series off to higher ratings. The name changed to *Emmerdale* after the plane crash, and in the last few years the programme has become one of the major successes of ITV and the first soap opera to be transmitted on five nights of every week in 2001.

Eldorado – a soap too far away

The vital importance of the regional identity of British soap opera can be seen in relation to programmes which have not been entirely successful. In the early 1990s the BBC launched its new soap opera set in Spain. The BBC publicity brochure for the programme beckoned viewers to a seductive location: 'Welcome to Eldorado: a coast of golden dreams and deep, dark secrets, a world of hedonism, hope and heartbreak – and the sun-drenched setting for BBC-TV's new three times a week drama serial' (BBC Enterprises 1992).

Unfortunately, the series was not successful and the world of hedonism and hope soon turned into heartbreak for the BBC and the production. There were many reasons for the failure of the series (discussed elsewhere), particularly relating to its launch date, but one of the most significant problems was that far from being attracted to the coast of dreams and the hedonism of life in southern Spain, the British audience exhibited their tendency to xenophobia and rejected the series in great numbers. The cast was European, with characters from Germany, Denmark, Sweden and France, and they all shared the life of expatriates in the newly built urbanization in the fictional town of Los Barcos on the Costa Eldorado. The series began badly, but after six months it had begun to establish itself and some more British characters had entered the series with more stories to reassure the audience. However, one of the problems could be that the series was supposed to be about a section of British characters, but there was little with which the audience could identify. It was not like going on holiday to Spain, because then you returned home after the holiday. The experiences of being an expatriate were not the experiences of the audience and there were no means of identification. The series had little reality for the audience, and there were too few points of shared reference to encourage the audience into making a commitment to the series.

Soaps and ethnic representations

Soap operas on British television have consistently been criticized for not representing ethnic characters. While the country is multicultural, and the soap operas do claim to reflect everyday life in Britain, they have sometimes struggled to incorporate black and Asian characters across their range of representations. For years *Coronation Street* was at the forefront of such criticism, particularly because the location which is fictionally represented in the series would have had a number of ethnic residents. Twenty years ago when it was first criticized the reason given by the producers was that if they included ethnic characters, then some of their existing characters would be racist and they did not want to portray racist characters – an example of the producers being aware of their fictional representations being different from the reality they portrayed. This became even more evident as an omission in the 1980s when the newer soap operas of *Brookside* and *EastEnders* were including black and Asian characters. However, in recent years *Coronation Street* has included characters who have been very carefully chosen to give positive representations. Fiona Middleton, the young black hairdresser, was one of the most attractive and positive characters in the series. Dev Alahan, who owns the corner shop which is part of a group of retail outlets has enabled the production to introduce more ethnic characters into the *Street* and to show their positive characteristics. Dev is one of the wealthiest and most charming characters of any series, and through the character the series has introduced an exploration of the positive aspects of

Asian culture and family relations, and the problems attached to some of the cultural norms. The reason why this character is important is because he exists as a rounded character, and the stories or issues which are handled in relation to him grow naturally out of his experiences. There is not a sense of issues being grafted onto the character.

EastEnders has included a number of characters from various ethnic backgrounds in many different jobs. Characters have been from a wide range of cultural backgrounds and have had jobs as diverse as social worker, café owner and doctor, and there have been ordinary families with undefined jobs. Audrey, who owned the guest house in Albert Square, had two sons, one a doctor and one a wheeler-dealer. Audrey died in September 2001, the father has returned and the production has included major storylines concentrating on this family. One of the strongest black characters as part of her own family and as part of the community of Albert Square was the character Blossom, who was the grandmother of Alan Jackson, father of Billy. Alan moved to the Square with his common-law wife Carol Jackson. She had three other children and Billy was her youngest child and their only child. Alan was already established as a strong, loving father and partner. When Blossom appeared in the series he showed the strength of the love of his family and Blossom became part of the extended family. The character was grandmother to all of Carol's children and acted as a confidant and loving friend to them all. She also had friends and her own relationships within the Square and eventually she left for a romantic visit with a male admirer. What was positive about Blossom was that her strength as a character was not gained by trying to give her an ethnic storyline. She was black, and she was a strong loving woman whose value as a character was that she united with members of the audience. They responded to her as a woman who was a grandmother and who loved her family and provided support and stability in their lives.

Brookside has also included ethnic characters throughout the life of its transmission, and has certainly tried to integrate black Liverpudlians into its drama – indeed it retained the character of Mick and his family over a number of years. This has been one of the positive representations because it has lasted and the characters have been allowed time to develop and explore different aspects of their lives in the same way that other characters have progressed. Mick has had many relationships and brought up his children as a single father, and the audience have seen the children grow up and deal with many issues which have related to them as children, teenagers, young people and being black. Some of their problems are ones which they shared with other young people in the series, and others have been related to the serious race issues which the programme has explored. Unfortunately, Mick and his family have now left the Close, and *Brookside* has Jerome as its one young black character.

The main criticism which can be made about soap operas is that it sometimes appears as if they include ethnic characters because they think that is what they should be doing or, worse, that they introduce ethnic characters in order to run storylines which they think are ethnically 'suitable'. The only way for the successful inclusion of any characters in any soap is that they are an integral part of the series and the storylines reflect aspects of their lives which the audience will find believable and with which they will connect. Representation of ethnic characters continues to be a difficult area within soap operas and one with which productions can easily make mistakes. They are still learning how to integrate characters successfully into the series without falling into the trap of making the issues, rather than characters, their *raison d'être*. While the productions have all included many characters, the problem is that no characters from ethnic backgrounds have remained as long-standing characters in any of the series.

Emotional stories – love, sex and other emotions

The history of the drama of soap operas is the history of emotions – universal feelings which are known and shared by the audience and with which they can connect. Sexuality and sexual relations are one of the driving forces of the soap opera, and love is the overriding emotion which fuels many of the actions of the characters. Whether it is maternal love, paternal love, familial love or sexual love between couples of all ages and genders, love and the search to find it is the emotion which drives many of the characters in soap operas.

Over the years soap opera has spanned there have been thousands of storylines which have involved sex and, in more recent years, the recognition of changing sexuality. Sexual attractions and the gratification of lustful desires have driven many of the storylines. While these may also be seen as natural couplings, there are numerous occasions when the proximity of characters within the locations of the dramas can be seen as the major reason for romantic and sexual relations. For every passionate love story which evokes the empathy of the audience there are affairs which are so unlikely that they can only be seen as the efficient use of characters and the available locations for them to meet. The great love stories of soap operas stand out and are remembered in the minute detail of the rise and fall and frequent recurrences of passion in the emotions of the characters. Memories of romances from soap operas are often of broken hearts for there are few long-lasting romances in the genre. There are also few long-lasting marriages. Vera and Jack Duckworth are an example, but unfortunately their marriage appears to work because, although Jack still loves Vera, sex is something of which he is terrified! Soaps do concentrate on romances which have been much more dramatic and in which characters have been filled with doubt, guilt and an ability to make the audience scream at the television set, 'Don't do it!' – as they engage with their favourite characters and will them to self-preservation. At the same time, they anticipate the potential excitement and sexual gratification which might just result from the proposed liaison.

While many of the younger characters in soap operas are extremely attractive and their liaisons are vibrant and interesting, there are some characters who have to work very hard to be seen to be at the forefront of sexual attractiveness. Some characters have led particularly active sex lives and yet never managed to appear as sexually attractive. Ken Barlow in *Coronation Street* has been much married and has had numerous relationships over the forty-two years of the series. Ken has spent at least nineteen years unable to cope with the sense of rejection and betrayal caused by the brief affair between Deirdre and Mike Baldwin. The catalogue of his relationships could give the impression that Ken is a Lothario, a great romantic, but viewers who have watched the series for either a short or a long period will know that Ken is neither a great romantic nor someone with whom you would be wise to trust your romantic or emotional future. In fact, he is one of the characters about whom audiences would tend to want to warn any female characters to 'stay away, it'll end in tears'. Ken has had many romantic liaisons and although it might now appear that he has settled again with his ex-wife Deirdre, who knows what the scriptwriters may have in store for him?

Indeed, many sexual relationships in soap operas do end in tears and the audience see that many of them are totally unsuitable as they are developing. Soaps are sometimes criticized for having too much sex included in their storylines, but in fact there is very little explicit or visual sexual activity in any of the soaps. This is because the transmission times for all of the soap operas are within the period of 'family viewing', before the nine o'clock watershed, and there are restrictions on what can be shown. Sex may be a vital aspect of what drives the characters in soap operas, but there is little evidence of the sexual activity taking place in the actual programmes. In fact, there are very few signs of any physical affection, and hugging and kissing – let alone moving further along towards the physical contacts leading to sexual activity – are rarely seen in British soap operas.

Sexual activity may not be explicitly shown in the various soap operas but it is an ever-present emotion and the engine of character and plot development. Many of the sexual couplings are unsuitable, and many result in highly charged emotional disasters. If one of the main tenets of the soap opera is the stories of families, then the sexual liaisons between partners of members of families is another major theme. Consider the Mitchell brothers in *EastEnders*: the affair between Phil and Sharon, while Sharon was married to Grant, resulted in a major fight between the brothers and has had storyline repercussions ever since. Kathy was married to Phil but slept with Grant, and when Sharon returned to the Square she slept with Phil. In another set of sexual liaisons, Phil slept with Lisa and also with her best friend Mel. Mel married Steve, and when he discovered that Phil had slept with her his violent retaliations culminated in his final act of revenge – he slept with Sam, Phil's sister. The sexual attractions are always believable and they drive the drama through some of its most exciting storylines. Viewers may disapprove of the activities of some of the characters, but the producers and writers know that it is conflict which drives the dramatic action along, and sex and its repercussions are one of the main themes which they use to fuel their productions.

The practicalities of everyday life: work – just around the corner

Many of the storylines in soap opera deal with the practicalities of everyday life. Work, unemployment, changing working lives, illness, crime and punishment are all parts of the storylines, although not the major engines which drive the narratives. The concept of work is not one of the main themes of the soap opera, although work is handled on British television in a number of separate drama series, particularly the medical and crime series. However, characters in soap operas do work and many of their places of work are unusually close to their homes.

In *Coronation Street* characters work in the Rover's Return, the corner shop, the café; in *Brookside* all the working activity takes place around the corner where the hairdresser's, the garage, the solicitor's, the doctor and Bev's bar all employ residents from the Close. They only have to walk a short way for work, medical attention, legal advice and for their social entertainment and liquid refreshment.

In Albert Square the residents work in the Queen Vic, Beale's Plaice, the café, the laundrette, the video shop, the car lot and the e20 Club. The location of work is an unrealistic aspect of soap operas, but it is the requirements of the production and the available locations which make this necessary. Characters need to be able to interact in locations other than their homes, the streets or the public spaces, and if their work is local, then there are more places where they can interact and more opportunities for dramatic situations.

Medical issues, but not too gory – serious illnesses – sensitive storylines

Considering the number of medical dramas on television, the importance of health in the national political debate and the everyday interest in medical matters, there is relatively little representation of illness in soap operas. Few characters complain of everyday aches and pains and those who do are usually defined as being over concerned about their ailments. As in real life, everyday illness is not the stuff of drama; it is only when life-changing or life-threatening illnesses become part of the lives of the characters in soap opera that illness or medical matters form major storylines.

When soap operas treat serious illnesses they perform at their best. Not only the serious illness discussed in chapter 5, but also the treatment of major illnesses which are extremely serious and potentially life-threatening and are, unfortunately, common to many members of the audience. There have been many examples of such storylines throughout the decades, and their treatment reflects the style of the soap. Sometimes illness can result in death, as a way of writing out characters, but the fatal demise of characters has usually been through accidents, which provide less harrowing but more dramatic viewing than terminal illness. Tiffany was run over by a car driven by Frank Butcher, Alan Bradley was hit by a Blackpool tram as he pursued Rita, and many characters met their demise in *Emmerdale* when a plane dropped out of the sky. (A moment of rare intertextuality deserves mention here. After that incident in *Emmerdale*, one of the characters in *Brookside* was seen reading a newspaper which had a headline referring to the plane falling out of the sky. This intertextuality was not an accident. It was possible only because Phil Redmond was the consultant on *Emmerdale* for this particular storyline; he was aware of its transmission date and was able to incorporate the nice reference within his own production of *Brookside*.)

Older characters have featured in storylines which have included dying from illnesses relating to old age. *EastEnders* famous matriarch, Lou Beale, died of heart disease, but not before she could talk to all of her family and leave instructions as to how they should behave. One of the most famous deaths in *EastEnders*, and the one which sustained a major storyline, was the death of Ethel, a character who had been in the series since it began and played one of the older East End women who had lived through the Second World War and had lost all her family in one attack by a doodlebug. She represented those women who had been young and newly married during the war and whose whole lives had been changed by the devastation of the effects of the war. Ethel was a character who, although comic, was also a poignant representation of the generation whose lives had been lived in the East End and who – just as the older trio of women carried the northern values in *Coronation Street* – carried the values and traditions for the East End. Perhaps the biggest storyline for the character was in the nature of her death. After the character had supposedly been living in sheltered accommodation away from the Square, she returned to the series in 2000 and sought out her old friend Dot Cotton. The initial reason was that she knew that she had cancer and she wanted to be near her friends as her illness became worse. The real reason was that she wanted to be near her friend Dot to ask her if she would assist her in euthanasia. Here was a storyline which enabled the production to set out all sides of the debate about the topic. The character was fully aware of what she was asking: she was asking her best friend, who was a very religious person, to assist her in the ultimate sin, to assist her in taking her own life. Dot suffered torment as she struggled with her conscience and she tried to resist the request, while Ethel prepared herself for enjoying the last days of her life and for what she chose to be her last evening. After her death, assisted by Dot, the repercussions were extremely serious. Dot suffered untold guilt and felt that she needed to be punished for the action. The series had tackled an extremely sensitive and serious issue and had tried to put all sides of the argument. In a similar, earlier, storyline *Brookside* tackled the management of terminal cancer when one of the characters was suffering from the end stages of cancer and asked other characters to assist in her euthanasia. Eventually this was executed by smothering her with a pillow and those involved were accused of manslaughter.

These storylines enable the series to examine the many different attitudes to serious illness and discuss some of the ethical issues which are part of the current debates around euthanasia. By bringing to the storylines those issues which could be part of the lives of the characters, it enables the characters that the audience know to express different perspectives on the arguments. In the event, both the terminally ill patients were aided in their death by other characters, and those who had helped had to suffer the intense emotional trial, and in the case of Mick the criminal trial, for complying with the request of their friends. It is a subject which evokes very different responses and, indeed, is illegal in Great Britain; nevertheless, the soap opera is one of the few ways in which there can be an exploration of the personal and emotional issues involved together with the unimaginable practical administration of the aid to death of the terminally ill patient.

Every woman's fear – breast cancer and its positive outcomes

Some of the major medical issues which have been tackled in poignant and moving drama have included life-threatening illnesses. The subjects have been addressed in a positive way and have provided some of the major examples of public service television (discussed at length in chapter 5). *EastEnders* handled both everyday and serious illnesses with great success, both dramatically and in terms of effective transmission of information.

A recent storyline involving a major character, Peggy Mitchell, tackled the issue of breast cancer. It progressed from her early suspicion when she found a lump in her breast, through her visits to hospital, keeping it to herself and eventually telling her family, having a mastectomy and up to her decision to have reconstructive surgery. Practical medical issues were handled but the devastating emotional factors were also a major part of the drama – how she felt about losing her breast and how it affected her own perception of her sexuality. In the scene when she first looked at herself in the mirror to see the scar and the terrible loss of her breast, the actress united both with women who had shared the experience and with those who feared they might have to share it in the future. In a further element of the story, *EastEnders* brought into the storyline the reaction of Frank, who was about to marry Peggy when she discovered that she had breast cancer. His reaction was not the conventional one which a soap opera might be expected to handle. He was, of course, devastated that Peggy had cancer, that she had to go through the operation and that she was facing a life-threatening illness. But what also dominated his response was that he had no idea how he would react after she had had her breast removed. How would he face her changed appearance and would his response be the same towards her? By pursuing this aspect of the illness, the production explored many of the fears felt by both men and women in relation to the emotional and sexual implications of the illness.

The inclusion of such issues in soap opera is one of the major strengths of the genre because it enables the audience to identify with the characters, to follow the progress of their problems and to see the possible outcomes. The possibility for the range of options, the exploration of the fears experienced by the character and the generous amount of time which can be devoted to the storylines make the soap opera an extremely positive vehicle for tackling the subject of serious illness.

Crime – a penchant for prisons

Criminality as a concept has been part of the drama of the soap opera. *EastEnders* have homed in on the real and imaginary images of the East End criminals and their influence on the daily lives of those in the district. In fact, an ongoing atmosphere of the threat of crime is part of the unspoken ambience of the series. Under the surface, for the most part out of view, there is always the possibility of a low-grade 'godfather' waiting to settle scores, call in favours or do a deed. There is even the questionable solicitor Marcus, who is brought in to help sort out the assorted 'problems' which occur.

Crime as a part of everyday life is not integral to the lives of the audience in terms of personal participation or intimate knowledge of family or friends who have been involved in criminal activity. Experience as a victim of crime, usually burglary or car theft, is much more common, but not the actual experience of committing, or being wrongly accused of committing, crime and eventually being committed for trial. In soap operas, however, there is likely to be a storyline which includes criminal activity or wrongful arrest. Some of the trials have been famous and some infamous, but all have produced dramatic storylines which have sometimes verged on the unbelievable. Part of the dramatic interest for the producers is that they can indulge their *penchant for prisons*. Various storylines over the years have included these excursions to prison and they have rarely been seen to fit 'easily' into the rest of the drama.

One high profile storyline was an example of how, even with the best acting and audience involvement with a character, a soap opera storyline can still not be entirely successful. This storyline took Den from his habitat in the Queen Vic pub to a prison where a totally unrelated parallel storyline was to unfold. While life continued in Albert Square, Den languished in gaol while a forgettable storyline ran its course. In a more poignant storyline Arthur Fowler went to prison and the distraught and guilt-ridden character was haunted by the shame of his crime of stealing money from the community. More recently, the Matthew and Steve story in *EastEnders* showed more of the horror of the conditions which exist in prison, but soap operas can really only touch on these elements. As with sex, the time slot for soap operas means that they are scheduled before the family-viewing watershed, and they are, therefore, restricted in the extent to which they can show extreme matters of any kind. But this does mean that scenes which are representative of prison life can never be as awful as the real conditions. This has an effect on the perception of these storylines by the audience. What is significant is that the audience never really feel as if they are part of the reality created by the production. The fictional sets and locations which form the aesthetic world of whichever series do not fit easily with the scenes inserted from prison. Coupled with portrayals of prison officers, police and legal officials which can never be any more than ciphers and stereotypes compared with their representation in other drama series, these incidents help to show why the other aspects of the soap opera are so familiar to their audience. While the genre works by revealing all aspects of the lives of the characters in the series, those scenes which are shot in the prison create a sense of 'unreality' when juxtaposed with the verisimilitude of the main action of the dramas.

When characters visit their friends and family who are 'banged up' there is even more of a mismatch. This could, of course, be seen to reflect the situation that prison visiting is a totally alienating experience in real life. However, this is not a valid argument because police and crime dramas do present completely realistic representations of such situations. In some cases, these storylines, albeit difficult to make credible, do have the effect of highlighting the injustices they seek to reflect. In the murder trial following the death of his wife Sarah, circumstantial evidence pointed to the guilt of Jack Sugden. However, eventually one of the characters changed his evidence and Jack was found not guilty.

It is not that the criminal acts perpetrated by the characters are particularly unrealistic; in fact, producers do base their storylines on actual cases that they or the writers are aware of, often from the press. However fantastic the story of the con man, John Bradley, who tricked Deirdre in *Coronation Street* and whose behaviour resulted in her being arrested and imprisoned for fraud, it was based on a true story. Similarly, the storyline (discussed in chapter 5), in which Beth and her mother Mandy Jordache were tried for the murder of the hated Trevor Jordache, was based on a story reported in the press. Soaps have a tradition of placing their characters in prison and have rarely been successful in fully integrating this into the overall drama. While Dirty Den and his dodgy dealings on the fringes of the London underworld may have meant that he was quite likely to end up in prison, the spectre of the character spending his time in a small cell did not enhance the dramatic credibility of the drama. These story-lines, while probably justified in statistical representation are never as successful as the production would hope and always create a cred-ibility gap in the fictional representation.

Education – not a major priority

Schooling and education have never been a major part of storylines in British soap operas. In contrast, Australian soaps have consistently included schools and education into their drama. Both *Neighbours* and *Home and Away* integrate education into the drama in main-stream storylines which do not split the generations into polar oppo-sites. The young characters have always had school as a major feature of their lives, and although the characterization of school has changed, the basic message of the series has always been aspirational and has stressed the importance of education, a perspective which has been positively reinforced by the young characters both within their own age groups and as peer groups to younger characters. Watching the storylines from *Neighbours* and the relationships between the younger characters and the other characters in the series reveals the ease with which education has been integrated into the series. In contrast, in British soap operas schooling is a minor part of the drama and although children are seen going to school, and mixing with their school friends, the actual role of education in their every-day lives is almost absent from the storylines.

Reflecting modern times

The strength of the soap opera is that it constantly changes to reflect the reality on which its stories are based. By the beginning of the twenty-first century it can be said that all the soap operas on British television are reaching the highest standard of dramatic representa-tion and are including storylines which have immediate resonance with their audience and with events which are happening with absolute frequency in their everyday life. One of the clues to the fact that soaps are based on the reality on which they draw for their story-lines is the similarity between issues which are handled at any one time by a number of soap operas. This is not because the writing teams confer with each other and decide what issues are to be included, but rather because the writers are aware of what are the issues of most interest, or likely to be of the most interest in the coming months. When storylines coincide it is clear that the series have chosen the right themes. In 2000 both *Coronation Street* and *EastEnders* tackled the theme of teenage pregnancy, concentrating on the effects on both girls and boys. This theme is discussed in chapter 5 but the issue was important enough to have been a major storyline in both soaps. Conversely, the heartbreak for those couples who wish to be pregnant and are not easily successful resulted in the 'Trying for a baby' stories – in *Coronation Street* with the young and newly married Maxine and Ashley, and in *Emmerdale* with Bernice and Ashley.

Similarly, but with rather less success as storylines, both *Brookside* and *Emmerdale* ran stories of gay couples. In both cases one of the partners was not British and wished to get married to enable him to stay in the country. In *Brookside* Bev agreed to marry one of the men and have a baby for the couple. In *Emmerdale* Trish agreed to marry the Australian boyfriend of Kirk in exchange for a cash payment to help with her own wedding plans. In a weak storyline, after the wedding the character left his boyfriend and left the district. These storylines did not sit well in the series. They may have been included to bring the facts of the difficulties faced by gay couples to the notice of the audience, but the treatment in both cases could not be seen to be doing anything positive for the subject. Both stories appeared to be grafted on to the characters and were good examples of issues which were not sufficiently organically integral to the characters and their situations.

Themes relating to the growing number of divorced couples and the repercussions for their children have also become major story-lines in all the soap operas. After the break-up of relationships between fathers and mothers, major parts of the storylines highlight the experience of the children in such circumstances. In *Coronation Street*, when Gail and Martin separated after Martin's affair with Rebecca, the effect on young David was devastating. He became disruptive and aggressive and the series worked through the problems and the difficulties all the characters had in negotiating the new relationship. Sally and Kevin have attempted to follow their separate lives while keeping Kevin's intensely close relationship with his daughters

Rosie and Sophie. Even though Kevin did remarry – only to lose his wife Alison and their baby in tragic circumstances – he was totally unable to cope with Danny, the new man in Sally's life, both because he still loves Sally and because he finds it impossible to accept that Danny would be attempting to become a substitute father to his children. When Danny and Sally broke up, the response of the children became a major theme in the drama. In *EastEnders* Beppe and his wife Sandra fought over their child Joe, and the harrowing effect on the child resulted in them trying to come to an amicable arrangement. The love of Laura for Ian Beale and his three motherless children has fuelled her determination to try to become a permanent part of their lives and take on the role of their mother. All these storylines, and others, do highlight the major significance of the changing nature of parental relationships and the delicate emotional and practical aspects of every individual case that has to be negotiated by the characters as they attempt to portray this aspect of their lives and reflect issues in the lives of their audience. These storylines have also been significant because they forefront the nature of the relationships between fathers and their children and confirm the already identified themes that men have become a major part of the soap opera. Whether for good or ill, they now have equal roles within the genre and carry many of the themes of the storylines.

Men behaving very, very, very badly

As fast as male characters attempt to show the intimate side of their natures, by talking and sharing their feelings, the scriptwriters have thrown them back to their expected behaviour patterns and let them carry on in ways we might have hoped they had grown out of. When three middle-aged men, Dougie Ferguson, Fred Elliot and Mike Baldwin, took over as licensees of the Rover's Return they almost destroyed the business, and when Dougie bought out his partners he began holding card games in the back of the pub and encouraged drinking and gambling and conventionally negative male behaviour. In *EastEnders* the outbreak of bad behaviour is a continuation of a theme which has been running throughout the series. Phil Mitchell was shot, albeit by his ex-partner Lisa in a crime of passion, when she was pregnant with his baby. But other activities around the Square have involved threats, beatings, demands for money, the calling in of 'heavies', the 'fitting up' of a character for a crime he did not commit (although he had committed many other crimes), the complete change of personality of one of the younger male characters (although this was perfectly credible given his background and the treatment he has had during his young life), and a general display of male aggression and anti-social behaviour – all of which makes you long for the days when Lou Beale would have sorted them out. Similarly, in *Emmerdale* Cain Dingle has shown there is no fury like a man scorned, and when his affair with Angie was over he told her husband and her employers, the local police force, that they had been having an affair. Now a new villain, Ray, has entered the series and it is obvious that more trouble will follow.

The entry of men into the genre has been positive, but it is very easy for the productions to get 'out of control' and to change the nature of the genre too much. Since the genre needs to retain its attraction for the audience – both male and female – it needs to retain the storylines that women find interesting and not simply become overloaded with aggressive behaviour.

This chapter has only touched upon a representative selection of aspects of the dramas and will have omitted major themes and concepts which are vital to the genre. What is important is that the soaps have consistently reflected areas of interest to the audience and have tried to reflect issues and concerns which have connected with their own experiences. Some of these themes have tackled some of the most important areas of our lives and brought them to the forefront of our consciousness. However, some of the most important issues in everyday life are the simple everyday pleasures, and these too have been the lifeblood of the series and brought laughter and tears to the audience. The strength of the characters and the exploration of relevant and changing themes has sustained the various soap operas through thousands of episodes, and they continue to address themes and issues which hold the audience and sustain their interest in and engagement with the genre.

5
The Big Issues

The unfamiliar as the everyday

The success of soap operas lies in their ability to make the familiar interesting and the mundane exciting. They reveal what we already know and acknowledge its value. While their success is in making the domestic dramatic, they do from time to time create stories which transport the genre into the realms of high drama. Some themes are of such significance that they achieve recognition and resonance outside the soap opera and unite or excite or trouble the nation as issues are revealed and explored. The strength of soap operas is that they can combine controversial content with the dramatic imperatives of the storylines to explore great themes. The way they handle these so-called big issues is the reason why soap operas are often held in high regard by campaigners who claim for the genre powers that are over and above the interests of entertainment or education. Soap opera producers are constantly approached by organizations of all kinds who ask them to include their own particular concerns or campaigns as part of the storylines. It is the ability to reveal, inform and engage which the soap opera has in abundance. The strength of handling serious issues in soap operas is achieved through the yoking together of characters who are totally familiar to the audience and giving them powerful storylines which explore issues that may be hardly known to the audience and enable all sides of the debate to be aired.

Revealing the unfamiliar – exploring the unknown

It is in the presentation and exploration of the unknown that soap operas reach their highest audience appeal, and the storylines based on issues which are, for the most part, unfamiliar to the audience are those which become the most talked about, and often the most influential. This chapter examines some of the issues which have been at the forefront of recent soap opera storylines, and explores and assesses their importance in the popularity and development of the genre. While the main thrust of soap stories is to make the familiar interesting, it is the ability to make the unfamiliar understandable and present the extraordinary as part of the everyday lives of the characters which separates the storylines that become outstanding. Of course, the issues are not extraordinary to those members of the audience who may have shared the experiences portrayed in the drama, but, unlike other issues portrayed in soaps, they are not personally familiar to all members of the audience. It is a remarkable skill because, within the context of mass popular drama, it enables the exploration of issues that might only be handled in other programme genres, such as documentaries, and these might not be as accessible or generate the same level of interest and interaction with the audience as is achieved in well-regarded, accessible and highly rated soap operas. These are not the familiar stories of family life, children, love, marriage, sex and sexuality, changing roles and the myriad of stories and themes discussed in chapter 4, – all of which are part of the lives of many members of the audience. The themes handled in these major storylines are part of the lives of some members of the audience, and they are well aware of every part of the story and its verisimilitude. However, for the majority of the audience, these same stories are never going to be part of their direct life experience; but they are part of the life about which they read and see reports on television. It is part of contemporary life and they can share in understanding it in greater depth by experiencing the representation in televisual form.

The issues discussed below are a part of recent soap opera storylines. They are selected as representative stories which have been at the forefront of the genre in the late 1980s, the 1990s and in 2000 and 2001. They are the extraordinary stories which stood out not only in dramatic representation, but also in view of the subjects which they handled and brought to the forefront of the consciousness of the viewing audience and the wider nation. The subjects were not new. The late twentieth century did not discover them; they were part of our lives. But we just did not talk about them and they were certainly not included in popular drama. The soap opera and its producers and writers brought these issues into the open, made them familiar and enabled the wider population to talk about them, maybe still with prejudice, but with the benefit of correct information and the ability to counter any arguments made by those who might still remain ignorant of the facts. The soap operas educated and informed us about important parts of other people's lives and helped us understand. These topics are also discussed in audience shows and daytime programmes like *This Morning with Richard and Judy* and *Trisha*, as well as on radio phone-ins, but it was through the soap operas that they moved towards being part of everyday discussions.

Sex and violence without voyeurism

Sex and violence are the areas which form the 'big issues' of British soap operas. Some of the issues explored in the big stories are concentrated on areas of sexuality and sometimes on the violence which emanates from sexual inadequacy. Two areas of television which, together with the use of 'bad' language, evoke the most criticism from viewers are these topics of sex and violence (ITC 1998: 43–6). Complaints about the inclusion of variants on these issues across many genres and programmes are many, but their handling within the genre can be a positive force for the imparting of information which might not otherwise be known. The issues have to be included in a way that is acceptable to the audience so that they do not become alienated from the content and refuse to watch the programme. Because the soap opera audience is highly appreciative and sophisticated about the genre, they will watch a story unfold precisely because it is connected with characters about whom they already have a great deal of knowledge. They will not be so offended by stories of sex and they will disengage the intricacies of violence emanating from sexual inadequacy. They will be interested in understanding the nature of the illness which can change the lives of the characters. Importantly, they will glean knowledge about the issues which are explored in the drama.

Homosexuality

Homosexual characters in drama have always caused comment, whether they are absent or present. If they are represented in a programme, some members of the audience will complain; if they are not represented in a programme, others will be concerned. The inclusion of gay characters in all forms of television has been a hard-won battle. Now that their inclusion in drama is at least more acceptable, there is far more which can be achieved. The groundbreaking Channel 4 series, *Queer as Folk* is perhaps the most progressive, entertaining, celebratory and ultimately positive drama to deal with the subject. The lobbies to include gay characters in soap operas have been critical of the genre for a number of years.

The first soap opera to include a character who was gay was *EastEnders*; Colin Russell was introduced in August 1986 and has been described as 'one of the most popular characters in the early years of the programme and perhaps the most controversial' (Brake 1994: 44). Working from home as a designer, Colin Russell was one of the 1980s yuppies who were part of the early cast of *EastEnders*. When he was introduced into the cast his homosexuality was not revealed, but within a few months he had a boyfriend, Barry Clark, a young man who worked on the market. Barry moved in with Colin and their relationship became one of the storylines on the Square. The storylines which addressed the question of homosexuality in the early years of *EastEnders* concentrated on the problems of class and age. Barry was much younger than Colin and a working-class lad. He had a connection with Dot Cotton's son Nick, who returned from prison and moved into Colin and Barry's flat. Inevitably, trouble ensued; Colin and Barry split up and Colin threw Barry out of the flat. In 1988 Colin met a new lover, Guido Smith, who he met through work, and this relationship became less controversial. However, Colin became ill and there was speculation as to whether he was suffering from AIDS. Apparently, this was never the intention of the production. Brake explains:

> Colin also had a health scare during the autumn and for a moment it looked like *EastEnders* might be about to do an AIDS story. In fact, this was never the idea – it was felt that the most simplistic and unhelpful 'message' that the programme could give out would be to have its only homosexual character become HIV positive. (Brake 1994: 64)

In 1989 Colin finally left the series; his illness had been diagnosed as multiple sclerosis. The character had been established; it did not cause any massive outcry and had set the standard for other characters to be introduced into soap operas. One of the most significant aspects of the introduction of the theme of homosexuality was that the character became familiar to the audience, and to the characters within the soap opera, without any revelation of his sexuality. Colin was known for his intelligence, kindness and social qualities before the knowledge of his homosexuality became part of the storyline. The character was liked, and as the storyline emerged about his homosexuality the audience were interested to learn of this aspect of Colin's life. Of course, prejudice is not immediately dispersed by the presence of an amiable homosexual character in a soap opera, but the skill of the production was that the audience already liked Colin before his homosexuality was revealed, so that any hostile feelings which were then experienced had to be seen as homophobic. The fear amongst other characters was that the age and class difference meant that Colin was vulnerable to being hurt by the younger man, and exposed to danger from some of his younger friends who were less law-abiding than the middle-class designer. In all, the character was extremely positive and, according to Brake, he was one of the most popular characters in the early years of *EastEnders* (Brake 1994: 44).

After *Sister George* and before the watershed – women in love

The recognition of lesbianism in British soaps came later than the inclusion of male homosexuality. While *EastEnders* did have a lesbian couple, Binnie and Della, in 1994, they were not major characters and did not last very long in the series. They were a missed opportunity because they had not been thought out sufficiently to become accepted as interesting characters. Della, who was black, entered the Square as a young hairdresser, opened a salon and moved in with her partner Binnie. The introduction of the hair salon gave the opportunity for a new location, with the possibility of casual characters as customers and of realistic everyday conversations. Instead of letting the character develop her career and explore her sexuality, the series let her sexuality dominate the character, long before the audience had had the opportunity to care about her as a person and hence be interested in her sexuality. It was one of the great missed opportunities.

However, the Yorkshire Television soap *Emmerdale* – which offered a realistic version of the pastoral dreams of many who live outside Yorkshire but which was considered by many to be a staid soap for nans – was actually the first soap opera to make one of its main female characters a lesbian. Through the summer of 1992 the soap opera developed a storyline which explored the sexuality of one of the main characters Zoe Tate. Zoe was the daughter of the landowner Frank Tate and had previously been in the series but had left for New Zealand, with a middle-aged lover, after objecting to animal experimentation in an earlier storyline. Slight, dark, attractive and feminine, Zoe, played by Leah Bracknell, was a vet. When the actress returned to the series, the character was already established as a part of the Tate family, one of the major families in the series. To introduce such a controversial element to the series, albeit at a time when the production was trying to attract a younger audience by presenting a definitely sexier image, was a gamble for the producer. However, the way that the story was introduced avoided sensationalist voyeurism.

Zoe is unsure about her own sexuality and she confides in another character, Archie, after they have had an unsuccessful date. He directs her towards a gay helpline in Leeds and the storyline takes a slight deviation when some of those living in the village believe that it is Archie who is gay. Thus the homophobia within the series was diverted to Archie before the fact that Zoe was a lesbian was revealed. When Zoe told her father that she was a lesbian, she explained to him what she felt about herself. His response was loving and supportive, and he promised to support her in whatever she wanted to do in her life. A professional woman working as a vet, who has gone through a number of romantic attachments with women since she 'came out', Zoe Tate was the first major lesbian character and has continued to be a well-rounded character who has storylines which relate to all aspects of her life and not merely a representation of lesbian issues. Her love life, of course, centres on her choice of partners, suitable and unsuitable. Their suitability, or more often their unsuitability, is about their age, class, personality, indeed, about whether they are the right one for Zoe. Their sexuality, albeit sometimes their *raison d'être* within the series, is irrelevant. It is their ability to be a love interest for Zoe, who is one of the loved and respected characters within the series, which over-determines their character's appeal to the audience. Zoe's sexuality is accepted within the series and her personality and professionalism remain at the forefront of the characterization. She is one of the most positive images and represents one of the major dramatic creations within all British soap operas.

Confusion – whom does he love?

Drama demands conflict, and once soap operas had become comfortable with including gay characters the disclosure of a character's sexuality was not in itself conflictual. It may be a dramatic moment when the revelation is made, but it is an exploration of the emotional issues that constitute the more in-depth storylines. Therefore, soap operas have needed to make gay characters have lives which are intrinsically interesting, or give them interesting storylines or create stories which make the drama out of their gayness. The question of unsureness about sexuality makes for more dramatic stories, and *EastEnders* ran a story which introduced bisexuality and involved major characters in dramatic and exciting storylines.

Briefly, Tiffany meets Tony and a teenage love affair begins. At the same time she is involved with Grant Mitchell. When her brother Simon appears in the series, Tony realizes that he is attracted to him. When Tiffany finds that she is pregnant this coincides with Tony feeling that he must choose Simon. Tiffany is thrown into marriage with Grant, whom she assures is the father of her baby. She grows to love Grant, with all the disastrous consequences that ensue. The story is complex and while it tackles the issues of social relations and sexuality, it employs conventions from the narratives of soap opera and literature. While Tony's attraction to the sister and brother, Tiffany and Simon, and his confusion over his sexuality is the major storyline, the uncertainty over the fatherhood is a major theme. However, this storyline resulted in bringing together two of the most explosive and successful characters in the series, Grant and Tiffany, and laid the foundations for major storylines to come. But, within the conventions of soap opera, the exploration of the nature of bisexuality and homosexuality is interwoven with the dilemma of a young woman who is pregnant and unsure of the father, who might either be a known wife-beater or a gay man. It is very dramatic and engaging, but within the drama the production has brought to the attention of the audience the facts of bisexuality and the nature of the experience of bisexuality in the young character of Tony. Again the skill of the soap producers is to make issues which are outside the experience of parts of the audience appear understandable and, though complex, not beyond the realms of reality.

This was one of *EastEnders'* strongest storylines and the fact that it incorporated two of its best and most popular characters, together with two new characters who had families living in the Square, set the fact of bisexuality and homosexuality, interwoven with hetero-sexuality, at the epicentre of the series. Everyone was involved and had an opinion on the events and incidents within the story. It enabled an exploration of all the various aspects of the themes, and gave rise to a totally integrated set of storylines which revealed how individuals were affected by and reacted to the themes. While the protagonists, Tony and Simon, could explore their own feelings, their parents had to confront their attitudes to the sexual orientation of their children, and the inevitable 'gossip' of Albert Square could put forward various prejudices and confusions about the situation. What was important was that once again the genre had introduced the topic of bisexuality and explored the subject without treating it in a sensational or voyeuristic manner.

Murder – Matthew is innocent

Murder is not as prevalent in soap operas as in the ubiquitous police series that vie for audiences with soaps. In soap operas murder is only of interest to viewers if the victim or murderer is a character in whom they are interested. If a character who has no intrinsic value to the series is murdered, then the audience is not interested. Similarly, if the murderer is someone who the audience would be happy to lose from the series, then the storyline is wasted. In *EastEnders*, Nick Cotton's criminal activities were only of interest in that they affected his mother Dot Cotton. The audience cared little when he murdered Eddie Royle, the landlord of the Queen Vic. Nick Cotton may have committed the murder, but Eddie Royle was not a character who had any specific appeal to the audience. Only when the murder is rooted in a character rather than treated as an issue does it move into the realm of 'super storylines'. While murder is outside the experience of most members of the audience, the possibility of wrongful imprisonment and the experience of prison life is what moves some stories into the league of 'super storylines'.

A recent murder story in *EastEnders* did achieve the status of a story which drew audiences into the detail of the events and provoked them to take sides while they waited for justice to prevail. Matthew Rose, a 17-year-old, lived in Albert Square with his mother and father. The marriage was far from idyllic and his mother was suffering from MS. The storyline took them away to live in the north, and Matthew was left alone in Albert Square. Meanwhile, Steve Owen, a 30-something, suave, maverick night club owner, befriended Matthew and gave him a job as a disc jockey at his club, the e20. When Steve was pursued by his ex-girlfriend, Saskia Reeves, who tried to get back into his life, he tried everything to get rid of her, but she persevered and tried to recapture his interest. In a fateful meeting one night at the e20 club, Saskia attacks Steve, and in the ensuing struggle he reaches for an ashtray and hits her on the head. Saskia is killed. Matthew witnesses the murder and is forced by Steve to help him get rid of the body by burying it in the countryside.

The storyline continued for many months. Matthew was terrified and lived in fear that they would be found out. His one alibi was that he had the security video which showed what actually happened. Eventually Saskia's body is discovered and they are both arrested for the murder. Steve tries to frame Matthew by implicating him in the murder, and they both spend months in prison awaiting trial. During this period the soap explores the horror and terror which Matthew experiences during this time in prison. It is a frightening, humiliating and ultimately life-changing experience for Matthew and for Steve, who is terrified of the whole experience. Ultimately, Steve is found innocent and Matthew is convicted of the manslaughter of Saskia. The horrors of his experience in prison have repercussions for Matthew, for when he is released on appeal, he terrorizes and stalks Steve and finally entraps him in the e20 club. In a harrowing scene Matthew subjects Steve to a terrifying ordeal, tied to a chair isolated in the middle of what appears to be a petrol-soaked floor. (In fact, the floor is soaked in water. This was revealed to the audience after Steve has begged for forgiveness and Matthew releases him. The illusion that the floor was covered in petrol was acceptable, but it had to be shown that it was in fact water because during the time of transmission, before the nine o'clock watershed, it is not permissible to show such a scene.) Apart from the obvious dramatic value of the storyline, a much deeper strength was that viewers saw how the young, vulnerable and innocent young man had been changed by his experience of prison. He had been taught to survive and to behave in a way that he would never have wanted to, and the horrors of what he had experienced in prison would stay with him for the rest of his life.

Domestic violence, child abuse, murder, lesbian love – everyday life with the Jordaches

Brookside has always thrived on hard-hitting stories: rape, gunfights, uncompromising drug dealing, death, explosions and every possible story of everyday life. Always at the cutting edge of soap drama, it has tackled some of the most sensitive and controversial issues and exploited the themes to create the most compulsive stories. It is difficult to choose stories to illustrate the big issues which have been tackled in the series, but for sheer dramatic impact and inclusion of issues of major importance the story of the Jordaches stands out.

In the spring of 1993 a family was introduced into the Close and was to have the effect of moving the soap opera into the national consciousness about the proposed storylines before the story had even begun. It all began with Mandy Jordache and her two daughters, Beth and Rachel. The house into which they moved was a safe house for battered wives. Mandy's husband Trevor was serving a prison sentence for wife battering. Mandy and her daughters were still very damaged and fragile from the effects on their lives of their father

Trevor, although the younger daughter Rachel was very hostile to her mother. After a short time in the safety of their new home, the horror returns to them. Trevor is released from prison and traces his family. Bryan Murphy, an actor who had played charming, lovable rogues, was cast as Trevor Jordache and was destined to become one of the most evil and hated characters in any soap opera. The story, spread over many months, took the production into one of the most horrific but important storylines ever produced in a soap opera. Through his fearful and frightening personality, Trevor forces his way back into the house and the terror begins. Beth is adamant that he should not be there, while Mandy is petrified by the terror she experienced as a woman who suffered in a violent marriage over many years. Worse, both she and Beth are aware that Trevor has sexually abused Beth, and Beth suspects that he had also begun to abuse her younger sister Rachel. Gradually, Trevor begins to practise his violence and sexual abuse. Beth and Mandy plot his demise. A cocktail of whisky and crushed aspirin fails to kill Trevor, who finally realizes that Mandy and Beth are trying to murder him. In a final struggle Mandy stabs him with a kitchen knife. Unable to go to the police to plead manslaughter in defence of her daughter, because they have been trying to poison him, Mandy and Beth have to think of another way to dispose of the body.

At this point it might be imagined that the wild creative imagination of the writers takes over. However, as with all of Phil Redmond's seemingly outrageous storylines, they are based on stories from 'real' life. Two years earlier there had been a court case when a mother of three had strangled her drunken, violent husband and then she and her teenage son had buried his body under the patio. Her daughter had told a friend whose father alerted the police, and later the woman admitted manslaughter and was sentenced to two years probation (Burke 1993: 3). No such appropriate sentence was in store for our characters.

Beth – a coalescence of television drama and cultural consciousness

Remembering that all soap operas are at the mercy of production needs, a new story was in store for the characters, and this was to transport the series and its young star into a whole new coalescence of television drama and cultural consciousness. With Trevor dead, buried in a bin-liner under the patio, the producers were not about to lose the momentum of a story which could stretch over the next few months and keep the audience glued to their screens to see if the unfortunate two were to be found out. The process of keeping the audience interested was begun in the mid-summer and the Jordache story reached another climax, presenting the most gothic and bizarre scene ever included in a British soap opera, and certainly worthy of any American daytime series.

When a badly decomposed and unrecognizable body was found, Mandy identified the body as Trevor's from the belongings. She then had to contend with Brenna, Trevor's sister, who wanted to bury his signet ring with the remains. Unfortunately Trevor had been buried wearing his signet ring, so Beth with Sinbad, a friend of the family, dug up the dead body of her murdered father to retrieve his signet ring and give it to Brenna. This is an example of how *Brookside* has a tendency to include storylines which stretch the credibility of the viewers. Beth survived this experience, and the audience was reassured to know that even though she had been in the process of helping to kill her father when she sat her exams, she had still achieved two 'A's and a 'B' in her A-levels. So Beth went off to university to study medicine and begin a whole new life experience. While at university, still concerned that her father might be discovered under the patio, Beth begins to have a fascination for one of her female lecturers and in fact discovers that she is lesbian. Beth also has a relationship with Margaret, a young friend on the Close. This relationship results in what has become famous as the first lesbian kiss in a British soap opera. While Zoe had the first storyline as a lesbian in August 1992, it was not until over a year later that the kiss between Beth and Margaret was screened. Beth became a star. Interestingly, Margaret did not go on to become such an icon, but left the Close to go to Bosnia to work with her original boyfriend, Derek the priest.

When I spoke to Mal Young, producer of *Brookside* at that time, he told me that the storyline which made Beth a lesbian was not an original part of the plans of the production team. In order to build the tension in dramatic terms, as the audience wondered whether they would be discovered, the team had to think of a new storyline to keep the suspense alive. What developed was the new storyline for Beth as she discovered that she was lesbian, and a strong story followed. Eventually, the body under the patio was discovered and Mandy and Beth stood trial for murder. The case was interesting because, through press interest, it brought to the notice of the public the plight of women who suffer at the hands of brutally abusive partners and parents. Although they do kill in a pre-meditated manner, they are in fact reacting to years of mental and physical abuse. In the event, Beth dies from an undetected heart condition on the eve of the verdict. *Deus ex machina* saved the day and allowed the actress, Anna Friel, to leave the series to pursue one of the most successful careers in film and television of any actress from a British soap opera.

Again, this was a powerful storyline and, even if rather sensational, it did bring to a mass audience a long-running story on the desperate plight of women and children who are subjected to abuse by those men who are supposed to be closest to them.

You make me feel like a natural woman – Hayley's story

One of the most surprising stories to have been included in soap operas on British television has been Hayley's story in *Coronation Street*. Traditionally not a series to handle controversial issues, in the late 1990s it became a leading exponent of the most controversial issues and handled them with impeccable care and attention to every detail. One of the storylines could be called 'Hayley's story'. It began when a young woman came to work at Bettabuys and attached herself to Alma. She was almost childlike in her attempts to make friends with Alma and the audience was intrigued as to whether she was sexually attracted to Alma, or whether it was a sign of a need for affection from someone who was much more likely to fit the role of a maternal figure for young Hayley. Hayley was a sympathetic and completely pleasant character. The audience liked her, and she was established as someone who may or may not fit into the street. She was a puzzle to Mike Baldwin, Alma's husband, but she was 'harmless', not a person who was about to cause trouble or problems for anyone. Hayley was a brilliant dramatic creation; her entrance into the soap and subsequent development meant that the series was able to introduce a topic which might have been expected to cause criticism, and possible alienation to the character, but turned out to be an extremely popular storyline that explored the subject and introduced a new character into British soap operas in an inclusive and sensitive manner.

It was gradually revealed that Hayley was in fact a man. S/he was a transsexual. As the story progressed, she became friendly with Roy Cropper and a romantic attachment ensued. The handling of the story and the issues was one of the triumphs of the soap opera. With dramatic licence, Hayley's father died and left her money, which enabled her to fulfill her dream to have a sex-change operation. The actress left the series and the character went off to Amsterdam to have the surgery necessary for her gender readjustment. When the actress returned to the series the storyline progressed and Roy, who missed Hayley being a part of his life, went off to Amsterdam to find her. The usual dramatic convention of a lover's misunderstanding ensued as Roy thought that the gay man, with whom Hayley was staying on the canals of Amsterdam, was a new boyfriend. Confronting the man whom he thought to be his rival, Roy learned that he was mistaken and eventually discovered the truth from Hayley, that she had had a sex-change operation and was now physically as well as emotionally living in her correct gender. Roy returns to Weatherfield and tries to come to terms with what he has learned. When Hayley returns they begin to build their relationship. The series had then to bring in the reactions of the other people who live in the area, and the reality base of the drama meant that there was a considerable amount of homophobia – albeit not as destructive and vindictive as someone in Hayley's position might have to deal with in reality. Eventually, the story was resolved in personal and professional terms. Hayley's workmates accepted her in her new gender.

Life was not without the expected homophobic banter. Some people were vindictive and some reacted out of ignorance, but eventually most of the members of the community accepted Hayley. Those who did not were those who were bigots and were recognized as such by their relations or neighbours, and certainly by the audience. Roy and Hayley's love affair blossomed and, without any attempt to mention salacious or intimate details, the storyline managed to integrate into British soap opera a character who had had a sex-change and was living in emotional harmony with someone of the, now, opposite sex. The question of a sexual relationship was always going to be part of the storyline. Roy Cropper was obviously not the most physically active man and he explored his feelings for Hayley and moved as far as he felt able towards physical consummation. After a romantic dinner the couple explored their feelings and reservations about their forthcoming night together. Hayley confided that she had never had a sexual relationship, neither when she was a man nor since she had become a woman. In a poignant response, Roy reassured her that this was also his 'first time'. The moment was almost complete and then, as they left the room to go to the bedroom, the soft strains of 'You make me feel like a natural woman' came from the CD player. Perfect production.

Granada had achieved the most sensitive handling of an issue which could have been portrayed in a prurient and lascivious manner. By introducing the character and letting the audience get to know her before the strong storyline became apparent, Granada were able to prepare the way for a story which was even more controversial by any standards. They wanted Roy and Hayley to marry. The subject was introduced, all the barriers that were in place were explored and the opportunities were revealed. The series examined the situation for transsexuals who wish to marry. The comedy elements of the series were maintained by showing some of the more outlandish versions of marriage that is available to couples who wish to marry. An on-line vicar offered a marriage which was bizarre. This was not the route for Roy and Hayley. What they wanted was a conventional marriage, where they could declare their love and intentions in a way that was the same as any other heterosexual couple. In the event, a female curate was willing to conduct the marriage ceremony in her own church. The wedding arrangements were made and the contradictions and problems were made a part of the storyline. The women at Mike Baldwin's clothing factory became completely involved in the preparations for the wedding – planning the wedding outfit, arranging the make-up, deciding on the 'hen night', making the wedding perfect for Hayley in confirmation of her new sexuality. Shared ideologies of femininity became the major driving force for the storyline. When a wedding was in the offing, the women were overcome with the shared aspects of preparing for the wedding and preparing the bride for her 'big day'. Eventually, after many setbacks – including revealing the bigotry of Les Battersby, the most bigoted member of the cast, and a foiled attempt by the press to sabotage the ceremony – Roy and Hayley were married and Hayley changed her name by deed poll to Cropper.

Making the 'unknown' understandable

Granada had achieved a major breakthrough in television drama. They had included in peak-time soap opera, ninety minutes before the watershed, perhaps one of the most potentially contentious storylines which could be included in a mass audience series. The reason why it could have been so contentious is that it is an example of an experience of life which is completely unknown to many people. In fact, it could be said that only those few individuals who are transsexual and who wish to pursue what they know is their natural sexuality have any real knowledge and experience of what is involved. It is easy for those who are ignorant of the facts of this aspect of sexuality to be cruelly bigoted and to see those involved as 'freaks'. What Granada achieved with this storyline was a representation of a man who knew that his correct gender was as a woman, albeit they were helped in the representation by the fact that the character was played by a woman.

By introducing the character and letting the audience accept her and feel empathy with her, they were able to take her through the most intimate change and bring the story to a conventional happy ending. The character, together with Roy Cropper, her husband, is now a major character in the series and she has emerged as one of the most popular characters. They had worked within the conventions of soap opera and taken their storyline beyond imaginable boundaries. It was a love story which triumphed over every obstacle and adversary – physical, practical and intellectual. Integrated into the love story, the production explored issues one would have thought would never have been explored on the main commercial channel. Information had been imparted, the audience had been educated and the level of entertainment had been of the highest.

'What am I? I'm not a kid and I'm not an adult.
I don't fit in anywhere' (Sarah Louise)

Unexpected and unwanted pregnancies have long been part of the everyday stories in soap operas. The way that individuals and their families cope with unwanted pregnancy and the way that their extended family and friends react to their situation is both part of everyday life and one of the most dramatic situations with which women have to cope. The realization that you are pregnant is either a cause for absolute joy or absolute despair, dependent upon any number of variables in your life. Perhaps the worst scenario for an unwanted pregnancy is when the mother-to-be is herself a child. The change from being a young teenager to the horror of the unbelievable fact that motherhood is inevitable is a catastrophic truth which overturns every emotional and physical essence of your existence. This is the stuff that nightmares are made of, not only for the pregnant young woman but also for her mother and father. It touches everyone she knows. It is possible to argue that it is a perfect topic to be explored from every aspect within the responsible world of soap opera; but it is equally valid to argue that such emotive and serious subjects should be handled only within a documentary or even a science or medical programme. But the discussion of such issues in soap operas does allow for a development of storylines and much longer-term representation of how they affect the characters. Also, in the changing world of television programmes, many of these issues are handled in the daytime audience shows when those involved have spoken about their lives after they have had babies (*Trisha*, January 2000).

In the early months of 2000 *Coronation Street* included a storyline which addressed the issues of a schoolgirl pregnancy. Sarah Louise is the 13-year-old daughter of Gail and her husband Martin. (Martin is not Sarah Louise's father and at the time of the story breaking, he was having an affair with one of his nurse colleagues. To add to the drama of the situation, he was thinking of leaving Gail for the younger Rebecca. The affair continues through the story of the pregnancy.) Granada has handled the issue of teenage pregnancy with great care and sensitivity. It has been a model of dramatic representation of an issue, which has all the ingredients for sensationalism and over-dramatic coverage. *Coronation Street* chose to handle the story in a responsible and ultimately very sensitive and informative way. They introduced the pregnancy not only to Gail and the audience but also to the character, Sarah Louise, at the same time. The fact that she was pregnant was a surprise to her and when the doctor confirmed that her sickness and weight gain were because she was pregnant, Sarah Louise was as surprised as her mother to discover her condition. Gail reacted in perfect character and exploded with shock and anger – probably the way that most mothers would react – and the audience was divided into those who sympathized or empathized with Gail as a mother, and those who wanted to shake her for not immediately comforting and reassuring Sarah Louise.

Each element of the storyline was handled with the expected care and attention to detail and presented a responsible attitude to the issues involved. However, the dramatic elements of the story had been interwoven into the lives of the characters and held the interest of the audience as well as providing one of the most poignant and pertinent stories to be handled in any soap opera. The sensitivity with which this theme was handled provides a model of how to include socially relevant issues in soap operas and create a dramatic situation to meet the needs of the series. While the various problems associated with teenage pregnancy were aired, the production also included the reactions of the immediate family, the relationship with the wider family unit and the reaction from the grandmother, Audrey, who had been an unmarried teenage mother herself some forty-odd years ago. It also included an exploration of the way some people were understanding and concerned, while other people in the community were prejudiced and outspoken in their condemnation of Sarah Louise and her family.

It was a frightening and painful experience for Sarah Louise and at no time did the production give the impression that it is easy to cope with the physical, practical and emotional effects of such a situation. After her baby, Bethany, was born, she had to cope with sharing the childcare with her mother Gail and continuing with her school work. She realizes that she is not free to do everything she might want to at school, and begins to re-build her own emotional life and resume relationships with boys. It has been an extraordinary storyline, which has been handled with sensitivity and the imparting of sensible information, and the acting from the young actress, Tina O'Brien, was outstanding. No one could accuse the series of promoting promiscuity among young teenage girls; what can be levelled at Granada is praise and commendation for handling such a sensitive story.

Mark's story – HIV/AIDS

When *EastEnders* began in 1985 Mark Fowler, the elder son of Pauline and Arthur, was a young rebel. He flirted with crime, ran away from home at 17, was involved with drugs and was sent to a detention centre for burglary. After leaving home Mark appeared infrequently in the series, and in 1990 Todd Carty – a young actor who was well established in children's drama through his role in *Grange Hill* and as the star of *Tucker's Luck* – took over the role of Mark. The choice of the actor was important, as became apparent when the storyline evolved to embrace the issues and prognosis which occurred with the discovery that Mark was HIV positive. Todd Carty was established as an actor with a strong following among young people. *Grange Hill*, written by Phil Redmond, was the premier and first children's/teen drama which tackled serious issues to which young people could relate. It handled issues which were relevant to them, and many of the young stars of the programme moved easily into the BBC soap and brought with them their own fans. The story of Mark Fowler's HIV has been ongoing since a short time after he returned to the series in 1990. Only a brief synopsis of the storyline can be given here but the relevant issues relating to this storyline permeated everything which Mark did – and does – following the discovery that he was HIV positive.

A year after he had returned to Albert Square, Mark Fowler had been 'going out' with Diane Butcher, the daughter of Frank Butcher. In January 1991 he revealed to Diane that he was HIV positive. She was supportive and took over the role of a friend, encouraging him to have counselling at the Terrence Higgins Trust. As Mark found out about the virus and the likely effects on his life, we found out the same information. As he attempted to come to terms with both the emotional and the practical aspects of the virus, we too learned about the way it was experienced by one character.

Popular drama, especially in the form of series and serials, remains perhaps the most effective and interesting method to disseminate information in a way which will reach large numbers of viewers. Soap operas in particular have thrived on storylines which explore all the social and emotional ills that befall their characters. However, they do not have a strong record in including illness in their storylines. While the ubiquitous 'doc' series include illness, accidents and death, these themes do not have a recognizable slot within the soap opera genre. Of course, there are exceptions and there have been illness and deaths to write out characters or to deal with the death of actors and actresses. Soap operas are perhaps the best way to spread information to viewers. Their consistent ability to gain the highest audiences, and a complete cross-section of age and social class, means that they are the most efficient way to reach large numbers of people with any form of information. To decide to cover a major illness, and one that, at the time of inclusion in the storyline, would almost certainly end in death, was a step which was considered very seriously by the production team.

While soaps remain the most likely vehicle for informing the audience about HIV/AIDS, there are problems for writers and producers. When *EastEnders* made their commitment to Mark Fowler contracting HIV, they took on the long-term commitment to a storyline which has continued to dominate Mark's life since he was aware that he had the virus. It is the need for long-term commitment which makes soap opera suitable and acceptable for developing storylines which can give information and unfold the reality of an illness as the pathology and treatment evolve. However, for the soap producer the dilemma is whether to introduce a new character in order to introduce the illness or make one of their existing characters the vehicle for the story. To use an already established character is always more effective, but the commitment for the theme to affect everything that the character does has not been tackled by any other soap. For audiences, the inclusion of the theme of HIV/AIDS in soaps is one which they see as beneficial:

> Positive and personalised coverage of people with HIV, such as Mark Fowler in the soap opera *EastEnders*, was shown to be important in allowing viewers to identify with people living with the virus and to enable them to develop a more complex picture of their own risk. (Miller 1992: 20)

While the decision to give a potentially fatal illness to an established character may present the best opportunity for informing audiences about the progression and outcome of an illness, once the commitment has been made to a long-term condition there is the potential for dramatic situations for the character, but the opportunities are ultimately finite. The dramatic trade-off should be that the actor has an opportunity to play scenes with emotional depth and communicate information of value to the audience. This has definitely been the situation in which Todd Carty has found himself. Mark Fowler has been living with HIV for a number of years and it is not possible to discuss every way in which the series has incorporated the elements of his personal experiences, portrayed the reactions of other characters and imparted information about the illness. What has been achieved is the foregrounding of the condition into a major popular drama, and the information – both medical and social – has become part of the shared knowledge of the audience. When the production first disclosed to the residents of Albert Square that Mark was HIV positive (omnibus edition, 14 July 1996) the production included many characters who asked questions and aired their opinions, prejudices or ignorance of the subject. As Mark answered all their questions, the audience learned about the issues at the same time as the characters were informed.

Public service and the soap opera

The conventional notion of 'public service television' is well known. The Reithian dictate that the BBC should educate, inform and entertain has been the guiding principle for BBC television and radio and for ITV and Channel 4. Traditionally, it is the genres of news, current affairs, documentaries, science, religion and the arts which have been perceived as carrying the remit of public service. However, it is in some of the more popular genres that public service is at its most powerful. The soap opera can claim to carry the mantle of public service and fulfil many of its requirements. While the conventional belief is that only the BBC carries the public service remit, both ITV and Channel 4 include it in their programming policies.

It is in the handling of both the everyday and the extraordinary that the soap opera moves into the realms of public service and provides one of the most effective examples of the way that television drama fulfils that remit. In concentrating on the areas which become 'big issues' within the genre, the soap opera can bring to the screen information which is complex, often includes moral and ethical considerations and, crucially, relates to the issue involved. The nature of the genre – thrice-weekly episodes, continuing, open-ended – means that there is time for the stories to unfold and for all the different aspects of the problem to be explored. As this happens the reactions of various members of the community are revealed and the debate ensues within the drama. However, the debate also moves out into

the audience and the wider community, and the issues are then discussed, initially in relation to the storyline in the drama but also
through a discussion of those same issues as they relate to the 'real'
world. Hence the soap opera can feed into a public sphere and
provide information of importance to the population; at the same
time, it fuels the natural interest of the public in these areas and
enables them to widen their discussion about the issues involved. This
is different from the issues which are routinely included in soap
operas. Audiences approach these subjects from the oblique angle of
their being embedded in a storyline to address their own problems.
These big issues may be embedded in the drama, but they immediately jump out from the screen into the national consciousness and
become part of a national debate, both at an individual level and also
through the media and collective discussions.

A prime example of this was the story of Mandy and Beth Jordache
and their trial for murder after they had killed the wife-beating,
child-raping husband and father, Trevor Jordache. As the two women
awaited trial, the story and its basis in reality were taken up by the
national press, women's groups and even discussed by Members of
Parliament, and it certainly related to the trial of a woman which was
taking place at the same time. The fictional issue was related to the
reality of the situation in which women who have been subjected to
domestic violence find themselves. If they retaliate and take defensive
aggressive action which can result in the serious injury or death of
their male partner, then they can be tried and convicted for grievous
bodily harm or murder. What the inclusion of such storylines in a
soap opera achieves is that it puts such issues into the level of public
service on a grand scale. It enables the issues and the intricacies of
the law and the reality of the situation which leads to the criminal
activity on the part of the women characters to be revealed and
understood in a much longer time context. The drama reveals every
aspect of the situations surrounding the family relationships, the violence experienced by the characters and the ultimate tragic reaction
to the abuses which have been tolerated. Again, it is in the exposure
of issues of great public interest and concern within the public arena
of the soap opera that the nature of public service is fulfilled.

The personal is also part of public service

Public service has to address issues of national concern, but these
issues are not the only issues which might be considered 'great
matters'. Just as the genre of the epic dealt with the heroic and the
universal, so the soap opera deals with the personal and the emo-

tional within the infinite boundlessness of the universality of the issues. This is why the form can be adopted so successfully to any country, either by exporting the form or, in the case of the American 'super-soaps', the actual programmes. The universality of emotional issues – and the transcendence of those emotions to practical effects and consequences – are the stuff of everyday life, of cultural studies and the drama of soap operas. Soaps embody the issues which are of personal and public concern in the late twentieth and the emerging twenty-first century. While in previous decades, and other lifetimes, the personal was constructed as private and unspoken, now the personal can be spoken, and it is at last being understood that the personal is not only political, but has practical outcomes, which may begin as being personal but soon become part of the everyday life of the nation or the global community.

The consequences, both personal and economic, of the impact of the HIV virus on the lives of individuals and their loved ones are global. Figures, statistics, medical and government experts can never inculcate the facts and consequences of the spread of the virus and the individual suffering which can ensue. Soaps can do that. Nick Farthing, Director of the British Aids Charity, The Terrence Higgins Trust, told me that the inclusion of the storyline in *EastEnders* about Mark Fowler being HIV positive achieved the most public awareness of any of the campaigns or education in which the high profile charity was engaged. He felt that their involvement with the series had been positive and had brought the issue and the true facts about the virus and its consequences, and how it could be managed, to more people than they could ever have reached by any other method.

The power of the soap opera and the inclusion of issues in their storylines are one of the most effective ways of transmitting information. It is one of the strengths of the genre and one to which the audience continues to respond, thus encouraging the broadcasters to provide even more storylines that embrace the more contentious and under-represented issues.

Part III

Soap Opera and its Audiences

6

A Universal Form

'What do you think of *EastEnders*?'
'That's better, that's more down to earth, that's more to do with real life. It has things that happen in your life. Proper places, like they understand our problems.'

Interview with young man in prison remand centre, September 1996

The importance of soap opera as a television and cultural form has so far been discussed in relation to broadcasters, producers and those involved in the production business of soap operas as well as through an examination of the texts which they produce. But there is a vital group of people who are essential to the production, for without them there is no understanding or completion of the 'circuit of production' (Hall 1997: 1). The audience for soap operas is vital for broadcasters. But the form itself is important to viewers for reasons which are often more than the entertainment value of the programme. Of course, the elements which are part of the soap opera attract viewers to the programmes, and the narrative and conventions of the serial form keep them watching and bring them back day after day, week after week, year after year and, in some cases, decade after decade. For the form enables the successful series to forge a link with its audience and to keep them watching. The form continues to be one which audiences *love*. It has evolved to include characters and stories that were not included in earlier programmes and it has expanded its audience and included them in the involvement with the characters and stories.

While soap opera is now accepted as a major form of television drama, it is recognized by television executives and held in high regard for its crucial role in the branding of channels and establishing viewer loyalty. However, it is only since the explosion of the programmes in the 1980s that the form became so well respected. As the growth of channels and the fragmentation of the audience took hold after the 1990 Broadcasting Act, the importance of any programme which was held in high regard by the audience became vital for the survival of the broadcasters. Audiences love soap operas. They are consistently at the top of the ratings and they command respect and loyalty, even through the inevitable troughs which every soap opera experiences. Audiences may stop viewing when their patience is exhausted, but they return when the producers remedy the shortcomings. Why do audiences continue to make the form the most successful on television? What is it about the genre which can keep audiences watching and interested over weeks, months, years of a production? And how can interest be sustained in the characters and their stories?

The active audience

The relationship of audiences to television programmes is a crucial part of media studies debate. How do audiences understand television programmes and what effects, if any, do the programmes have on audiences? Audiences for soap opera have long been perceived as being completely fooled by the programmes and the stories which they are told, but this has usually been by non-academic sources like journalists and critics, who see the audience as an easily duped mass. And although the 'hypodermic effects' model has been superseded in academic debate, there is, nevertheless, still a belief in journalistic circles that soap opera viewers believe everything that they see and are gullible and naive. Uses and gratifications theory, and particularly the work of McQuail (1977: 70–94) is readily applicable to the soap opera and its viewers, but it is the theories of the active audience (Brunsdon and Morley 1978; Hobson 1982; Morley 1992) that can best be considered as a starting point for any analysis of the form. Audiences bring their own experience, knowledge, preferences and understanding to every television text which they watch. They interpret the text according to what they choose to take from it and this may change according to their own circumstances and experiences. This does not mean that there is no overriding 'meaning' in the text – there is, of course, the meaning inscribed by the creators – but this is their meaning and what every viewer does is broadly read the text for the overall meaning and then distil it into their own particular areas of interest. My own audience research has shown that when talking about television programmes viewers always highlight areas which have interested them and discuss the programme in a way which is driven by their specific interest. This does not apply only to soap operas, for it has been evident when talking to the audience about any television programmes. This is not just a negotiated reading or a polysemic understanding, but rather an active choice of what aspect of the programme they wish to take. They subconsciously edit out stories and themes which are not of interest, and they see in every work aspects which are of interest to themselves. This chapter will look at the soap opera audience. Through a selection of extracts from various research projects which I have conducted since 1977, I will present and strengthen the case for the active and individual audience and its understanding of and contribution to the success of the soap opera genre.

I was first alerted to the importance of soap opera in relation to women viewers when I was conducting research about young women with children and the role that television and radio played in their lives (Hobson 1978). While conducting this research, which was in fact about the everyday life of these young women and not specifically about media consumption, I learned that television and radio played an important part in their lives and I heard from them of the differentiation which they made within their selection of types or genres of programmes. These women chose to reject the serious news and current affairs programmes, because they saw them as having no relevance to their own lives. In re-studying this work it must be remembered that news, current affairs and documentaries were different from what is now seen on television. These women designated the programmes as 'male' and certainly the style and content was much more male-orientated than similar programmes now. However, while they rejected the news and more serious programmes, they turned to drama, quiz shows, soap opera and serials as their chosen viewing. These programmes did not necessarily bear any resemblance to the lives of the young women who were aged between 18 and 21, living on a council estate and had very young babies to look after. However, the programmes which they found interesting were those which spoke to their interests as women. Many of the characters in the series *Coronation Street* and *Crossroads* were women who themselves had to confront 'problems' in their 'everyday' lives, and the resolution or negotiation of these problems within the drama provided points of recognition and identification for the women viewers.

Everything stops for Crossroads.

> If anybody comes here I say, 'Well, if you don't mind, I like to see *Crossroads*, I'm going to have it on.' Or when *Coronation Street* comes on, I say, 'Well if you don't mind I'm going to have it on.' But I don't keep viewing to interfere with company really, but I don't think it hurts anybody for half an hour to sit, do you? (Marjory, quoted in Hobson 1982: 111)

In 1981 I conducted research about the ATV soap opera *Crossroads* (Hobson 1982). The study involved watching the production of the series and then watching programmes on transmission, with the audience. The experience of watching programmes with the audience throws into sharp focus the way that they actually view and the reality of their relationship with the genre and, indeed, with all television programmes. For me one of the most important aspects of this work was that it exploded the myth of the passive viewer and revealed the complexity of the relationship between viewers and television programmes. This research also showed me for the first time the way that women as viewers saw the content of this particular programme as relating to their own lives, and how the inclusion of problems within the series had a resonance with problems which they knew within their own lives.

Most of the women with whom I watched *Crossroads* in 1981 had families and their viewing had to be fitted in around the other domestic duties which coincided with the transmission times of the series. However, some were older women who lived alone and could choose the programmes of their own interests and watch whenever they wanted. This research was conducted before the video recorder was widely available, and there were no omnibus editions to catch up on episodes which might have been missed. To watch the soap opera required a commitment on the part of the viewers and to miss an episode meant that it was more difficult to catch up. Time had to be made to watch the programme on a regular basis. One of the first indications of the importance of soap operas to women audiences came to light when they talked about the way that they watched the programme *Crossroads*. These extracts (Hobson 1982) tell of the way that women operated their domestic duties to enable them to watch the programme. At the time of this research *Crossroads* regularly had 15 million viewers and was hugely popular with its audience.

However, this was before soap opera was widely accepted as an interesting genre by critics, and although they might reluctantly admit to finding *Coronation Street* interesting, *Crossroads* was universally denigrated by critics and commentators (Hobson 1982: 15). The viewers of *Crossroads* were well aware that the critics, for the most part, did not like the programme. To ask viewers why they persist in watching a programme which had the reputation of being 'not very good' was to ask them to examine and admit why they were willing to stake their opinions against those of recognized critics or so-called 'experts'. Historically then, the audience for soap operas had to contend with the scathing opinion which critics had of the form. Some of the women to whom I spoke were not too troubled by the adverse criticism which the professionals made about *Crossroads,* forcefully preferring their own opinions.

DH: What do you think when you read about the critics and people moaning about the programme?
Mary: Well, I think that some of those critics moan for moaning's sake, don't you? I've read things up about various things the critics have said have been marvellous, and I've thought it's been tripe. So I mean, that's just someone else's opinion, isn't it? I mean, I'm not too enthralled about what critics say. I think my own thoughts – if I like it, I look at it. (Hobson 1982: 108)

Others were not so happy about the way that critics criticized the programme and also implied in their attacks that the viewers were indiscriminating if they watched *Crossroads*. In fact, it was as if they thought that the fact that they viewed the programme attracted as many derogatory opinions as those which were directed at the programme itself. Although one of the women I interviewed made an interesting observation about the critics, and at the same time identified some of the major qualities of soap opera and the nature of its appeal to their fans.

J: Well, I don't think the people who criticise it find it's good viewing because it's too near to their own sort of lives. It's not entertaining watching real-life situations. When they want to be entertained they want to see something different from like everyday life and it's too realistic in a way to be entertaining for them. . . . It's too close to home. (Hobson 1982: 109)

She later identified the content as being 'too emotional' for men to be able to watch the programme and confirmed that it was when women characters were talking about 'emotional' things that they think it is stupid and unrealistic because they are not brought up to accept such situations – a far cry from the current opinions on soap operas where men's emotions are often at the forefront of the drama.

> *In between half-past five and eight, that's my busiest time – feed him, change him, sometimes bath him, get Richard's dinner . . . I stop at half-past six to watch* Crossroads.

As well as coping with some of the attitudes which were held about the soap opera, I first learned from these women how they organized their domestic duties to enable them to watch soap operas. They would complete their work and meal preparation so that they could watch the programme. Some altered the time that they served evening meals to avoid clashes with the programme and others prepared the meal while they watched the programme on small black-and-white sets in the kitchen. They created a space so that they could watch the programme and fit it in around other duties.

Audience readings of the characters and their behaviour in relation to the problems in their lives were a major part of the enjoyment of the programmes. While some of the characters were working-class, as were the women I interviewed at this stage, other characters in the series were more middle-class, and the audience's assessment of their behaviour included a class perspective and a shared universally held view of how a character should behave as a woman. The most important elements in the storylines were the fact that they must relate to 'real' life and families. Marjory, a woman in her seventies told me why she enjoyed the programme:

Marjory: I like family stories and things like that, I like something with a story.

DH: So do you think that's the reason that you like it?

Marjory: Yes, because it continues, and personally I think it's a lot like real life.

DH: In what way?

Marjory: Well, I mean Jill had her ups and downs, didn't she, and so did Meg, and whatsit, with her kiddie who she wants from America, I mean that can happen in real life, can't it? To me it's things in there that can happen in real life. It's not fiction to me; to me it's a real family story.

DH: Now, when you say that, you don't mean you think they're real, do you?

Marjory: No, they portray that and they do it well. It's like we used to have in the pictures in the olden days, we used to have those kind of family stories in the pictures, but you never get them now. You see now, I like that kind of thing. (Hobson 1982: 122)

Marjory is clearly under no illusions that the programme is fiction; there is no hidden misunderstanding that these characters are anything other than fiction but a recognition that the incidents which make up the storylines are based on events 'that can happen in real life'. Similarly, in a storyline about 'mugging' another two women talked about the social problems which were addressed in the programme and which were more acceptable than if they had been covered in an abstract way in a news item:

Sheila: Oh, I'd say it's definitely to get a message over, to try to make people realise to check and all this business like, you know. Because you don't realise how typical of real life . . . it's the sort of thing you do, isn't it? You put it on after like. It is the sort of thing you do do in real life. You never think you are going to be the one who's mugged or burgled or anything like that.
June: I mean this is everyday news isn't it, muggings and murders and all this and that and the other. You expect to see that sort of thing on the news. . . . But you don't expect it on *Crossroads* . . . I think you get a lot of old people as well who do watch *Crossroads* and *Coronation Street,* whereas they are probably sick to death of the news on *ATV Today* because of the fact that it is all murders and muggings and that, and it would certainly come over to their age more in this programme. Certainly it would come over more to them, you know, the older age group, especially women living by themselves as well, which there is an awful lot of nowadays as well. (Hobson 1982: 123)

The argument that it was the unexpectedness of the events which happen within the serial is an interesting one. It seems from this perspective that the events which are reported within news programmes are so predictable that they cease to have such a strong effect on the audience. June is implying that such events can be seen as part of the genre of news. News contains muggings and murders and the audience expects it. It is 'everyday news'. But if there is a mugging in *Crossroads* then it is identified as unexpected in terms of what they expect to happen in the serial, and it therefore has a more dramatic effect and causes the audience to relate the incident to their own lives or the lives of other people they know. The combination of the familiarity of the characters and the unexpectedness of the events carries the 'message' more effectively than the same incidents happening to someone of whom the audience knows nothing, and which is reported and expected in a news programme. Looking at this extract in retrospect, it also shows how the content of soap operas has changed, because now its audience might expect that there would be violence within a soap opera as well as on the news.

> *Because if he was my husband, I would have kicked him out years ago, but that is obviously the character, not him.*

The interpretation of the behaviour of characters within the soap opera, the playful way in which audiences compare the behaviour of the characters in their storylines and the way that they would behave in their own lives was also made clear in these early interviews which I conducted. Behaviour of characters, whether in a serious or playful mode, was compared with the way that the women thought they would behave in similar circumstances. Sometimes they felt that the producers could make the lives of the characters more interesting, and they suggested solutions which were based on their 'real life' experiences and on how the production should be handled. One of the women spoke of the Brownlows, Kath and Arthur:

Linda: I dislike Arthur Brownlow, I can't stand him.
DH: And why don't you like him?
Linda: Because if he was my husband I would have kicked him out years ago – but that is obviously the character, not him. And his wife gets on your nerves, but then again they ought to be able to do something with her part, I think because she's either laying the table or unlaying it or they are eating . . . that gets on your nerves. (Hobson 1982: 128)

Linda's husband then joined in the discussion and I asked how the storylines could be improved:

Peter: Put more meat into it.
Linda: Yes, she seems sort of downtrodden.
Peter: Take a lover!
Linda: Get her husband to lay the table for a change. It's just the character. She's probably doing a very good acting job. (Hobson 1982: 128)

The suggestion from Peter is of a frivolous nature, but Linda has identified one of the significant characteristics of Kath. She appears downtrodden and accepts Arthur's chauvinism, but not without a certain amount of eyebrow raising at his behaviour. The character as portrayed by the actress is seen as 'realistic' but the viewers wanted stronger storylines to enable the character to develop.

Viewers have a remarkable amount of knowledge of what has happened in the series and make judgements about it, always based on 'real life'. Sometimes these are at a small or trivial level; others are much more complex opinions. The set for the Brownlow family was very basic, with teak-effect furniture and a rather shabby brown-and-cream-striped lounge suite. One woman commented on the shabby state of the furniture and said that it was about time that Kath Brownlow had a new three-piece suite because the old one was getting to look old: She then added the postscript, 'She will be able to when she's having the digs money from Kevin'. The comment was at a light-hearted level but it did indicate that she was working with her own notions of realism and her judgement on the series was from the same perspective. Now that the character would have a little money of her own, she would be able to buy herself a new suite, indicating a reading of the issue which recognized that not all women had access to the family wage and if she wanted luxuries, or something which her husband did not think necessary, then the only way to get it was to take work outside or within the home.

Another example of the way that these women interacted with the text came when they talked about one of the characters, Jill, who was going through a storyline in which she had taken to drink when her current relationship had broken up. Jill had had a previous broken marriage and tumultuous affairs but she had a very attractive country cottage home and a pleasant job working for her mother at the motel. Idyllic conditions compared with the lives of the audience to whom I was speaking. One woman commented:

> I thought when Jill was going through this drunken phase, you know, not so long ago, after this other fella ditched her, I thought she was pathetic actually. Because she's been through it all before. It's about time she . . . you know. It is – it's part of life. We could all turn to the bottle but you just don't, do you, in real life? Some do, I agree some do, and I suppose that this is what they are trying to get over, that some do turn to the bottle. But there again, from the type of family that she's supposed to belong to, you wouldn't imagine that she would. (Hobson 1982: 120)

The woman was certainly not tolerant towards Jill. The fact that the character had been through many problems in her life meant, in the eyes of this woman, that she should have learned to cope with them better, and her class position should have stopped her from taking such a course. Even though there were areas of the character's life of which the woman had no knowledge, there were assumptions that were based on a view that all women of whatever class should be able to cope with such problems. She says, 'We could all turn to the bottle, but you just don't, do you, in real life, but then again, some do! We could all be weak and drink to drown our problems, but we carry on with our lives.' However, she then preserves the authenticity of the production by confirming, in unspoken condemnation, that some women do turn to drink.

What I first learned from the viewers was the way that they worked with the series to make comparisons with the way that they thought characters should behave and the correct or expected behaviour in everyday life. When the series handled social issues – and at the time they were much the most forward of any of the series – the viewers saw the airing of the problem as being of as much value as the resolution. Everyday life, its problems and whether the way the characters reacted was similar to the way that the audience felt that they should behave was one of the ways in which these women judged the soap opera. They fitted in their own working routines to enable them to watch the programmes and they saw them as part of their working day. Within their homes and while they pursued their everyday lives, they made time to watch the series and within their domestic realms they had the confidence to judge the series and pitch their opinions against the producers.

Soap operas at work

> *It's like Gail in* Coronation Street . . . *it's almost as if you know her, so I think, 'I wonder what she'll do about this baby?' – almost like someone you work with in the office.*

After my initial research into how women watched television in their homes and fitted it into their other responsibilities, in the late 1980s I conducted two pieces of work which looked at the way that women watched and talked about, in particular, soap operas outside their homes, in the workplace (Hobson 1989, 1990). Soap operas are part of the lives of their audience and while they depict everyday happenings in the fictional form, they also form part of the detailed cultural exchanges which go on both in the home, while watching the programmes, and in the workplace. A large part of the enjoyment of watching soap operas is derived from talking about them with other people, sharing opinions and, perhaps as important, using opinions and stories taken from the soap opera to talk about aspects of their own lives. This aspect of the television communication process is, of course, true of other programmes, but it is the nature of the form and content of soap opera which makes it a genre that audiences use to discuss their own life stories. Talking about television is part of the everyday work culture of both men and women. It is fitted in around their working time or in lunch breaks. The process takes the form of storytelling, commenting on stories, relating the incidents and assessing them for realism, and moving from the drama to discussing the incidents which are happening in the 'real' world and in their own lives. The process of watching soap operas is not a passive operation; it continues after the viewing time and is extended into other areas of everyday life. Talking at work is the way that these two groups of women reveal the place which soap opera has in their everyday lives. It also confirms the totality of the active viewer.

The first group of women all worked at a local authority in the Education Department and were aged between 23 and 35; they shared their working lives and also spent some of their social time together. They would go out for meals in the evenings, visit each other and occasionally go out to the theatre. As a work group, they are at ease with each other and this is evident in the way that they speak about events in the programmes and in their own lives. They are so 'in touch' with each other's opinions that they interrupt each other and finish each other's sentences. They speak in unison when they have shared opinions, as do the young men discussed below. And in so doing they reveal the collective views which many members of the audience feel about characters. When one of the women is talking about *Brookside* she says, 'There are certain ones in there that get on your nerves'. In unison, the other women in the group interrupt with 'The Corkhills'. They are all so aware of how each other feel that their responses are simultaneous. During this discussion, they are talking among themselves rather than answering questions. I might ask the first question, but they would move on to other topics as they took the discussion to areas which they would discuss naturally amongst themselves.

During the time that this interview was conducted the American series *Dallas* and *Dynasty* were being shown and it is interesting to see how they differentiated between the British and American series.

They also specify the importance of male characters, and identify their attractions and fascinations within the genres, indicating the importance of male characters in the American series which was then taken up in the British soap operas:

Di: The fantasy Americans and that, you can't relate to. I mean they're on a different planet really.
Mary: But they're nice to watch because of the clothes and their houses.
DH: And what about the characters in American soaps? I mean, why do you like them or don't you really like them and do you feel you can identify with any of them?
In unison: No!
Mary: I don't think you can relate to them in that respect, no. (Hobson 1989: 155)

I continued by asking if it was mainly the women to whom they related and all of them said that it was the women that they found more interesting, but not one mentioned any of the female characters, and they voluntarily proceeded to discuss the male characters. The following extract shows how the male characterization, while not uniformly attractive either physically or emotionally, does hold a fascination for the women.

Mary: I like to watch Bobby.
Wendy: I like J.R. though. When he's sort of scheming and he'll sort of turn his back on whoever he's playing up and this smile comes on his face and I think, 'Ooh, he's at it again', you know.
DH: Why do you like people like J.R?
Wendy: Well he's a very clever bloke, isn't he?
Vijya: He's very crafty.
Di: You've got to admire him though, the way he – he knows his business, sort of thing. He knows.
Wendy: And it's sort of the power that money can have, you know, that really comes across. He'll say, 'It don't matter what the price is, I'll pay it but you do your job'. And I respect the way he says, 'I want a good job done', you know. I just like him.
Di: I suppose most people want to stand up to people in their life but they haven't got the power that he has, have they?
DH: Do you think the women in *Dallas* are weak?
All: They all are.
Mary: They are really.

Di: If J.R. was my husband, I wouldn't marry him again. That sort of thing.

DH: But you just said you find his portrayal of power is quite attractive.

Di: Yea, on the telly but I don't think I'd like to be married to him. [Laughter]

Mary: But perhaps she means to other people and not necessarily to whatsername?

Di: Sue Ellen.

Mary: I don't think she comes out very well in it, she's a bit of a cry-baby really, isn't she, she's always . . .

DH: What about the men in the American soaps?

Vijya: Geoff in *The Colbys*. I quite like Miles as well.

Wendy: I quite like Jack Ewing. (Hobson 1989: 155–6)

This exchange of views begins to differentiate between the British and American soap operas. The 'down-to-earth' realism of the British soaps and the 'fantasy' of the American series. Fantasy or reality, it is characters who hold the key to appeal for viewers. The women interviewed were unanimous when they said that it was the women who were the most interesting characters in the American soaps. However, after being unanimous in supporting the women, the group then went on to discuss the devilish attraction of J.R. and the magnetism of power, and the physical attractions of Bobby and Jack Ewing and Geoff Colby. The only woman mentioned by name is Sue Ellen and she is categorized as a 'cry-baby'. Clearly, the attractions of male characters in American soaps added to the fantasy element in the series, and throughout the interviews there is hardly a mention of men in British soap operas. There was a clear differentiation between the attractions in the fictional form and the prospect of knowing any of the characters in the 'real' world. J.R. was good value as a character in a fantasy soap opera like *Dallas* but not someone to be desired as a husband, despite his worldly goods. Even the sexually attractive males were not someone to be desired in everyday life. And their whole *raison d'être* seemed to be to provide glamour and sexual attraction to the series.

British realism and the strong women of the 1980s

The American supersoaps offered fantasy, but it was to the British series that the women turned for 'realism'. The subject of soap operas and their relationship to everyday life has always been one in which the audience carried a vast amount of knowledge. They make judgements to decide how well the production has portrayed the fictional representation of characters and their lives. The audience feel that their knowledge is superior to that of the producers. In the 1980s the then newly created *EastEnders* was aiming to represent the characters of the time. When it began the characters were either conventional East End working-class or the newly emerging yuppies (young upwardly mobile – into a middle class defined mainly by money, often 'loads of money'!) who themselves in reality were beginning to star as the fantasy of the British television and advertising executive. Most of the rest of the population outside London had only seen or heard of the new species through the media! In assessing the British soap operas of the 1980s, these women identified the women as the major characters and the strongest in the series. The women characters who were seen as the most popular were those who had to struggle against the vicissitudes of life. It is their ability to 'cope', which is seen as admirable, and women's behaviour was not expected to be 'wimpish'. If the characters are seen as keeping on top of their own lives, that is judged as admirable and only in extreme cases did the audience excuse lapses in strength from the women in soap operas.

DH: What about the English soaps then? What do you think about
   the characters in those?
Mary: They're very realistic.
Di: Women seem to be much stronger in them, don't they?
DH: Who do you think are strong characters in British soaps?
Di: Well, in *EastEnders* it's Pauline. (Hobson 1989: 158)

The discussion moved to discussing the physical appearance of the characters and a clear distinction was made between the actress and the character that she plays. As with the women who had talked about the characters in *Crossroads*, there was absolutely no confusion as to whether the characters were the same as the actresses. The distinction was always made between the two. Viewers were also well aware of the separate existence of the actors and actresses, as they appeared on other television programmes, particularly chat shows, and at charity events. The women referred to the difference between the actress Wendy Richards and her character in *EastEnders*:

Di: While you were up the bar, we was talking about Pauline in
   EastEnders and said doesn't she look old – look awful.
DH: You mean as an actress or the character?
Di: Character – looks old – not the glamour part, is it?

DH: Is anybody glamorous in British soaps?
Di: Don't watch *Crossroads* regularly, but Nicola Freeman, she's attractive in a funny sort of way.

Actresses are playing a part and when they refer to Wendy Richards they are clear that she is playing a role when she appears looking 'old and awful' in *EastEnders*. Characters are judged for realism, as are storylines, and as always these women reveal that they have no misunderstanding as to the difference between the fictional character and the actress who is playing the part.

Pleasure at work – talking about television

One of the areas of particular interest in talking to audiences is the way in which soap operas, and indeed television in general, are discussed by women at their workplace and the way that they bring the interest of the private sphere into the public domain. Indeed, it is the fusion of the two areas which characterized much of our discussion. The following extract also illustrates the importance of television in the everyday exchanges within the working environment.

DH: So how does television in general come into your conversation at work?
Mary: It's almost every morning, isn't it really. We tend to say; 'Did you see such and such last night?' It depends on the plot in the programme at the time.
Diane: If it's been a gripping episode then even those who haven't seen it talk about it.
Mary: The Michelle and Lofty episode was quite a talking point.
Diane: But also we come in when we miss one and say, 'What's happened?'
DH: What do you do if you miss something – do you ask at work the next day?
Mary: Yes.
Diane: But whether that's because of the way we are, the way the office is set up. We get on with our work but we've got a relationship where we can and do talk about these sorts of things. The general banter going on in the office that allows us to be able to do that.
DH: If you are at work you're talking about other things as well. You are saying that your work enables you to chat at the same time as you work?

Mary: No, you fit it in.
Diane: It's the way we can get on with our work.
Mary: It may be in between phone calls. If someone rings. It can go
   dead for half an hour – if the phone rings you say 'Hang on a
   minute – don't say any more.'
Diane: Conversation might take all morning.
Mary: You stop, then when you put the phone down you start again
   and someone else's phone will go and you stop again. (Hobson
   1989: 160)

This discussion indicates the way that these women are able to discuss
what happened the previous evening and carry on with their work.
They do not talk while they are working but rather they carry on the
general conversations about the soaps in between their work. The
storytelling carries on with breaks while they take and make telephone calls. They also respect the need for some of them to catch up
on viewing and will wait to talk about the episode until they have
watched the video. They will ask if their colleagues have watched the
episode before they start talking about it. Sometimes the episodes
have not been recorded and then the 'catching up' will happen, when
they tell the stories to those who might have missed it. It is clear that
soap opera producers are served exceptionally well by their viewers
because they act as the bridge between episodes. The narrative form
of storytelling which the soap opera employs makes it simple for the
audience to re-tell the stories to their friends and colleagues. It is beneficial to the producers and broadcasters because it helps ensure that
the viewers do not lose interest and stop watching a series because
they have missed what is going on. In one sense retelling soap opera
stories gives everyone the opportunity to be a storyteller without
needing to write their own stories. In some instances it is the talking
about soap operas at work or among families and friends that determines whether someone begins watching the series in the first place.
When a storyline is so strong that it is the main topic of conversation in the office, it is reason enough to get someone watching so as
not to be out of the conversation which takes place at work.

A special knowledge – Asian culture

*They are trying to arrange a marriage but it wouldn't work.
They wouldn't send him round and try to fix them up together
like that. It wouldn't work like that.*

Vijya

One of the women in the group, Vijya, was Asian and had a specific knowledge of the culture which was represented in the series *EastEnders*. The fiction did not satisfy her ideas of the way that her people should be portrayed. At the time of these interviews, there was a storyline running in which the character Naima did not get on with her husband from an arranged marriage and stayed on in England while he returned to Bangladesh. Her family has kept a check on her and they had then sent her cousin to take control of the shop and ultimately to marry her. The women in the office had no way of knowing whether the story was realistic. This was not their culture and they had nothing against which to make their judgements. They had no way of knowing whether the production had 'got it right'. In their discussions with Vijya, they could satisfy their curiosity as regards the storylines and also learn more about Vijya's own culture, without having to ask her directly. When I spoke to my friend who was my original contact to meet these women, she told me that Vijya had herself had an arranged marriage the previous August and this marriage had not worked out. Her husband had returned to Bangladesh and she had returned to live with her parents. Her superior knowledge was both cultural and personal, and the storyline in the series helped her colleagues to be able to talk to her about her own life without feeling they were intruding.

Talking to this group of women who worked so closely together gave an insight into the way that audiences use the information and the dramatic interest in the soap opera to discuss aspects of their own lives and to make their working days more pleasurable. Speaking about the narratives of the soap operas gives them the ability to discuss matters of interest without the intrusion and painful repercussions of office gossip. A second piece of research (Hobson 1990) was based on an account which one young woman, who worked as a telephone sales manager for an international pharmaceutical and feminine hygiene company, gave of the way that the women in her office spent their working day – selling, talking and as she terms it 'putting the world to rights'. The women were graphically described:

> The eldest was Audrey who was 56, two children, both gone to university, husband has a good job, staying there till she retires, quite quiet, just talks about curtains and things like that, but will contribute to discussions. The youngest person, who is the office junior, is little Tracey, who gets a black eye from her boyfriend every five weeks or whatever – 17 and very young in her ways. And then you've got all the ages in between and all the different marital statuses and all the different backgrounds, different cultures and classes which were just

mingled together. Which was so nice because it was so different but they all came together in one unit and discussed openly different issues and topics, which were sometimes, but not necessarily, triggered off by television. (Hobson 1990: 62)

What became clear from the stories was the way that the women used the television programmes to trigger conversations and inter-weave stories of their personal interests, current affairs, social and philosophical debates and media events. They fitted work in around their conversations, which were sometimes triggered by television programmes or newspaper articles. Some television programmes would draw the whole group into the conversation. Once the people in the office were talking about a television programme, they quickly adapted the conversation to include topics which were about their own lives and interests. After the initial catching up on storylines, the women who worked in this office would extend the stories of what had already happened in the series to speculating as to what was likely to happen next. The next phase was to extend the conversa-tion to discuss what they would do if they were in the same circum-stances as the characters. Jacqui explained:

> As I was saying you might be talking about an episode of *Coronation Street* or *EastEnders* and after you had said, 'What happened?' then you would say, 'What do you think is going to happen next?' 'Well, I think Angie's going to run off.' [She did.] 'No she won't.' 'Well, I think she will.' It's all a bit of a laugh really, a bit of gossip, nobody really takes it seriously but then you might move on to talk about Kath and Willmott-Brown and someone will say 'I think Kath is going to go off with Willmott-Brown' and then they would start putting things in relating it to themselves, but doing it in a joking way. Like saying, 'Well, if my Alan was as vile as Pete, I think I'd go off with Willmott-Brown!' (Hobson 1990: 64)

The comments about whether they would actually have an affair if their husband behaved like the character in the television serial are offered only in a joking manner. For some of the women who had difficult marriages, the events in the series were close to their own lives and they did not comment as to what they would do in similar circumstances. One particular woman revealed not only her interest in soap operas but also what Jacqui terms 'her own particular domes-tic hell':

> Vicky, who hardly ever contributed to discussions, if you talked about soap operas then she was at the forefront of the conversation. She lived in this sort of domestic hell with this bloke who was not her husband.

She'd never been married and she lived with this bloke and it was his house and her philosophy was that she had to do what he said because he could throw her out because it was his house. She used to say she loved all the soap operas. 'I watch them all, *Coronation Street, Cross-roads, EastEnders, Dallas,* I watch them all and I love them.' But if Brian came in she could not watch them. She used to say, 'Brian hates them and if I'm watching them he'll come in and turn them off and I'm not allowed to watch them. He turns the telly off and I'm not allowed to watch them, I have to go and get his tea.' (Hobson 1990: 64)

This story of how Vicky was not allowed to watch soap operas is not unique. Other women, whether by fear or collusion, do allow their partners to control their viewing habits and choice of programmes. Many other women have told me that they are restricted in what they are allowed to watch. This is not the issue of men having control of the remote control (Morley 1986) but rather a case of the man controlling what the woman is allowed to view. But Jacqui continued to explain that although Vicky never speculated what she would do if she were in the position of someone in a television drama, it did provide a means for her to talk about the way that she experienced her own life.

Using an event which had happened in a television programme to talk about events in their own lives was a common practice amongst the group. I asked directly if they moved from topics or situations that were seen on television to talking about how those events might figure in their own lives or lives of their acquaintances. Jacqui responded:

Well it would be quite funny actually, what would happen would be somebody would talk about something that had happened in a programme. The hypothetical situation that they might be in is that their husband had been unfaithful and they found out. And they would be coming out with this and that of what they would do. 'Well, I'd pack his bags, send him off, put him outside, wouldn't have him back!' And there would be all this big palaver going on. And then you would have people who it had actually happened to or it was happening to and they would begin to talk in the abstract, as in, 'But what if you loved him?' 'But what if he said?' They would try to get the reactions from the other girls. I suppose it was a way to assess their own feelings and situations. (Hobson 1990: 65)

The use of events within fiction to explore experiences which were perhaps too personal, too painful, to talk about to a complete work group is beneficial and a creative way of extending the value of the programme into their own lives. Again the women combined discussing areas of interest in their personal lives with creating a cultural space within their work time to share the narratives of the programmes and assist their working day.

Soaps are not only white and female – the experiences of young black men

Not all viewers are soap opera fans and in another series of interviews which I conducted with various audience groups, completely different opinions emerged in relation to the soap opera and the television audience. (These interviews formed part of a study (unpublished papers) which I made in *Perceptions of Channel 4 Television* during the first six years of its transmission from 1982–7 when I worked as a consultant to Channel 4. Part of the work was an audience study and I conducted a number of interviews across a wide range of audiences to find out about their views on television in general and Channel 4 programmes in particular.) Questions about soap opera were often introduced spontaneously by the viewers as they talked of their preferences and dislikes across the whole of the television schedule. Many of those who spoke were not fans of the genre, and their reactions reveal some of the reverse side of the coin in the appreciation or obverse of the genre. Naturally, the purpose of these interviews was to discover what various groups thought about Channel 4 and I approached the subject via discussions of television in general, partly to learn more about their views across all four channels, but also to approach Channel 4 in an oblique manner and not to load their opinions by moving straight into this topic. Many of those who were interviewed in these groups had very little interest in soap operas. Some of them mentioned individual programmes and some wrote off the whole genre in a dismissive phrase. What was interesting was that they had definite views on why the programmes in the genre did not meet their taste.

The first group were a number of young black men who worked in small engineering workshops in the Handsworth area of Birmingham. These men had very little interest in soap operas; indeed they had very little interest in television in general. They did not feel that the medium had very much to offer to them although they were certainly well aware of the programmes which were available. At this time there was, indeed, very little which was directed at black people and although the BBC made *Ebony* from their Pebble Mill studios in Birmingham, and Central made *Here and Now*, these programmes had made little impact on these men. Aged between eighteen and early twenties their interests were not met by the type of programme which they were offered. Channel 4 was beginning to fare a little better because it had specifically targeted ethnic minorities as part of the fulfilment of its remit. They had two specific programmes directed at black and Asian viewers – *Black on Black* and *Eastern Eye*. Some of them were aware of *Black on Black* and they appreciated the recognition of their specific interests. However, one group of men were certainly the target audience for the sports coverage, and since Channel 4 had taken American football and basketball as their chosen sports, it might have been expected that they would watch these. They watched basketball, but did not see it as of particular interest. What was of interest was the recognition that Channel 4 had made an effort to target their own interests through their black programmes. However, they were not particularly enamoured by these programmes and would have preferred to have been given black films and other entertainment from Jamaica than the offerings from London Weekend Television, the broadcasting company who made the programmes for Channel 4. However, the appearance on the channel of a black station announcer, albeit one who only worked part-time, was a cause of great interest. One young factory worker told me:

> Like it has a main presenter telling you what's coming on. I have seen a coloured person presenting the main thing, what's coming on, like saying what's next. That's different to me. . . . I was shocked when I first saw him.

To be shocked that a black person is a station announcer reveals the alienation that must have been felt by black viewers in their experience of viewing British television. The lack of black people in general can be seen as one of the reasons that these young men all rejected television as a form of entertainment. It is not relevant to the topic of soap opera to go into detailed discussion about the provision of programmes for black viewers, but two examples of opinions from these interviews serve to illustrate the way that the channels were perceived at this time and present a clue to why these young men hardly mentioned soap operas in their choice of viewing. The first man was indulgent to BBC1 in its attempts to address the black audience:

Dennis: They are trying to get good, but I can't see them, how can I say . . .
DH: Do you feel you can relate to any of their programmes?

Dennis: No, not at all. They are things that are either too way up or too down. They are like the Third World; they are always showing programmes about that, fair enough. And if there is something bad, they always found out about it, but nothing good, they try to show relating to our kind of people, always bad. Or high class films.

What this young man is asking for is a representation of normality, his normality. Another interviewee promised that if the programmes were shown, he would surely watch them. He, like others interviewed, said that if programmes for black viewers were shown on Channel 4, he would adjust his lifestyle to watch them:

> If they had programmes on blacks all the time, like *No Problem*, if they had that on every day, I'd watch it every day. *Black on Black* should come on every week, and I'd watch it every week. [It alternated with *Eastern Eye*.] If there was a film on tonight, I'd go home and watch it and if it was boring, I'd go to bed, but if it was good, I'd stop up all night to watch it.

Dennis had a great deal of knowledge about television in general and watched across a range of programmes. He gave a list of black films which could be shown and would attract black audiences and identified performers who should be given more airtime on television. Dennis was adamant that he would not watch soap operas, a response gained by enquiring if there were any sort of programmes he would never watch.

> Same as Winston, *Coronation Street* and *Crossroads*. I don't go into the house to watch them, like if I go in and one of them is on, I'll go and turn the TV over because I don't think anybody in my house watches them; there's my mother, she used to watch it, she watches now and then.

Dennis does not elaborate on why he does not watch soap opera, but later in the interview he talked about watching *Empire Road* a few years earlier and how his family had watched the programme:

> We used to come in and my dad and my brother would say, 'I'm watching *Empire Road*,' that was good.

I asked about his views on representation of black people on television, whether any programmes really showed how he experienced life. His reply gives a clue as to why at that time the young black audience was not watching soap operas:

Dennis: Well, I think none of them show what black people are really like. Especially in this area [Handsworth in Birmingham]. They show them in Jamaica where the programme *The Harder They Come* will be realistic. And *Empire Road* a few years back. Was that ITV or BBC1?

DH: That was BBC2. It was made by the people at Pebble Mill; it was made out of that studio and they used to come and do all the filming round Handsworth.

Dennis: That was something near it.

There was a recognition that, at that time, rare programmes were beginning to get near any sort of acceptable representation of everyday life for young black Britons. Winston, whom Dennis referred to when talking about soap operas, was not a great fan of the genre but he did select within those programmes on offer and chose to watch *Brookside* on Channel 4. He too was a very knowledgeable viewer who had opinions on programmes ranging from politics to documentaries and news programmes. He was a fan of Channel 4, which by this time had established itself as a channel that was trying to meet the needs of ethnic minorities. He was a benevolent viewer.

Winston: I can't say I dislike anything. I haven't seen anything really bad to say. I like *Brookside* and I watch *Brookside*, but I don't like *Crossroads*. I can say I don't like that, but I can't say anything that I don't really like. There's things that I'm not interested in, but I don't dislike them.

DH: So why do you like *Brookside*?

Winston: Because it's more modern, it caters for people of our age. *Crossroads* is definitely for the middle-aged to me. *Coronation Street* is for the older aged, but *Brookside* has got teenagers in and things that I'll do, mischief that I'm up to, like stealing the carpet, not really!

DH: So do you relate to the characters?

Winston: Yes.

DH: Like Barry and Terry?

Winston: Yes, if I can see myself doing it, I can relate to it.

While the picture which emerged through these interviews reflected that a complex set of negotiations were going on between these viewers and the attempts of the broadcasters to begin to serve them, it was clear that the relationship of viewers to soap operas was one where they did not relate to the characters in general, so there was no possibility that they would engage with the storylines. There was nothing to which they could relate and only *Brookside* was making any connection. Interestingly, the characters who had attracted Winston were the young 20-year-old Liverpool scalleys – Barry Grant and his friend Terry Sullivan, who at this time were generally into minor skirmishes and scams. They were not black but they united with Winston because of their youth. In fact, at this time *Crossroads* did have a black character, Carl, who was a garage mechanic and had a wife and child, but since the programme was defined as for the middle-aged, Winston had not been attracted to it to find the character. The rejection of the genre, albeit not in a particularly negative way, by these young men was a reflection of their attitude in general to most of the programmes which they were offered. It was the representation of the youth in *Brookside* which meant that at least one of them found areas of interest.

Soap opera and unemployment

I don't watch things to do with the family.
　　　　Mark (16-year-old, unemployed, at the drop-in centre)

Being a young male and unemployed rapidly became a feature of life in the 1980s and beyond for many young men who faced a life with little chance of a job and a society which increasingly sought to blame them for their own situation. Out of work and out of school, one of the few places where some of them found a place to meet and pursue interests, like pool, or 'just hang around', was a 'drop-in centre' funded by the leisure services departments of local authorities. One such centre was a location where I went to 'talk to' rather than 'interview' some of the boys. These young men visited the centre, actually located within an old building in a suburban shopping area. In a tiny room, filled with a pool table, and with barely enough space to walk around and handle the pool cue, a group of young boys played the game, sat on wooden window sills and talked to me about what they thought about television and its role in their lives. They were heavy viewers who watched television to help fill the empty hours in their lives. In answer to the question as to whether there were any programmes he would never watch, Mark quickly responded: '*Dallas, Coronation Street* and *Crossroads* – I don't watch things to do with the family.'

While many watch soap operas for the very reason that they deal with family issues, this was the reason why he was adamant that he would not watch. Another young man playing pool was Neil, also aged 16 and engaged in a Youth Training Scheme (YTS – a government scheme for 16-year-olds whereby they worked for an employer who was paid by the government to employ them) with the hope of employment as a plumber at the end of it. While I sat moving my legs out of the way, the boys stalked the room playing pool, and they held forth with considerable expertise on the schedules across four channels and the time of every programme which they watched. They switched channels to seek programmes which would both appeal to them and fill their endless empty hours. Neil did have an interest in soap opera, was a Channel 4 fan and was viewing the programmes with which Channel 4 had specifically targeted him. His viewing was wide-ranging: films, plays, documentaries, particularly if they were about animals and insects. His choice in drama was to select those programmes which particularly concentrated on issues which had a resonance for him – *Boys from the Blackstuff*, Phil Redmond's ground-breaking series *Going Out* and a significant drama transmitted by Channel 4 called *One Summer*, which told the story of young men from a northern city who found freedom and understanding with a farmer in the Yorkshire countryside. His choice of soap opera was, not surprisingly, *Brookside* and his comments locate its appeal: 'I've been watching from the start. It's funny. It's like real life in it.'

This was the only comment which Neil made about the programme, but his intense praise for the other dramas which he watched and his location of *Brookside* within these areas indicate that it was the content which attracted him. All of these series told stories of young people and the unemployed and the various aspects of their lives. All were working class and all shared elements of their lives with Neil's own life. Mark, another young man at the pool table, also singled out *Brookside* in spontaneous response to a general question, 'What programmes do you watch?' His answer was a long list of genres with a heavy emphasis on sport and along with *The Young Ones* and *Man About the House*, *Brookside* was the only other programme named as one which he watched. What was interesting about these three young men was that, interviewed in 1984, they did not even mention any of the other leading soaps. These interviews were conducted before *EastEnders* began and it was clear that at that time none of the soap operas, save for *Brookside*, was offering any characters or storylines which had a direct interest to this section of the audience. In another series of interviews, which I will not discuss at length here, I interviewed a group of firemen aged between 25 and 40 and, apart from remarks which indicated that sometimes they were forced to watch soap operas with their wives, they again spontaneously mentioned soap operas as programmes which they would never watch. Even a group of students, interviewed in the common room at Birmingham University, revealed that the only soaps they saw were those they watched with their nan. What has become for me the hallmark of the close relationship between grandmas and their grandchildren is the number of people, in both formal and informal interviews, who over many years have told me, 'I used to watch *Crossroads* with my Nan'.

These brief comments about soap opera from members of the audience for whom the genre was neither a favourite nor one to which they would naturally be attracted are included as examples of the way that audiences related to the programmes. During 1983 and 1984, when these interviews were conducted, there was no shortage of women who could be interviewed about soap operas, but this was a time when young men did not have any interest in the genre, since there was very little to appeal to them in the characters or their storylines. Only *Brookside* with its young male characters was attracting young male viewers and it was not until 1985, when *EastEnders* provided a new range of young characters, that the genre began to appeal to the young audience and its storylines reflected their own everyday lives. Ten years later, in the mid-1990s, the soap opera was sufficiently established as a form to appeal to the apparently toughest of young men, who identified the genre as one of their favourite types of programme.

Fantasy and reality

Everything's all cushy, there's no one there [in Home and Away*] who signs on the dole. They all get jobs and everybody's willing to help everybody else . . . It's a paradise there, paradise.*
                                        Rudy, man in young offenders' prison

The notion of a negotiated reading of a television text was never more clearly demonstrated to me than during research which I conducted with young men in a young offenders' institution. The interview was with twelve young men, aged between 16 and 20 and from different ethnic groups, who had been convicted or were awaiting trial for various criminal offences. This was a group interview, so personal details were not part of the preliminary aspect of this research. They shared an age and background which had exposed them to mass media of different forms from their childhood through their adolescence. The interview and discussion, which had a different focus, ranged over a wide area of mass media but for the purpose of this book I will concentrate on their views on soap operas and their understanding of, relation to and opinions of the various programmes which they discussed.

The nature of the research needs explanation and the context of the interview deserves consideration. In September 1996 I conducted a pilot study for research on whether young offenders thought that the mass media had had any effect on their behaviour and whether they felt that their experience of and viewing of violence had had any effect on their own criminal activities. I arranged to visit a young offenders' institution and to talk to some of the young inmates, ostensibly to ask for their views on the mass media – although as the discussions progressed they became aware of my interests as questions relating to violence entered into the discussion. Arranging to gain entry to the prison was very difficult and was only possible because I was introduced by a member of the Board of Prison Visitors. Visiting the prison was a harrowing experience because prisons are frightening places and I was there to talk to young men who would not leave at the end of the interview. My heart raced and, more than with any other interviews that I have conducted, I felt that I was completely at the mercy of my interviewees. Of course, that is always the case for the researcher, but here I knew I had to convince them that I really needed to know what they thought and I wanted to listen to their opinions. They did not disappoint me and this is just a tiny part of the fascinating insights which they gave into their relationship with the mass media and its role in their lives. While my questions were wide-ranging, their discussion about soap operas came early in the interview and they talked openly about their preferences and opinions. Before we discussed soap opera, we had talked about their background at school, their entry into crime, their newspaper reading habits, their opinion of tabloid journalism, their childhood television viewing, their opinions of political parties (a topic introduced at their instigation) and their opinion of soap operas. I asked, 'Do you watch, or did you watch soap operas on television?' In unison they replied, 'Yes, yes'. They then listed their programmes. The programmes they liked were *Neighbours, East-Enders, Home and Away. Home and Away* was cited as a programme watched and liked by young offenders (Hagell and Newburn 1994), so I probed their interest in the series.

DH: Why do you like *Home and Away*?
Rudy: There's a lot of humour there, 'cos things like that . . . it's hard to imagine like what it would be like to be there.

DH: Someone who talked to young people who had been in trouble found that they liked *Home and Away*, but the people who did the interviews didn't talk about television programmes, they were only interested in the crime. As you know, *Home and Away* is all about, well most of the characters there have been in trouble or they . . .

Steve interrupted my attempt at setting up the themes of the programme as he and the others were well ahead of me in knowing what the programme was attempting to represent:

Steve: Yes, but they are all like, it's all like these pretty people, like with the mothers, they try to make out they are like us . . .

The boys interrupted in unison with a clear analysis of the programme:

All: Yes, stereotyping!
Rudy: Everything's all cushy, like there's no one there to sign on the dole. [Laughs] They all get jobs like, and everybody's like willing to help everybody else, you know what I mean. [Laughter from all the boys]
DH: So do you think that it's nothing like what life is like here?
Rudy: No. It's a paradise there, imagination – what, living there, next to the beach, living next to a beach, mm, paradise, paradise.

As one, the young men signified their assent to his proposition. If only they could be there, that would truly be paradise. This brief insight into the reading which these young men made of the series reveals their superior knowledge of the subject and their interest in the representation of life portrayed in the series. Their words highlight the oppositional reading of the representations portrayed in the series. However, what was revealed was that while they disagreed with the 'reality' represented in the programme, at the same time it was the subject, the content and the fact that they had superior knowledge of the reality which was being represented that added to the attraction of the series. Also they longed for the fictional reality that was portrayed to be a reality for them. For these young men, the life in the series is 'cushy'; no one has to sign on and they all get jobs. This is paradise and in unspoken contrast to their own lives on the estates, of which they have previously spoken, where crime and drug dealing was everyday life. Living next to the beach would be paradise to everyone, but to these boys it was the same level of fantasy as not having to sign on the dole, getting a job, everyone being willing to help everyone else and everyone being pretty, including the mothers.

The simple thesis of the programme is that if you were young and in trouble and your own family had difficulty or were not willing to look after you, you could be taken into foster care and all your problems would be dealt with – and not only that, but you would live in an idyllic community, next to a beach. Not like their lives; nevertheless, a favourite programme which they chose to watch, perhaps because it did offer an alternative dream of how life could be. When Rudy said 'Mm, paradise, paradise', there was a moment when they all united in thinking about how life could be if that were the reality for them rather than the reality which they had lived and were continuing to live.

Their ability to watch programmes in the remand centre was confined to the time when they had 'association', a time when they can join with each other and choose, within restrictions, what they can do. They watch television and the choice of programmes is determined by the most powerful of the group. In prison they are not fully in charge of what they watch, yet soap operas are their collective choice of programmes during this early evening period. We moved on to talking about prime-time British soap operas:

DH: What do you like about *Brookside*?
Wesley: Stories, all what's going on.
DH: What do you think about the way they are into . . .
Wesley: Drugs.
Steve: It's more closer to life.
DH: Is it well done; do you think it is like real life?
All: Yes, yes.
DH: What do you think about *EastEnders*?
Many voices: That's better, that's more down to earth, that's more to do with real life.
Unidentified voice: It has things that happens in your life. Proper problems like, they understand our problems.
Rudy: The Mitchell brothers.
Many voices: Yes, yes. [all laugh]
DH: Who are your favourite characters then in the soaps?
All: Grant, Grant, the Mitchells [all laughing], Grant.
DH: What about the stories they have in *EastEnders*, if you think it is good why do you think it's good?
Steve: Like it's got drugs in there and it's got like that Grant Mitchell's mom knocking that bloke off and he's like well bent and he's like supplying E's and nicks cars and all that and he's a bit shady like.
DH: Does she know?
Steve: She doesn't know . . .

DH: When do you know that from?

Steve: A while back. Like that club he was behind it. He knew how
  to organize everything . . . Like, there's things like that in my area
  and people like that who are into E's and all that.

The choice of *EastEnders* as the most realistic soap and the Mitchell
brothers as the favourite characters – and especially the lauding of
Grant who is an ex-offender and embodies the essence of tough male
aggression and vulnerability – shows the selective reading which they
have made of the programme. Also, they have chosen storylines
and themes which are directly related to their own knowledge and
experience. Their knowledge of drugs was far superior to my own
and they had ascertained that the character was supplying E's before
I had. The designation of the character as the 'bloke that Grant
Mitchell's mom was knocking off', would not have been the way that
every viewer would have described Peggy Mitchell. She was a
character in her own right but Steve described her only as 'Grant
Mitchell's mom', designating to the character a reading which would
indicate that, as the mother of Grant Mitchell, her behaviour was
inappropriate – because she was 'a mom' and that is not how 'moms'
should behave. He goes on to say that the realism of the series relates
to happenings in his own home area, in 'real life'. So he prefers
characters and storylines that are close to his own experiences and
beliefs. I moved on to questions about the purpose of soap operas,
whether they are purely entertainment or if the issues included in the
storylines have a purpose:

DH: Do you think that the stories in soaps are a help to people or
  do you think that they are just entertainment?

Steve: I think they could be, it depends how people look at it. Like
  your age group or how old you are and the way you see things
  like. Someone younger will look at, you know, like the Mitchell
  brothers or whatever, and think – 'Yes, I want to be like that'. Or
  how like that Cindy buggered off with Ian's kids but people from
  an older age group will see that as bad, it like influences both ways.

Again, the 'kids' in question are designated as 'Ian's kids' and it is
Cindy who has 'buggered off' with them; they are not described as
'their kids'.

Wesley: That could give people ideas to get rid of their husbands or
  whatever. [Laughter]

DH: Well, do you think people get ideas from television programmes then?
All: Oh yes, yes.

We then moved into an area of discussion which arose naturally out of the comments about soap opera, but which introduced extremely revealing, and from my point of view original, information about the way these young men saw the influence which violence on television may have had on their lives. Following on from their comment that you could be given ideas for crimes from watching television, I asked if they had ever got any ideas. But before I could finish my question I was interrupted by James: 'No 'cos *Crime Stalker* never show you how a robbery is done like.' There was then a general discussion, not clear enough from the tape for exact transcription, about whether you can tell from a television drama or reconstruction how to commit a crime. The general consensus was that it was not possible to see from television programmes how to commit criminal activities, because they do not show you enough. Eventually Rudy, who was clearly the toughest and biggest of the young men said in a very knowing tone: 'It's not that easy man.' The mood changed slightly and became rather serious and I posed the question which was the main point of the research, but which I would not have introduced at this point had not the young men brought up the subject of violence and the influence of television on their lives. My questions moved the discussion temporarily from soap opera to the influence of television in their lives. I asked: 'Do the things that you see on television have an influence on you?' After a pause for consideration:

Steve: It can put you in a different train of thought. Like say something might happen, like say somebody got beat up or was ill and it gets you thinking, like things out of your life, why they happen, you know what I mean? And it gets you thinking about things, you know what I mean? And if you have been thinking about these things. It brings out things from your life and gets you thinking about them. So, like, say after a programme you go out and have a few bevies and you see someone you don't get on with and you've got a grievance with them – it gives you ideas for a punishment.
DH: Has it ever done that with you?
Steve: When I was younger, yes.
DH: Younger being?
Steve: Fourteen, thirteen. Seeing things like you retaliate like – car thefts. Where I grew up they were all into car thefts and crime and

that to me at that age seemed exciting, something I wouldn't mind doing.

At their instigation, we moved back to talking about soap opera. I asked: 'Do you watch *Coronation Street*, what do you think about that?' There were general mutterings of 'Yes', and someone said, 'Boring, if you miss an episode, like you have lost it again'. And then someone said *Emmerdale*. I followed the lead:

DH: What do you think of *Emmerdale*?
Many voices: Good, good.
Rudy: It was crap at first but it's got exciting.
Steve: Since the plane crash it's gone up, it's started to get more exciting.
Rudy: Armed robberies and that and scandals. It's good.

There was then a general discussion about the merits of *Emmerdale*, and I asked if they had seen the programme the previous evening. Their response was surprising since they had expressed approval and knowledge of the current storylines. One of the boys said: 'Nobody really watches it, can't watch that, they'd say "get that off".' I asked if that meant that they had to watch what the majority wanted. Rudy, who had acted as my translator for prison jargon throughout the interview, continued his attempts to educate me in the ways of prison life. He explained:

Rudy: I wouldn't recommend it though, 'cos some people still say 'get that off it's crap'.
DH: So you might like to watch it but you wouldn't like to say.

Rudy persevered with my innocence and confirmed his position in the group. With a quiet firmness he told me again, 'I would watch it' and laughed. At last he had got his message through to me and I respond with the right answer to confirm that I have at last understood by confirming what I think he is telling me: 'So, depends on how tough you are whether you can pick. Is it that the ones who pick the programmes are the toughest?' Rudy smiled his acquiescence, confirming that I now understood, both the principle of selecting the programme and the fact that he was, in fact, the one who could, if he wanted, choose for the group to watch *Emmerdale*. He was the most important person in the room and his sitting next to me was clearly to indicate his importance. He was the one explaining to me those comments made by the group which I didn't understand. He was not the most voluble in the group, but certainly one of the most interesting and intriguing. He had chosen to watch *Emmerdale* because the recent storylines had included some elements of crime and the characters of the Dingles, who were much more struggling on the poverty line than characters in the other soap operas at the time. They had become major characters in the series and their lives skirted around crime. They were poor and lived by their wits as they struggled to survive. Their presence had proved more attractive to these young men than other characters in the series.

We moved towards the end of the discussion about soap opera and they said: '*Coronation Street* is for middle-aged people, there's not much exciting.' Steve concluded that soaps were 'women's programmes', and I asked if they thought any of them reflected life as it is. Steve volunteered that *EastEnders* is probably the closest, but *Brookside* because of the drugs with Jimmy What's-it, and then they spontaneously moved me on to the next area of interest by announcing, 'Nearest to life is *The Bill*!'

This brief discussion about soap operas as part of a much longer discussion about the life of these young men and their relationship with various parts of the mass media, revealed their spontaneous selection of characters, storylines and themes as well as the effects of the programmes which they had chosen as being of most importance to them. While these elements were part of the soap operas, they were only part of the entire miscellany of characters and themes which form the programmes. What these young men indicate is evidence that viewers, active as ever, select areas of interest and make their judgements primarily about areas which are of greatest interest to them. Other elements of the series were not discussed and only matters of direct interest to them were mentioned. In their current circumstances certain things united them. In some areas they had far superior knowledge to mine. Their assessment of the verisimilitude of the drugs stories and the criminal elements was beyond my experiences. This was how they chose to judge the programmes and compare the realism of the programmes to what they knew from their own experiences. While Steve may designate soap opera as 'women's programmes', they have managed to talk about the various series without ever considering women as being any part of them – except for describing Peggy Mitchell as Grant Mitchell's mom and defining her as 'knocking off' the criminal, and discussing Cindy in her capacity as a trophy for Whicksy and as 'taking Ian's kids from him'. Certainly they were making selective readings of the characters. They have seen the characters from the perspective which interested them, and have ignored, or edited out of their perception, any other features. The character of Peggy Mitchell is perceived only from the perspective of what interests her to Steve. Grant Mitchell is the character who is of interest to him, and Peggy is his mom. Not surprisingly, for men of his age, a middle-aged woman, however glamorous, bouncy or feisty, is only of interest in the way that she relates to people who are of interest to him. Describing her through her sexuality, as 'knocking off the criminal', is a comment on her inappropriate sexual activity and a recognition of the 'criminal' who owns the club where the drugs are sold. Defining her as 'Grant Mitchell's mom', also includes the unspoken comment that as the mom of a major character, or as a representation of a 'mom', she should certainly not be spending her time 'knocking off' anyone!

> *Soap opera speaks to millions of individuals and mirrors aspects of their lives back to them.*

Contrast the detailed knowledge which these young men had in 1996 across the wide range of soap operas with the superficial mention of the genre by the young men in the interviews in the 1980s. Now the soap opera has evolved to capture the widest audience by including characters and stories which reflect their lives. Remember the aspects of each soap opera which various members of the audience related to me as being important: they have selected the moments of greatest interest and appeal and have repeated them in their fictional form and sometimes told how they have related to their own lives. Each has taken individual moments, many of which are of universal appeal, and they have shown how individual readings may concur with millions of other readings, but nevertheless remain individual. The appeal of the genre to the audience is that soap opera speaks to millions of individuals and mirrors aspects of their lives back to them. It may be reflecting values shared with millions of others but it speaks to the individual and unites them with their own cultural history. Soap operas tell our stories and we respond because, if they do it well, they give reassurance that we are not alone in our thoughts and experiences. It is an affirming genre, and the audience responds to the productions by recognizing that affirmation and completing the circuit of production by accepting the version of their lives which the soap opera presents.

7

The Cultural History of Soap
Opera and the Audience

I remember I used to watch Crossroads *with my Nan.*

All successful soaps have a history which is part of the cultural history both of its audience and of the population as a whole. Generations have watched soaps in their respective countries and the characters and stories are part of the shared knowledge of the audience. Young children have grown up watching soap operas with their siblings, their parents and often their grandparents and their friends. For many the experience of watching television programmes in general, but specifically soap operas because of their regularity in the schedule, has a resonance which connects with other aspects of their lives and often contains points of reference which merge the experience of watching television with other, often pleasurable, experiences: 'having your tea while watching *Crossroads*', 'watching *Coronation Street* in your pyjamas', 'watching *EastEnders* with your friends' and, in specific circumstances, 'watching *Emmerdale* in association time in a young offenders' institution'. It is not simply the experience of the memories of the programme but also the association of the surrounding circumstances that makes for the intensity of the relationship with the genre. You don't only remember the characters and the storylines but also the personal memories which locate them in a certain time and place.

Television has been part of our collective lives, not only because its content is part of our entertainment and knowledge, but also because, crucially, it has been a feature of what we have been doing. It is a part of our lives. In the UK we watched *Neighbours* after *BBC*

Children's Television in the afternoon, or before we watched the *Six o'clock News*, or began to prepare the evening meal, or eat it, depending on our age. Or if we were true soap fans, we might switch from BBC1 to ITV if we lived in a region where *Home and Away* was shown at six o'clock. We watched *Crossroads* while we ate our tea, and if we were housewives we often scheduled the teatime in order to be able to watch the programme. We watched *Dallas* and *Dynasty* mid-evening at eight o'clock, in 'prime time', or 'peak-viewing time' as it was termed in the UK, and we often knew that we were settling down with 20 million other viewers to watch the same programme. In the case of the American super-soaps, we were sharing the cultural experience with millions of people in a global context. One crucial element of this shared experience is that it binds the audience with shared knowledge and cultural capital. If you have the knowledge, you can exchange stories with others the next day, or you can update those who missed the episode. You can talk in the shorthand of those who know the programmes and you can confer, argue and parody scenes, accents and stories which you have seen. In the 1980s we watched *Brookside* and *EastEnders* and we knew all the storylines and all the characters, who had to speak to a younger audience and still keep faith with its older viewers. As soap viewers we became part of a national and global audience who watched, enjoyed, criticized and knew every nuance of the personalities of the characters and their stories.

No other form has lasted and had such resonance with the audience. While we remember films and music as significant entities in their own right, we may also remember at what time in our lives they were significant, what we were doing when the music was around or we went to see the film. However, because soap opera is an ongoing form, we identify many more significant events and storylines as they connected with events in our lives. We see the changes in the lives of characters and relate those events to our own lives. Conversely, events which might not seem of interest at one time may have a resonance in a future time. Soap opera, together with other significant cultural icons, particularly television programmes, are part of the 'structure of feeling' (Williams 1971: 64) which unites the television audience and links the experience of watching cultural forms with our own life experiences. They are readily brought to mind and we associate the stories in soap operas with the times when they were current. Associations differ and just as audiences make differential readings, so the memories of specific stories will not only be triggered by the actual storylines but by the importance they had to the individual. When the process of communication has extended to talking about programmes with friends or work colleagues, those stories and characters are remembered as part of those exchanges.

This connection with memories of our lives is not only relevant to the soap opera. Of course, it can be related to other popular forms. Each generation has its own particular set of cultural icons. It may be that you know all the words to *The Young Ones* because you knew the words when you were at school and you and your friends would recite them to each other and in unison on the morning after you had watched the programme. You may share knowledge of the significance of the current popular television programmes and the words of pop music, which often carry more meaning and recognition with young audiences than any television programme. All of these media forms are part of both our individual and our collective memories. We not only remember cultural artefacts from our own lives but from those of our younger siblings or our own children.

As an exploration of the important issues in everyday life, the soap opera provides a set of representations which can be seen as vibrant reflections of reality. They work because they reflect important issues and they connect with the experiences of the audience; unless they make that connection they will not succeed. The writers of soap operas often have shared experience with that of which they write. More importantly, the issues that formed the basis of stories were those which were important and relevant at the time when they were conceived and had a place within the planned storylines. Millions of examples exist. While the story of Ian Beale could be seen as a *Bildungsroman* in its narrative form, it also speaks to the audience of experiences, if not their own then certainly those of many people they know and of whom they read regularly in the press. Divorce and bankruptcy are two of the most distressing social realities for the 1990s and the personal experience, as portrayed in the representation of Ian Beale, was a powerful example of how the genre can link with every aspect of the lives of the audience. When Peggy Mitchell discovered the lump in her breast and underwent emotional and physical suffering, she united with women who had shared that experience and with those women who feared that they may experience the same. These are the ways in which the soap opera can and does unite its audience with the experiences explored in the drama.

Known communities

We are aware of the communities of soap operas in the same amount of detail as our own communities and in some cases in more detail

– not more than we know our families but, for many people, more than they know about their neighbours and neighbourhoods. The idea that the audience would like to 'inhabit' the world of their favourite soap operas is, for the most part, hardly a rational idea. The young offenders, may 'dream' of the unobtainable paradise of living in Summer Bay next to the beach, with a job and with a mother to look after them, but for most of the audience the thought of living in Albert Square with the constant noises of the market and The Vic, will not be appealing. Some women were not even enamoured at the thought of living with the wealth of the Ewings if it meant living in a house with your in-laws. It is not the notion of inhabiting the soaps that has appeal for audiences, but rather the idea that they know the location and the sets so well that they could find their way around the physical location, and they also 'know' the characters who inhabit the fictional reality. Familiarity with the form enhances the pleasure when watching. The audience knows what to expect and the drama fulfils that expectation and sets up new expectations to anticipate. The setting and fulfilling of expectations of the genre and the pleasure of that experience are a crucial key to the appeal and success of the soap opera. And to this can be added the formal effect of the narrative offering *recurrent catastasis*, which creates a relationship with the audience of ongoing and endless pleasure in the text, and the *intimate familiarity* with everything that is happening within the drama. This is not escapism, but an engagement with a cultural form which connects with experiences and recognizable emotions and situations from the lives of the audience.

Soap opera and new television forms – hybrids and hydra

Soap opera is a living form. It has been shown how vital the genre is to the broadcasting industry, and the future of soap opera is intricately interwoven with the power and desires of the audience. A beneficial effect which the soap opera has had on the broadcasting business is in the way that it has changed the content and areas of concentration in other drama series. In many forms, the concentration on personal relationships has become perhaps the paramount theme in dramas across the schedules. While the staple major soaps need to retain their substantial audience appeal, the broadcasters need to develop new programmes. Developing a new soap is one of the most difficult areas of drama – not because the form is too difficult but because the expectations of the audience are so great and so fuelled by press speculation that it is difficult for any soap opera to establish itself and build a relationship with the audience. Attraction must be instant. There is no hiding place for gently getting to know characters or becoming interested in their lives. While the existing form still holds great appeal, it is in the development of new versions that part of the success for the future of the genre will lie. There have been a number of direct extensions of the form which have stayed within the confines of the basic dramatic integrity of the original series but have made slight dramatic diversions.

Soap bubbles and spin-offs

During the 1980s Phil Redmond initiated a new form of spin-off from his soap opera *Brookside*. Soap 'bubbles' set storylines outside the conventional locations and took the characters away to have adventures and misadventures in unfamiliar regions of the country. Damon and his girlfriend went to Newcastle, and in a horrific and totally pointless incident Damon was stabbed and died in Debbie's arms. A dramatic way to write out the character, but an episode which stands out for its portrayal of death in a quiet and terrifying manner.

The form of the 'bubble' has become a feature of the soap opera genre and each series has its own version. They sometimes tackle storylines which have to be transmitted at a later time because of the content. They also have the ability to tackle the stories of characters who might not currently be a part of the drama. *EastEnders* returned Nick Cotton to the series by producing a half-hour bubble which allowed him to renew his relationship with his son Ashley and plan their return to Albert Square. As a form it has not been used very often but there is a possibility for further development. The problem is that it asks the audience to commit to a different, unallocated, time, and it does, of course, put new demands on the production teams. It also means that the storylines need to be picked up in the main programmes so that the audience never loses track of progress.

Daytime – protecting and nurturing the product

One of the best ways to develop a new series which may evolve into a soap opera is for the programme to begin in the more protected daytime slots so that the series can find its feet as well as its audience. The most successful established soaps were not set up as soap operas but as drama series which were only expected to last for thirteen episodes. When *Coronation Street* first began it was planned as a thirteen-week series. *Emmerdale Farm* was first transmitted in the

protected lunchtime slot and it was not until it had become established with a loyal audience that it moved to seven o'clock on ITV.
Brookside, *EastEnders* and the ill-fated *Eldorado* all began their
transmissions in the full glare of publicity, with the press waiting
to comment on their every weakness. *Brookside* and *EastEnders*
survived because the executives of both Channel 4 and the BBC were
totally in support of the programmes and withstood the attacks by
the press. When *Eldorado* was under attack it failed to gain support
from the senior management, and, indeed, cancelling the contract
was the first action of Alan Yentob when he took over as Controller
of BBC1 in March 1993. It would now be very hard to launch a new
soap opera in prime time because the voracious appetite of the press
would certainly be likely to devour the programmes as they try to
find an audience.

To launch and support a new soap opera now requires nerves of
steel and indifference to the slings and arrows of outrageous criticism
which might be hurled at your programme. It is better to let the fledg-
lings take root in the daytime schedule where the viewers can learn
about the characters, and the writers and actors can become established in the consciousness of their audience. But now the daytime is
also a ground for contestation in scheduling and to have a successful drama series in a daytime slot will also bring audiences to the
channel. In 2000 BBC1 launched a new daytime series, *Doctors*.
Although its form is not that of the soap opera, it does have a core
set of characters and ongoing storylines through a number of episodes
as well as storylines relating to patients which are complete in each
episode. The programme is transmitted every day and has been so
successful that it is scheduled to become a daily continuous series.
For while the programme is part of the genre of medical series it does
concentrate heavily on the everyday life and loves of the professional
medical staff within the practice. It is an example of a hybrid which
is taking positive elements from the basic soap opera genre and
developing it into a new dramatic form.

Soap opera is massively influential in all aspects of television
production. The most recent manifestations of the influence of soap
operas on other genres within television is in the inclusion of themes
from soap operas. While domestic and personal relationships are at
the forefront of the soap opera, they have been extended into
other forms of television drama. The police and medical series, the
ubiquitous 'Cops and Docs' are ostensibly about the working lives of
the characters in crime or medicine, but they have become more and
more to be about the personal relationships of the characters. The
BBC1 series *Casualty*, now in its fifteenth series, has always addressed

the personal lives of nurses and doctors in the Accident and Emergency Department of Holby General Hospital. Personal relationships have always been a part of the series, and love affairs have flourished in traditional stories of 'doctors and nurses'. In the recent series the personal lives of the staff are almost as important as the stories of the patients who pass through the department, and their emotional highs and lows are the stable ingredients of the current series. The change in emphasis in the series is reflected in the opening titles, which no longer feature the ambulance and the signifiers of medical care, but the characters who are the main focus of the storylines.

Similarly, the ITV series *The Bill* evolved from being a one-hour series, to spending nine years as a twice-weekly half-hour series transmitted at 8.00 p.m., and now to being a one-hour series which runs from 8.00 to 9.00 p.m. The changes are significant because the series has changed its direction. The concentration used to be solely on the crime and the police interest in solving the crime, and there was little involvement with the personal lives of the officers. The inevitable personal lives came into everyday contact but were never central to the action. The big change now is that a concentration on the personal lives of the officers has taken its theme from soap operas. It does not make the programme a soap opera, but it does show that one of the major ingredients which has made soap operas successful has been taken to revitalize other forms of drama. The personal has become essential to the success of the series form of television drama.

Hydra – the many-headed docusoaps

While the hybrids of soap operas mean that there are new drama series which take the themes of personal relationships at their heart, the most potent manifestation of the form has been the importation of themes from soap operas into the ubiquitous 'docusoaps'. The form is a hybrid from the documentary genre, taking its credentials from the conventional fly-on-the-wall documentary, but it has little in common with that form other than that it appears to follow its subjects around while they pursue their daily lives. It purports to show its subjects in 'real life' situations, and the film makers give the appearance of observing their subjects. The programmes feature 'ordinary' people in their jobs, as opposed to most soap operas where personal relationships are paramount even when jobs are part of the storyline. In fact, docusoaps are one of the most constructed of programme genres. The participants in the documentary who 'perform' the most are made into the 'stars' of the series. This is partly because the audience responds to their extrovert or extreme behaviour, but only after the director has constructed the seemingly natural appearance through the editing of the footage. Their persona is created and their story is enhanced into a narrative which will make the best programme. The opening titles imitate the titles of American or Australian soap operas, with the 'ordinary' people being featured as 'stars' of the programme.

The form of the docusoap could be mistaken for a sporidesm, which perpetually give birth to new programmes with little to differentiate between them. It has become very popular but is rarely praised, except in exceptional circumstances, and on British television the term 'docusoap' would now seem to add to the derision which is still attached by some to the soap opera. Of course, the form does have its exceptions and some programmes are of a higher standard than the more tabloid style of some of the series within the form. The BBC series *Vet School*, *Vets in Practice* and *The Cruise* followed the lives of their subjects without treating them like freaks. Out of these series came the professional vets who continue to be part of the television landscape, and the talented Jane MacDonald, who was already a professional singer, was made into a 'star'. But the series *Traffic Wardens* revelled in the fact that the main participant saw part of his job description as being to take pleasure in imposing fines on motorists. In some of these programmes those who become the leads are chosen for the 'star' treatment because they are eccentric or outrageous. They are, in fact, the opposite of the characters in fictional soap operas, which are created to be 'ordinary' and believable. We never feel that the stars of docusoaps are 'people like us' or people we know. They are usually such that we watch them as a form of voyeurism, not for the recognition of shared characteristics but for the smugness of seeing people not like us. The term docusoap is a misnomer because the form has so little in common with the genre of the fictional soap opera. There is already evidence that the audience is growing tired of the apparently everyday lives of the 'stars' of the docusoap, but they never seem to tire of the everyday stories of fictional folk.

Reality television – *Big Brother* – watching real people in an unreal situation

In the summer of 2000 a programme was transmitted on Channel 4 which was defined by the programme makers as a game show. The idea behind the programme, which was devised by the Dutch independent production company Endemol, put ten contestants into a warehouse, purpose-converted into open-plan living accommodation, where they lived under the constant scrutiny of the cameras. It was not a docusoap but a game show, with a prize of £70,000 to the contestant who was voted to stay in the house until the end of the contest. Indeed, during the course of the transmission, at a particularly stressful time, the contestants made up a song, which confirmed, 'It's only a game show, it's only a game show'. The programme became a summer phenomenon and was heralded as a new form of programming. It imprisoned its participants and their activities were available for viewing on the Internet twenty-four hours a day, whereas with the soap opera the audience had to imagine what was happening for the hours when they were not watching. Again, this concept was not a representation of 'reality' but rather a total hyper-reality.

To be fair to the producers, the concept of the programme was that it was a game show and that each person involved was a contestant. What made it interesting in the evolution of television was that, once again, it was the most interesting participants who became the stars of the series. And while there was the obvious selection of what to portray for the television series, it was much more difficult for the production team to 'select' its stars. This programme was one of the genuine innovations in television; it took the personal life elements of soap opera and fused them with the competitive elements of the game show to create something totally fresh. What it did not do was 'pretend' to be a soap opera. It acknowledged that its participants were in extraordinary situations and gave its contestants tasks to fulfil to win the rewards of more food or entertainment. In fact, the contestants did not talk very much about their lives outside the programme and there was a limited amount of information available to the audience about their lives in their 'real' homes. What was significant about the contestants in *Big Brother* was that these were extraordinary people, who were able to survive in the house for a long period of time with virtually 'nothing to do'. No writers, no scripts, and yet, even here, the directors were in the business of constructing the story of the house as it had happened during the day.

The link to the soap opera was that the cameras had indeed been observing what had happened even when the viewers were not watching, but, even then, the version which was presented to the viewers was as constructed by the producers. An interesting development in the form was the *Celebrity Big Brother*, produced as part of the BBC charity fund-raising programmes for Comic Relief. In contrast to the ordinary contestants of *Big Brother*, in *Celebrity Big Brother* minor celebrities were at first of interest because of their celebrity, but as the programme progressed they became of interest as they revealed their 'ordinariness'. It could be said that *Big Brother* made minor celebrities out of ordinary people, and *Celebrity Big Brother* made ordinary people out of minor celebrities.

Soap opera and television drama in the twenty-first century

The influence of the soap opera on many television forms was extremely powerful at the end of the twentieth century as television producers searched for new forms in desperate attempts to gain new audiences. Many of these forms can be seen as transitory and ephemeral. Like the ephemera itself they are lightweight, without the power to survive, and live only for a short time. They may have been inspired by elements of the personal which have been taken from the genre of the soap opera, but they can never sustain the commitment and involvement of the audience. For these programmes are ultimately voyeuristic. They look in on the version of the 'real' life of the participants which the production team chooses to portray as their reality. There is little room for engagement because it is such a limited version which is presented: watered-down soap opera with diluted drama. When the possibility of heightened drama is imminent, it is, quite properly, the duty of the production to withdraw from the personal feelings and emotions of the protagonists.

Only within drama can personal themes be fully explored without impinging on the privacy of the participants. Agreement to participate is no solution because self-exploitation is so easily condoned and encouraged both by producers in search of interesting topics and audiences in search of voyeuristic entertainment. In soap opera the representation of the 'ordinary' person has a role and a function in the drama, as in everyday life. However, in the docusoap only the 'extraordinary' find a role. For what the docusoap lacks is a narrative conceived by an artist. While the writer constructs the narrative of the soap opera and the storyline includes the interesting elements and nuances of behaviour, in the docusoap the director has to construct the narrative after the event, and naturally only those participants who behave in an extraordinary manner are chosen for leading roles in the pseudo-dramas. So soap opera as other drama has the advantage over other forms in its ability to explore every aspect of everyday life and to retain an integrity which is based on the skills of the creative power of the writer and not on the manipulation of specific elements of the character of ordinary people.

Soap opera and public service – popular culture, popular programmes and public service

The concept of public service broadcasting, originally formulated by Lord Reith when he was Director-General of the BBC, was based on certain well-defined criteria. Public service broadcasting should inform, educate and entertain. The philosophy of public service television is sometimes seen as only being applicable to the more 'worthy' or 'serious' television programmes. News, current affairs, education, documentaries and arts programmes easily wear the mantle of 'public service'. It is less obvious how popular programmes such as soap operas, popular drama and comedy series fit the remit. However, while these are a crucial element in the provision of programmes which attract large audiences, the quality and range of popular programmes is as important in the provision of public service. In the summer and autumn of the year 2000 the ITC conducted a public consultation about the future of public service broadcasting. Public service is currently the subject of public debate and a redefinition of the concept is in progress. In spite of the discussions about redefinition, there are certain well-defined tenets of public service which should remain as 'absolutes'. Public service provision as defined by the Broadcasting Research Unit (BRU 1985) gives eight principles for public service. Of these, five are directly addressed by soap operas:

- Universality – programmes must be available to the whole population.
- Universality of appeal – broadcast programmes should cater for all interests and tastes.
- Minorities – especially disadvantaged minorities should receive particular provision.
- Broadcasters – should recognize their special relationship to the sense of national identity and community.
- Broadcasting – should be structured so as to encourage competition in good programming rather than in competition for numbers.

The role of soap opera as a vehicle for the public service remit of UK television is at first not obvious. Soaps have been perceived as frivolous, as pandering to the lowest ambitions, but it is perfectly possible to see the soap opera as having a crucial role to play in the provision of public service broadcasting. Soap operas are among the most popular programmes on television, are availability [...] certainly have universality of appeal. Any programme [...] audience figures has to be satisfying a wide range of [...] only. Soap operas address the largest audiences of relevance, and because of their availability through BBC and ITV the requirements of 'universality' for public service. They had of address and perhaps a unique line of communication audiences and they thus have the ability to perform the role of service broadcasting through their accessibility. There is fierce competition among the most popular programmes, and the race top slot between the two major soap operas, *Coronation Street* and *EastEnders*, illustrates this rivalry. Neither wants to fall behind the other and the constant jostling for top position ensures that standards are kept high and the genre is constantly developing.

It we concentrate on the original concept of public service, educate, inform and entertain, then the role of popular television and the soap opera in particular can be seen as the epitome of public service. The elements which are necessary to make a successful soap opera combine also to fulfil the public service remit. Soap operas work because of the strength of their characters. If the characters are well drawn and believable, then the storylines which interweave to form the drama will include many elements of public service concepts. It is in the social elements of soap storylines that public service can be perceived. Soap opera is the perfect genre to educate, inform and entertain. As a genre it is constantly imparting information and educating its audience about a myriad of issues; at the same time it is essential that the audience is entertained, otherwise they would not watch the programme. The premise of 'issue-led' soaps has been discussed in chapters 4 and 5. The importance of the hundreds of storylines which have dealt with social and personal problems has added to the dramatic impact, but also had immeasurable effects on the audience. The list of issues is impressive: recent episodes of the leading soaps have had storylines which have addressed domestic violence, murder, gay and lesbian sexuality, race, drugs, child abuse, transsexuality, divorce, breast cancer, male impotence, menopause. The list is endless and the effects endlessly positive.

Recently *EastEnders* ran a story of child abuse within the Slater family. Eighteen years ago, when she was 13 years old, one of the daughters, Kat, was sexually abused by her uncle, her father's brother. She told her mother, who helped her through the pregnancy and then took the new baby, Zoe, and brought it up as her own. The mother has since died and the secret has never been revealed. It was kept from her father, Charlie, and only one of the sisters knew the true story. In a storyline which also involved other members of the family, Harry, the uncle, who does not know that a child resulted from his sexual intercourse with Kat, invites Zoe to go to stay with him and his new partner, Peggy Mitchell, in Spain. Kat is desperately adamant that Zoe cannot go and, in a moment of terror, she tells Zoe that she is her mother. Through tears, fighting, passionate emotions and the revelation of secrets which will change the lives of all the members of the family and their friends, this particular drama reached its first catastasis and the move to the next phase of their lives was set in motion. The writing and acting was of the highest standard and the production had taken yet another fact from life stories and explored its myriad of characteristics, and its consequences for those involved. The public service element is perfectly illustrated in this storyline. After each of the four episodes, the programme gave a helpline telephone number for viewers who might have been affected by such events in their own lives. On the evening of 6 October 2001, by chance, I met Mal Young at an awards ceremony. He told me that 5,000 people had telephoned the helpline after the programmes. Five thousand people who had watched the programme had a personal reason to telephone to talk about the way that they had been affected by the issues raised within the drama. It is this crucial connection with the audience that makes the soap opera a perfect vehicle for public service.

The way that soap operas work to fulfil a public service remit is to impart information in an acceptable and accessible form. Viewers are able to discuss issues because they are aired within the drama. Popular television has to be more accessible and the issues are discussed in colloquial language by characters with whom the audience is familiar. The issues discussed often become part of public debate, as the press take up the storylines and other television programmes augment the issues in their discussions. Viewers are able to include their own opinions and fears in the debate and expand their knowledge of the issues. The form can be popular, democratic and accountable and can be seen as a particularly potent form of public service broadcasting.

Soap opera and the narrative of our lives

The cultural significance of the soap opera is greater than the significance of the drama, because they integrate with all aspects of our lives. They become part of the narrative of our lives. They are part of our individual memories and the memories of our shared relationships. While some have called them surrogate communities, and some soaps may certainly have that function and quality for certain members of the audience, this is not the normal function of the soap opera. It is in fact as part of our own lives and community, in a wider sense than our immediate neighbourhood, that their great strength and significance rests. For those who have watched them they are part of the 'structure of feeling' of our cultural development and memory. Rock music may be the 'soundtrack of our lives', but soaps are not, as Mal Young believes, 'the movie of our lives', for that would leave them in the realm of fiction. The importance of soap operas is that they are certainly part of the reality of our lives. They have intertwined with events which have happened in our own lives and they have become part of our memories. This is not because we are confused that the characters are real and that events actually happen to them; rather, like Forster's rounded characters, it is because they have the quality of verisimilitude which enables them to exist outside their fictional location. What happens when the stories are merged with our own experiences is that they become part of the memories of our own lives. They exist in our imagination and through our remembering. They are not 'the movie of our lives', but they certainly have a major role in that movie. They are part of what form our experiences and, as with other major cultural forms, they become part of how we experience and remember our lives.

References

Allen, R.C. 1985: *Speaking of Soap Operas*. Chapel Hill, NC: University of North Carolina Press.

Allen, R.C. 1992: *Channels of Discourse, Reassembled: Television and Contemporary Criticism*, 2nd edn. Chapel Hill, NC: University of North Carolina Press and London: Routledge.

Allen, R.C. (ed.) 1995: *to be continued . . . Soap Operas Around the World*. London: Routledge.

Ang, I. 1985: *Watching 'Dallas'*. London: Methuen.

BBC Enterprises 1992: *Eldorado*. London: BBC Enterprises Ltd.

Brake, C. 1994: *EastEnders: The First 10 Years*. London: BBC Books.

Broadcasting Act 1981: London: HMSO.

Broadcasting Research Unit (BRU) 1985: *The Public Service Idea in British Broadcasting: Main Principles*. London: Broadcasting Research Unit.

Brown, M.E. (ed.) 1990: *Television and Women's Culture*. London: Sage.

Brown, M.E. 1994: *Soap Opera and Women's Talk*. London: Sage.

Brunsdon, C. 1981: *Crossroads*: Notes on Soap Opera. *Screen*, 22 (4), 32–7.

Brunsdon, C. 1990: Problems with Quality. *Screen* 31 (1), 69–70. In C. Barker, *Global Television*. Oxford: Blackwell, 1997.

Brunsdon, C. 2000: *The Feminist, the Housewife and the Soap Opera*. Oxford: Oxford University Press.

Brunsdon, C. and Morley, D. 1978: *Everyday Television: 'Nationwide'*. London: British Film Institute.

Buckingham, D. 1987: *Public Secrets: EastEnders and Its Audience*. London: British Film Institute.

Burke, M. 1993: Brookside Fury as Bosses Stage Horrific Murder. *People*. 14 March.

Cantor, M.G. and Pingree S. 1983: *The Soap Opera*. Beverley Hills, CA: Sage Publications.

Chambers Twentieth Century Dictionary 1972. Edinburgh: W & R Chambers.

Drabble, M. (ed.) 1985: *The Oxford Companion to English Literature*. Oxford: Oxford University Press.

Dyer, R. 1977: *Gays and Film*. London: British Film Institute.

Dyer, R. 1979: *Stars*. London: British Film Institute.

Dyer, R. 1987: *Heavenly Bodies: Film Stars and Society*. London: MacMillan Education Ltd.

Dyer, R., Geraghty, C., Jordan, M., Lovell, T., Paterson, R. and Stewart, J. 1981: *Coronation Street*. London: British Film Institute.

Forster, E.M. 1971: *Aspects of the Novel*. Harmondsworth: Pelican.

The Future of the BBC: A Consultation Document 1992: London: HMSO.

Gambaccini, P. and Taylor, R. 1993: *Television's Greatest Hits*. London: BBC Books.

Geraghty, C. 1991: *Women and Soap Opera*. Cambridge: Polity.

Gillespie, M. 1995: *Television, Ethnicity and Cultural Change*. London: Routledge.

Grade, M. 1999: *It Seemed Like a Good Idea at the Time*. London: MacMillan.

Hagell, A. and Newburn, T. 1994: *Young Offenders and the Media*. London: Policy Studies Institute.

Hall, S. (ed.) 1997: *Representation of Cultural Representations and Signifying Practices*. London: Sage.

Hobson, D. 1978: A Study of Working Class Women at Home: Femininity, Domesticity and Maternity. Unpublished MA thesis, Centre for Contemporary Cultural Studies, University of Birmingham.

Hobson, D. 1980: Housewives and the Mass Media. In Hall, S., Hobson, D., Lowe, A. and Willis, P. (eds), *Culture, Media, Language*. London: Hutchinson.

Hobson, D. 1982: *Crossroads: The Drama of a Soap Opera*. London: Methuen.

Hobson, D. 1987: Perceptions of Channel 4 Television 1982–87. Unpublished papers.

Hobson, D. 1989: Soap Operas at Work. In Seiter, E., Borchers, H., Kreutzner, G. and Warth, E. (eds), *Remote Control: Television Audiences and Cultural Power*. London: Routledge.

Hobson, D. 1990: Women Audiences and the Workplace. In Brown, M.E. (ed.), *Television and Women's Culture*. London: Sage.

Hobson, D. 1992: Eldorado's Buried Gold. *The Guardian*. 10 August.

Hobson, D. 1997: *The Daily Telegraph*. 17 March.

Hoggart, R. 1973: *The Uses of Literacy*. Harmondsworth: Penguin.

ITC, 1998: *Television: The Public's View*. London: ITC.

Isaacs, J. 1989: *Storm Over Four*. London: Weidenfeld and Nicolson.

Katz, E. and Lazersfeld, P. 1955: *Personal Influence*. New York: Free Press.

Liebes, T. and Katz, E. 1989: On the Critical Abilities of Television Viewers. In Seiter, E., Borchers, H., Kreutzner, G. and Warth, E. (eds),

Remote Control Television: Audiences and Cultural Power. London: Routledge.

Livingstone, S.M. 1990: *Making Sense of Television: The Psychology of Audience Interpretation*. Oxford: Pergamon.

Lock, K. 2000: *EastEnders: Your Ultimate Guide to Who's Who*. London: BBC Worldwide.

McQuail, D. 1977: The Influence and Effects of Mass Media. In Curran, J., Gurevitch, M. and Woollacott, J. (eds), *Mass Communication and Society*. London: Arnold/Open University Press.

Miller, D., Kitzinger, J., Williams, K. et al. 1992: Perspective. In *Times Higher Educational Supplement*, 3 July, p. 18. Quoted in Gunter, B., Sancho-Aldridge, J., Moss, R. 1993: Public Perceptions of the Role of Television in Raising AIDS Awareness, *Health Education Journal* 53 (1), 20.

Morley, D. 1986: *Family Television*. London: Comedia/Routledge.

Morley, D. 1992: *Television Audiences and Cultural Studies*. London: Routledge.

Nown, G. (ed.) 1985: *Coronation Street 1960–1985*. London: Ward Lock.

O'Donnell, H. 1999: *Good Times, Bad Times*. London: Leicester University Press.

Seiter, E., Borchers, H., Kreutzner, G. and Warth, E. (eds), 1989: *Remote Control: Television Audiences and Cultural Power*. London: Routledge.

Smith, J. and Holland, T. 1987: *EastEnders – The Inside Story*. London: BBC Books.

Walton, K.L. 1992: Pretending Belief. In Furst, L., *Realism*. London: Longman.

Watt, I. 1972 [1957]: *The Rise of the Novel: Studies in Defoe, Richardson and Fielding*. Harmondsworth: Pelican.

Williams, R. 1971: *The Long Revolution*. Harmondsworth: Pelican Books.

Index